ORGANIZATIONAL LEARNING: A THEORY OF ACTION PERSPECTIVE

Chris Argyris   *Harvard University*

Donald A. Schön   *Massachusetts Institute of Technology*

ADDISON-WESLEY PUBLISHING COMPANY

Reading, Massachusetts • Menlo Park, California
London • Amsterdam • Don Mills, Ontario • Sydney

ISBN 0-201-00174-8
ABCDEFGHIJ-AL-798

Preface

This book has grown from our earlier inquiry into the theories of action which individuals bring to their interactions with one another. In *Theory in Practice,* we described the theories-in-use which guide our interpersonal behavior, create the behavioral worlds in which we live, and influence both our long-term effectiveness and our capacity for learning. Originally, we had planned in a chapter of that book to apply the theory of action perspective to the problem of organizational capacity for learning. But we could not write that chapter; it called for a conceptual bridge which we had not yet built—a bridge between the world of interpersonal behavior and the world of the organization. The effort we had projected for a few months has become a four-year enterprise; what began as a chapter has become a book.

In the present work, we argue that organizations are not collections of individuals which can be understood solely in terms of the social psychology of group behavior. Neither are they understandable only as structures of authority and information-flow, or as instruments for the achievement of social purposes, or as systems for communication and control, or as cultures, or as theaters for the play of conflicts of interest. Social psychologists, sociologists, management theorists, systems analysts, anthropologists, and political scientists have examined organizational phenomena, each inquirer using the perspective current in his discipline. Each perspective offers a unique and interesting view of organizational action and of the ways in which organizations may be said to learn. In the Appendix, we have described these perspectives and the approaches to organizational learning which may be derived from them. But no single perspective gives a workable basis either for diagnosing the impediments to organizational learning or for designing interventions which would increase organizational capacity for learning.

An intervention-oriented perspective on organizational learning depends upon a synthesis of other perspectives. It is necessary, we believe, to show how organizations, which act only through the agency of individuals, cannot be reduced to collections of individuals. It is necessary to explain how organizations themselves are theories of action—theories of action which are maintained and transformed by individuals who occupy roles within organizational structures and live in the behavioral worlds draped over those structures. It is necessary to show how the behavioral world may constrain or facilitate the joint inquiry through which error in organizational theory of action may be detected and corrected.

We believe that a preoccupation with a normative theory of intervention provides the best starting point for a theory of organizational learning. Such a theory, we hope, will be of use both to practitioners and to scholars—of greatest use, perhaps, to the small band of scholar-practitioners on whom the future of research into organizational learning most depends.

In the early stages of our work, we have profited from seminars held at M.I.T.'s Division for Study and Research in Education, especially from discussions with Sir Geoffrey Vickers, Tom Burns, and Martin Rein. Clay Alderfer, Lee Bolman, Bernard Cullen, Steve Ehrmann, Richard Hackman, Elliot Jaques, William Ronco, Roger Simmonds, and John Van Maanen have all read our manuscript and we are grateful to them for their criticisms, as we are to Scott Cook for help in preparing the Appendix.

Cambridge, Mass.   C.A.
October 1977   D.A.S.

Contents

v

Introduction

Several years ago the top management of a multibillion dollar corporation decided that Product X was a failure and should be disbanded. The losses involved exceeded one hundred million dollars. At least five people knew that Product X was a failure six years before the decision was taken to stop producing it. Three of those people were plant managers who lived daily with the production problems. The other two were marketing officials who realized that the manufacturing problems were not solvable without expenditures that would raise the price of the product to the point where it would no longer be competitive in the market.

There are several reasons why this information did not get to the top sooner. At first, the subordinates believed that with exceptionally hard work they might turn the errors into successes. But the more they struggled, the more they realized the massiveness of the original error. The next task was to communicate the bad news upward so that it would be heard. They knew that in their company bad news would not be well received at the upper levels if it was not accompanied with suggestions for positive action. They also knew that the top management was enthusiastically describing Product X as a new leader in its field. Therefore, they spent much time composing memos that would communicate the realities without shocking top management.

Middle management read the memos and found them too open and forthright. Since they had done the production and marketing

1

studies that resulted in the decision to produce X, the memos from the lower-level management questioned the validity of their analysis. They wanted time to "really check" these gloomy predictions and, if they were accurate, to design alternative corrective strategies. If the pessimistic information was to be sent upward, middle management wanted it accompanied with optimistic action alternatives. Hence further delay.

Once middle management was convinced that the gloomy predictions were valid, they began to release some of the bad news to the top—but in carefully measured doses. They managed the releases carefully to make certain they were "covered" if top management became upset. The tactic they used was to cut the memos drastically and summarize the findings. They argued that the cuts were necessary because top management was always complaining about receiving long memos; indeed, some top executives had let it be known that good memos were memos of one page or less. The result was that top management received fragmented information underplaying the intensity of the problem (not the problem itself) and overplaying the degree to which middle management and the "techies" were in control of the problem.

Top management therefore continued to speak glowingly about the product, partially to assure that it would get the financial backing it needed from within the company. Lower-level management became confused and eventually depressed because they could not understand this continued top management support, nor why studies were ordered to evaluate the production and marketing difficulties that they had already identified. Their reaction was to reduce the frequency of their memos and the intensity of their alarm, while simultaneously turning over the responsibility for dealing with the problem to the middle-management people. When local plant managers, in turn, were asked by their foremen and employees what was happening, the only response they gave was that the company was studying the situation and continuing its support. This information bewildered the foremen and led them to reduce their concern.

We should like to use this case to explain a view of organizational learning, but first we must define a few concepts. Organizational learning involves the detection and correction of error. When the error detected and corrected permits the organization to carry on its present policies or achieve its present objectives, then that error-detection-and-correction process is *single-loop* learning. Single-loop learning is like a thermostat that learns when it is too hot or too cold and turns the heat on or off. The thermostat can perform this task because it can receive information (the temperature of the room) and take corrective action. *Double-loop* learning occurs when error is detected and corrected in ways that involve the modification of an organization's underlying norms, policies, and objectives.

The case we have described illustrates many of the important problems that we have found in private and public organizations as they strive to learn. Most organizations do quite well in single-loop learning but have great difficulties in double-loop learning. For example, the participants, acting as agents for organizational learning, were able to detect and correct error as long as the original objective—to produce X—was not questioned. Difficulties with and barriers to organizational learning arose as it became clear that the original decision (and hence the planning and problem solving that led to the decision) was wrong. Questioning the original decision violated a set of nested organizational norms. The first norm was that policies and objectives, especially those that top management was excited about, should not be confronted openly. The second norm was that bad news in memos to the top had to be offset by good news. These two interdependent norms require behavior that would be disloyal to the espoused theories of management and to the formal organizational policies. Hence, the fact that these two norms existed had to be camouflaged. And, at least one layer of camouflage on top of the original camouflage would help the participants to feel more secure that they would not be caught.

When the participants camouflaged the norms, and camouflaged the camouflage, they did so because they knew that to hide information violated organizational policies. Thus the participants were in a double bind. If they exposed the errors, they would call into question a set of nested norms that were supposed to be kept covert. If they did not expose the errors, they created and/or reinforced processes that inhibited organizational learning.

But there were also organizational norms against discussing double binds. Hence games of deception were played in which everyone knew that the realities were being hidden, but no one discussed them. So they became undiscussable.

Such procedure means that the very information needed to detect and correct errors becomes undiscussable. If one wanted to design a strategy to inhibit double-loop learning and to encourage error, a better one could not be found. One of our major assertions will be that organizations tend to create learning systems that inhibit double-loop learning that calls into question their norms, objectives, and basic policies.

In a previous book we concluded that individuals created similar conditions in their interpersonal relationships (Argyris and Schon 1974). We suggested that people held theories of action that they used to design and carry out their behavior in any situation in which they were embedded. These theories of action had to be based on a form of logic, otherwise those using them would be creating new theories in every situation. This would violate the information-processing limits of human beings (Simon 1969). We developed a model of this logic and called it Model I. Once it was built, it became apparent that people who held Model I theories of action tended to be unable to reflect and question either their own governing values or the theories of action and governing values of others.

The predisposition of organizations to inhibit double-loop learning (which calls into question fundamental objectives, and norms) is therefore reinforced (and, as we shall see, caused) by the theories of action with which most people are acculturated in modern industrial societies. This mutual reinforcement of processes to inhibit double-loop learning exists, we believe, in all modern organizational societies regardless of their beliefs.

Our ultimate goal is to help individuals unfreeze and alter their theories of action so that they, acting as agents of the organization, will be able to unfreeze the organizational learning systems that also inhibit double-loop learning. In defining this goal, we realize that we are probably biting off much more than we can possibly chew. Not only do we have the temerity to question underlying human theories of action and organizational learning systems, but we are calling into question some of the most basic societal norms and values. Moreover, we even strive to present new models of action for individuals, organizations, and society.

One reason for taking the risk that some readers may view our goals as premature or naive is that we believe that social scientists should explore possible resolutions of these learning issues. Unless people acting as agents for organizations and societies are able to learn how to detect and correct double-loop errors, the survival of the society may be in doubt.

At this point, we should like to make explicit another perspective that underlies the entire book. As a result of our previous work (Argyris 1976a, 1976b; Argyris and Schon 1974) we have concluded that theories created to understand and predict may be quite different from theories created to help people make events come about. The latter, which we have called theories of action, must lead to understanding and prediction, but they must go beyond these two important functions.

For example, certain theories of leadership have recently shown important gaps and inconsistencies as their creators attempted to apply them (Argyris 1976a). We maintain that it was not accidental that these inconsistencies arose while attempting to produce the theories. We believe that theories of action whose purpose is primarily to discover problems may be quite different from those whose purpose combines discovery of problems with the invention and production of solutions.

We question the current model that first there is basic research and later there is applied research. It is our view that basic research is needed about applications, and that theories should be developed around these issues as well as research methodologies to test the theories. As a result, the reader will find that our perspective includes both descriptive and normative models. The model of organizational learning in Part V is descriptive; it purports to give an account of actual organizational learning systems. The model of organizational learning systems in Part III is normative, in that it suggests how the world might be rearranged in order to enhance double-loop learning.

Having made this differentiation according to existing practice, we should now like to question it. The descriptive model is also a normative model not only because most actors will agree that it describes the world the way it is, but also because it describes, from their theory-of-action perspective, the way the world ought to be. In other words, from a theory-of-action perspective, all models that are valid are both descriptive and normative.

THE ORGANIZATION OF THE BOOK

In Part I we concern ourselves with what we mean by organizational learning and how it differs from individual learning. In Part II we develop our theme that individuals are programmed with Model I theories of action, and hence they create organizations with learning systems that facilitate single-loop learning and inhibit double-loop learning.

A model of an organizational double-loop learning system is described in Part III. Also, we describe two kinds of intervention that may be used to solve organizational problems. The first type is a comprehensive intervention strategy and the second is more limited.

In Part IV we examine six cases of other approaches to intervention. We will strive to show how each approach is self-sealing, how it tends to lead to its self-deterioration, and hence how it fails to achieve its intended objectives.

A FRAMEWORK FOR ORGANIZATIONAL LEARNING

Our aim in Part I is to define the terms and to describe the conceptual framework which we will use in our further discussions of organizational diagnosis and intervention. Chapter 1 examines the senses in which an organization may learn or fail to learn, and sets out the kinds of organizational learning we believe to be most important. Chapter 2 presents a case of limited learning capacity in an industrial corporation and describes an intervention aimed at enhancing that capacity; the case serves to introduce the key concepts of limited learning system and of good organizational dialectic.

CHAPTER ONE

What is an organization that it may learn?

THE QUESTION

There has probably never been a time in our history when members, managers, and students of organizations were so united on the importance of organizational learning. Costs of health care, sanitation, police, housing, education, and welfare have risen precipitously, and we urge agencies concerned with these services to learn to increase their productivity and efficiency. Governments are torn by the conflicting demands of full employment, free collective bargaining, social welfare, and the control of inflation; we conclude that governments must learn to understand and accommodate these demands. Corporations have found themselves constrained by a web of increasingly stringent regulations for environmental protection and consumer safety, at the same time that we are most sensitive to the need for jobs and for economic growth. Government and business must learn, we say, to work together to solve these problems.

Sometimes our demands for learning turn back on our history, as when politicians and planners ask, "What have we learned from the last 20 years of housing policy?" "What have we learned from the Great Depression?" "What have we learned from Vietnam?" In a bicentennial article on "The American Experiment," Daniel Moynihan begins by asking, "What have we learned?" (Glazer and Kristol 1976)

It is not only that we are poignantly aware of our dilemmas and of the need for learning. We are also beginning to notice that there is nothing more problematic than solutions. Some of our most agonizing problems have been triggered by our solutions to slum eradication and urban renewal, by the success of the Labor Movement in achieving income security for workers, by rising expectations consequent to our economic growth, by the unwanted consequences of technological innovations. We begin to suspect that there is no stable state awaiting us over the horizon. On the contrary, our very power to solve problems seems to multiply problems. As a result, our organizations live in economic, political, and technological environments which are predictably unstable. The requirement for organizational learning is not an occasional, sporadic phenomenon, but is continuous and endemic to our society.

Nevertheless, it is not all clear what it means for an organization to learn. Nor is it clear how we can enhance the capacity of organizations to learn.

The difficulty has first to do with the notion of learning itself. When we call for learning or change, we seem to be calling for something good. But there are kinds of change which are not good, such as deterioration, regression and stagnation. And there are kinds of learning, such as government's learning to deceive and manipulate society, which are no better. So we need to spell out both the kinds of change we have in mind when we speak of learning, and the kinds of learning we have in mind when we call for more of it.

Further, it is clear that organizational learning is not the same thing as individual learning, even when the individuals who learn are members of the organization. There are too many cases in which organizations know *less* than their members. There are even cases in which the organization cannot seem to learn what every member knows. Nor does it help to think of organizational learning as the prerogative of a man at the top who learns *for* the organization; in large and complex organizations bosses succeed one another while the organization remains very much itself, and learns or fails to learn in ways that often have little to do with the boss.

There is something paradoxical here. Organizations are not merely collections of individuals, yet there is no organization without such collections. Similarly, organizational learning is not merely individual learning, yet organizations learn only through the experience and actions of individuals.

What, then, are we to make of organizational learning? What is an organization that it may learn?

THEORY OF ACTION

In our earlier book, *Theory in Practice* (Argyris and Schon 1974), we set out to understand how practitioners of management, consultation, and intervention might learn to become more competent and effective. Our concern was especially directed to learning about interpersonal interaction. In that context, we found it useful to look at professional practice as informed by *theories of action:*

> All human beings—not only professional practitioners—need to become competent in taking action and simultaneously reflecting on this action to learn from it. The following pages provide a conceptual framework for this task by analyzing theories of action that determine all deliberate human behavior, how these theories are formed, how they come to change, and in what senses they may be considered adequate or inadequate. (p. 4)

When we attributed theories of action to human beings, we argued that all deliberate action had a cognitive basis, that it reflected norms, strategies, and assumptions or models of the world which had claims to general validity. As a consequence, human learning, we said, need not be understood in terms of the "reinforcement" or "extinction" of patterns of behavior but as the construction, testing, and restructuring of a certain kind of knowledge. Human action and human learning could be placed in the larger context of knowing.

We found it necessary to connect theories of action to other kinds of theory:

> . . . whatever else a theory of action may be, it is first a theory. Its most general properties are properties that all theories share, and the most general criteria that apply to it—such as generality, centrality, and simplicity—are criteria that apply to all theories. (p. 4)

And we also found it necessary to differentiate theories of action from theories of explanation, prediction, and control:

> A full schema for a theory of action, then, would be as follows: in situation *S*, if you want to achieve consequence *C*, under assump-

tions *a . . . n*, do *A*. . . . A theory of action is a theory of deliberate human behavior which is for the agent a theory of control but which, when attributed to the agent, also serves to explain or predict his behavior. (p. 6)

Because we wished to do empirical research into human learning in situations of interpersonal interaction, we distinguished espoused theory from theory-in-use:

When someone is asked how he would behave under certain circumstances, the answer he usually gives is his espoused theory of action for that situation. This is the theory of action to which he gives allegiance and which, upon request, he communicates to others. However, the theory that actually governs his actions is his theory-in-use, which may or may not be compatible with his espoused theory; furthermore, the individual may or may not be aware of the incompatibility of the two theories. (p. 7)

From the directly observable data of behavior, we could then ground our construction of the models of action theories which guided interpersonal behavior. And we could relate these models to the capacity for types of learning in professional practice.

It is tempting to apply this line of thought to the problem of understanding organizational learning. Perhaps organizations also have theories of action which inform their actions, espoused theories which they announce to the world and theories-in-use which may be inferred from their directly observable behavior. If so, then organizational learning might be understood as the testing and restructuring of organizational theories of action and, in the organizational context as in the individual one, we might examine the impact of models of action theories upon the capacity for kinds of learning.

But this path is full of obstacles. It is true that we do apply to organizations many of the terms we also apply to individuals. We speak of organizational action and organizational behavior. We speak also of organizational intelligence and memory. We say that organizations learn, or fail to learn. Nevertheless, a closer examination of these ways of speaking suggests that such terms are metaphors. Organizations do not literally remember, think, or learn. At least, it is not initially clear how we might go about testing whether or not they do so.

It is even puzzling to consider what it means for an organization to act or behave—notions which are essential to the construction of organizational theories of action. Does an organization act whenever one of its members acts? If so, there would appear to be little difference between an organization and a collection of individuals. Yet it is clear that some collections of people are organizations and others are not. Furthermore, even when a collection of people is clearly an organization, individual members of the organization do many things (such as breathe, sleep, gossip with their friends) which do not seem, in some important sense, to be examples of organizational action.

If we are to speak of organizational theories of action, we must dispel some of the confusion surrounding terms like organizational intelligence, memory, and action. We must say what it means for an organization to act, and we must show how organizational action is both different from and conceptually connected to individual action. We must say what it means for an organization to know something, and we must spell out the metaphors of organizational memory, intelligence, and learning.

PERSPECTIVES ON ORGANIZATION

Let us begin by exploring several different ways of looking at an organization. An organization is:

- a government, or *polis,*
- an agency,
- a task system.

Each of these perspectives will illuminate the sense in which an organization may be said to act. Further, an organization is:

- a theory of action,
- a cognitive enterprise undertaken by individual members,
- a cognitive artifact made up of individual images and public maps.

Each of these descriptions will reveal the sense in which an organization may be said to know something, and to learn.

Consider a mob of students protesting against their university's policy. At what point do they cease to be a mob and begin to be an organization?

The mob is a collectivity. It is a collection of people who may run, shout, and mill about together. But it is a collectivity which cannot make a decision or take an action in its own name, and its boundaries are vague and diffuse.

As the mob begins to meet three sorts of conditions, it becomes more nearly an organization. Members must devise procedures for: (1) making decisions in the name of the collectivity, (2) delegating to individuals the authority to act for the collectivity, and (3) setting boundaries between the collectivity and the rest of the world. As these conditions are met, members of the collectivity begin to be able to say "we" about themselves; they can say, "We have decided," "We have made our position clear," "We have limited our membership." There is now an organizational "we" that can decide and act.

When the members of the mob become an identifiable vehicle for collective decision and action, they become, in the ancient Greek sense of the term, a *polis,* a political entity. Before an organization can be anything else, it must be in this sense political, because it is as a political entity that the collectivity can take organizational action. It is individuals who decide and act, but they do these things *for* the collectivity by virtue of the rules for decision, delegation, and membership. When the members of the collectivity have created such rules, they have organized.

Rule making need not be a conscious, formal process. What is important is that members' behavior be rule-governed in the crucial respects. The rules themselves may remain tacit, unless for some reason they are called into question. So long as there is continuity in the rules which govern the behavior of individuals, the organization will persist, even though members come and go. And what is most important for our purposes, it now becomes possible to set up criteria of relevance for constructing organizational theory-in-use. Organizational theory-in-use is to be inferred from observation of organizational behavior—that is, from organizational decisions and actions. The decisions and actions carried out by individuals are organizational insofar as they are governed by collective rules for decision and delegation. These alone are the decisions and actions taken in the name of the organization.

Through such a process, a mob becomes an organization. But if we are interested in organizational theory of action, we must ask what *kind* of an organization it becomes.

If a collection of people begins to decide and to act on a continuing basis, it becomes an instrument for continuing collective action, an *agency*. In this sense, the collections of workers involved in the labor movement organized from time to time to form unions, and collections of individual investors organized to form limited liability corporations. Such agencies have functions to fulfill, work to do. Their theories-in-use may be inferred from the ways in which they go about doing their work.

Generally speaking, an agency's work is a complex task, continually performed. The agency—an industrial corporation, a labor union, a government bureau, or even a household—embodies a strategy for decomposing that complex task into simpler components which are regularly delegated to individuals. Organizational roles—president, lathe-operator, shop steward—are the names given to the clusters of component tasks which the agency has decided to delegate to individual members. The organization's *task system*, its pattern of interconnected roles, is at once a design for work and a division of labor.

An agency is thus the solution to a problem. It is a strategy for performing a complex task which might have been carried out in other ways. This is true not only for the design of the task system, the division of labor, but also for the selection of strategies for performing component tasks.

We can view a sugar-refining company, for example, as an answer to questions such as these: What is the best way to grow and harvest cane? How should it be refined? How is it best distributed and marketed? For each subquestion the organization is an answer. The company's way of growing cane reflects certain strategies (for the cultivation of land, for harvesting and fertilizing), certain norms (for productivity and quality, for the use of labor), and certain assumptions (about the yields to be expected from various patterns of cultivation). The norms, strategies, and assumptions embedded in the company's cane-growing practices constitute its *theory of action* for cane-growing. There are comparable theories of action implicit in the company's ways of distributing and marketing its products. Taken together, these component theories of action represent a theory of action for achieving corporate objectives. This global theory of action we call "instrumental." It includes norms for corporate performance (for example, norms for margin of profit and for return on investment), strategies for achieving norms (for example, strategies for plant location and for process technology), and assumptions which bind strategies and norms together (for example, the assumption that maintenance of a high rate of return on investment depends on the continual introduction of new technologies).

The company's instrumental theory of action is a complex system of norms, strategies, and assumptions. It includes in its scope the organization's patterns of communication and control, its ways of allocating resources to goals, and its provisions for self-maintenance—that is, for rewarding and punishing individual performance, for constructing career ladders and regulating the rate at which individuals climb them, and for recruiting new members and instructing them in the ways of the organization.

Like the rules for collective decision and action, organizational theories of action need not be explicit. Indeed, formal corporate documents such as organization charts, policy statements, and job descriptions often reflect a theory of action (the *espoused theory*) which conflicts with the organization's *theory-in-use* (the theory of action constructed from observation of actual behavior)—and the theory-in-use is often tacit. Organizational theory-in-use may remain tacit, as we will see later on, because its incongruity with espoused theory is *undiscussable*. Or it may remain tacit because individual members of the organization know more than they can say—because the theory-in-use is *inaccessible* to them. Whatever the reason for tacitness, the largely tacit theory-in-use accounts for organizational identity and continuity.

Consider a large, enduring organization such as the U.S. Army. Over 50 years or so, its personnel may turn over completely, yet we still speak of it as "the Army." It is no longer the same collection of people, so in what sense is it still the same? Suppose we wanted to discover whether it was in fact the same organization. How would we proceed? We might examine uniforms and weapons, but in 50 years these might have changed entirely. We might then study the 50-year evolution of military practices—that is, the norms for military behavior, the strategies for military action, the assumptions about military functioning. We would then be studying the evolution of the Army's theory-in-use. And we might learn that certain features of it—for example, the pattern of command, the methods of training, the division into regiments and platoons—had remained essentially unchanged, while other features of it—battle strategies, norms for performance—had evolved continuously from earlier forms. We might conclude that we were dealing with a single organization, self-identical, whose theory-in-use had evolved considerably over time.

It is this theory-in-use, an apparently abstract thing, which is most distinctively real about the Army. It is what old soldiers know and new ones learn through a continuing process of socialization. And it is the history of change in theory-in-use which we would need to consult in order to inquire into the Army's organizational learning.

In order to discover an organization's theory-in-use, we must examine its practice, that is, the continuing performance of its task system as exhibited in the rule-governed behavior of its members. This is, however, an outside view. When members carry out the practices appropriate to their organization, they are also manifesting a kind of knowledge. And this knowledge represents the organization's theory-in-use as seen from the inside.

IMAGES AND MAPS

Each member of the organization constructs his or her own representation, or image, of the theory-in-use of the whole. That picture is always incomplete. The organization members strive continually to complete it, and to understand themselves in the context of the organization. They try to describe themselves and their own performance insofar as they interact with others. As conditions change, they test and modify that description. Moreover, others are continually engaged in similar inquiry. It is this continual, concerted meshing of individual images of self and others, of one's own activity in the context of collective interaction, which constitutes an organization's knowledge of its theory-in-use.

An organization is like an organism each of whose cells contains a particular, partial, changing image of itself in relation to the whole. And like such an organism, the organization's practice stems from those very images. Organization is an artifact of individual ways of representing organization.

Hence, our inquiry into organizational learning must concern itself not with static entities called organizations, but with an active process of organizing which is, at root, a cognitive enterprise. Individual members are continually engaged in attempting to know the organization, and to know themselves in the context of the organization. At the same time, their continuing efforts to know and to test their knowledge represent the object of their inquiry. Organizing is reflexive inquiry.

From this perspective, organizational continuity is a considerable achievement. But we could not account for organizational continuity if the cognitive enterprise of organizing were limited to the private inquiry of individuals. Even when individuals are in face-to-face contact, private images of organization erode and diverge from one another. When the task system is large and complex, most members are unable to use face-to-face contact in order to compare and adjust their several images of organizational theory-in-use. They require external references. There must be public representations of organizational theory-in-use to which individuals can refer.

This is the function of organizational maps. These are the shared descriptions of organization which individuals jointly construct and use to guide their own inquiry. They include, for example, diagrams of work flow, compensation charts, statements of procedure, even the schematic drawings of office space. A building itself may function as a kind of map, revealing patterns of communication and control. Whatever their form, maps have a dual function. They describe actual patterns of activity, and they are guides to future action. As musicians perform their scores, members of an organization perform their maps.

Organizational theory-in-use, continually constructed through individual inquiry, is encoded in private images and in public maps. These are the media of organizational learning.

ORGANIZATIONAL LEARNING

As individual members continually modify their maps and images of the organization, they also bring about changes in organizational theory-in-use.

Not all of these changes qualify as learning. Members may lose enthusiasm, become sloppy in task performance, or lose touch with one another. They may leave the organization, carrying with them important information which becomes lost to the organization. Or changes in the organization's environment (a slackening of demand for product, for example) may trigger new patterns of response which undermine organizational norms. These are kinds of deterioration, sometimes called organizational entropy.

But individual members frequently serve as agents of changes in organizational theory-in-use which run counter to organizational entropy. They act on their images and on their shared maps with expectations of patterned outcomes, which their subsequent experience confirms or disconfirms. When there is a mismatch of outcome to expectation (error), members may respond by modifying their images, maps, and activities so as to bring expectations and outcomes back into line. They detect an error in organizational theory-in-use, and they correct it. This fundamental learning loop is one in which individuals act from organizational theory-in-use, which leads to match or mismatch of expectations with outcome, and thence to confirmation of disconfirmation of organizational theory-in-use.

Quality control inspectors detect a defect in product, for example; they feed that information back to production engineers, who then change production specifications to correct that defect. Marketing managers observe that monthly sales have fallen below expectations; they inquire into the shortfall, seeking an interpretation which they can use to devise new marketing strategies which will bring the sales curve back on target. When organizational turnover of personnel increases to the point where it threatens the steady performance of the task system, managers may respond by investigating the sources of worker dissatisfaction; they look for factors they can influence—salary levels, fringe benefits, job design—so as to reestablish the stability of their work force.

Single-loop learning

In these examples, *members of the organization respond to changes in the internal and external environments of the organization by detecting errors which they then correct so as to maintain the central features of organizational theory-in-use.* These are learning episodes which function to preserve a certain kind of constancy. As Gregory Bateson has pointed out (Bateson 1972), the organization's ability to remain stable in a changing context denotes a kind of learning. Following his usage, we call this learning single-loop. (Bateson 1960) There is a single feed-back loop which connects detected outcomes of action to organizational strategies and assumptions which are modified so as to keep organizational performance within the range set by organizational norms. The norms themselves—for product quality, sales, or task performance—remain unchanged.

These examples also help to make clear the relationship between individual and organizational learning. The key to this distinction is the notion of *agency. Just as individuals are the agents of organizational action, so they are the agents for organizational learning.* Organizational learning occurs when individuals, acting from their images and maps, detect a match or mismatch of outcome to expectation which confirms or disconfirms organizational theory-in-use. In the case of disconfirmation, individuals move from error detection to error correction. Error correction takes the form of inquiry. The learning agents must discover the sources of error—that is, they must attribute error to strategies and assumptions in existing theory-in-use. They must invent new strategies, based on new assumptions, in order to correct error. They must produce those strategies. And they must evaluate and generalize the results of that new action. "Error correction" is shorthand for a complex learning cycle.

But in order for *organizational* learning to occur, learning agents' discoveries, inventions, and evaluations must be embedded in organizational memory. They must be encoded in the individual images and the shared maps of organizational theory-in-use from which individual members will subsequently act. If this encoding does not occur, individuals will have learned but the organization will not have done so.

Suppose, for example, that the quality control inspectors find a product defect which they then decide to keep to themselves, perhaps because they are afraid to make the information public. Or suppose that they try to communicate this information to the production engineers, but the production engineers do not wish to listen to them. Or suppose that the interpretation of error requires collaborative inquiry on the part of several different members of the organization who are unwilling or unable to carry out such a collaboration. (Indeed, because organizations are strategies for decomposing complex tasks into task/role systems, error correction normally requires collaborative inquiry.) In all of these instances, individual learning may or may not have occurred, but individuals do not function as agents of organizational learning. What individuals may have learned remains as an unrealized potential for organizational learning.

From this it follows both that there is no organizational learning without individual learning, and that individual learning is a necessary but insufficient condition for organizational learning. We can think of organizational learning as a process mediated by the collaborative inquiry of individual members. In their capacity as agents of organizational learning, individuals restructure the continually changing artifact called organizational theory-in-use. Their work as learning agents is unfinished until the results of their inquiry—their discoveries, inventions, and evaluations—are recorded in the media of organizational memory, the images and maps which encode organizational theory-in-use.

If we should wish to test whether organizational learning has occurred, we must ask questions such as these: Did individuals detect an outcome which matched or mismatched the expectations derived from their images and maps of organizational theory-in-use? Did they carry out an inquiry which yielded discoveries, inventions, and evaluations pertaining to organizational strategies and assumptions? Did these results become embodied in the images and maps employed for purposes such as control, decision, and instruction? Did members subsequently act from these images and maps so as to carry out new organizational practices? Were these changes in images, maps, and organizational practices regularized so that they were unaffected by some individual's departure? Do new members learn these new features of organizational theory of action as part of their socialization to the organization?

Each of these questions points to a possible source of failure in organizational learning, as well as to the sources of organizational learning capacity. So far, however, we have limited ourselves to the kind of learning called single-loop. Let us now consider learning of another kind.

Double-loop learning

Organizations are continually engaged in transactions with their internal and external environments. Industrial corporations, for example, continually respond to the changing pattern of external competition, regulation and demand, and to the changing internal environment of workers' attitudes and aspirations. These responses take the form of error detection and error correction. Single-loop learning is sufficient where error correction can proceed by changing organizational strategies and assumptions within a constant frame-work of norms for performance. It is concerned primarily with effec-tiveness—that is, with how best to achieve existing goals and objec-tives and how best to keep organizational performance within the range specified by existing norms. In some cases, however, error correction requires an organizational learning cycle in which orga-nizational norms themselves are modified.

Consider an industrial firm which has set up a research and development division charged with the discovery and development of new technologies. This has been a response to the perceived impera-tive for growth in sales and earnings and the belief that these are to be generated through internally managed technological innovation. But the new division generates technologies which do not fit the corpora-tion's familiar pattern of operations. In order to exploit some of these technologies, for example, the corporation may have to turn from the production of intermediate materials with which it is familiar to the manufacture and distribution of consumer products with which it is unfamiliar. But this, in turn, requires that members of the corporation adopt new approaches to marketing, managing, and advertising; that they become accustomed to a much shorter product life cycle and to a more rapid cycle of changes in their pattern of activities; that they, in fact, change the very image of the business they are in. And these re-quirements for change come into conflict with another sort of cor-porate norm, one that requires predictability in the management of corporate affairs.

Hence, the corporate managers find themselves confronted with conflicting requirements. If they conform to the imperative for growth, they must give up on the imperative for predictability. If they decide to keep their patterns of operations constant, they must give up on the imperative for growth, at least insofar as that imperative is to be realized through internally generated technology. A process of change initiated with an eye to effectiveness under existing norms turns out to yield a conflict in the norms themselves.

If corporate managers are to engage this conflict, they must undertake a process of inquiry which is significantly different from the inquiry characteristic of single-loop learning. They must, to begin with, recognize the conflict itself. They have set up a new division which has yielded unexpected outcomes; this is an error, in the sense earlier described. They must reflect upon this error to the point where they become aware that they cannot correct it by doing better what they already know how to do. They must become aware, for example, that they cannot correct the error by getting the new division to perform more effectively under existing norms; indeed, the more effective the new division is, the more its results will plunge the managers into conflict. The managers must discover that it is the norm for predictable management which they hold, perhaps tacitly, that conflicts with their wish to achieve corporate growth through technological innovation.

Then the managers must undertake an inquiry which resolves the conflicting requirements. The results of their inquiry will take the form of a restructuring of organizational norms, and very likely a restructuring of strategies and assumptions associated with those norms, which must then be embedded in the images and maps which encode organizational theory-in-use.

We call this sort of learning *double-loop.* There is in this sort of episode a double feedback loop with connects the detection of error not only to strategies and assumptions for effective performance but to the very norms which define effective performance.

Single-loop learning, as we have defined it, consists not only of a change in organizational strategies and assumptions but of the particular sort of change appropriately described as learning. In single-loop learning, members of the organization carry out a collaborative inquiry through which they discover sources of error, invent new strategies designed to correct error, produce those strategies, and evaluate and generalize the results. Similarly, double-loop learning consists not only of a change in organizational norms but of the particular sort of inquiry into norms which is appropriately described as learning.

In organizational double-loop learning, incompatible requirements in organizational theory-in-use are characteristically expressed through a conflict among members and groups within the organization. In the industrial organization, for example, some managers may become partisans of growth through research and of a new image of the business based upon research, while others may become opponents of research through their allegiance to familiar and predictable patterns of corporate operation. Double-loop learning, if it occurs, will consist of the process of inquiry by which these groups of managers confront and resolve their conflict.

In this sense, the organization is a medium for translating incompatible requirements into interpersonal and intergroup conflict.

Members of the organization may respond to such a conflict in several ways, not all of which meet the criteria for organizational double-loop learning. First, the members may treat the conflict as a fight in which choices are to be made among competing requirements, and weightings and priorities are to be set on the basis of prevailing power. The "R & D faction," for example, may include the chief executive who wins out over the "old guard" through being more powerful. Or the two factions may fight it out to a draw, settling their differences in the end by a compromise which reflects nothing more than the inability of either faction to prevail over the other.

In both of these cases, the conflict is settled for the time being, but not by a process that could be appropriately described as learning. The conflict is settled not by inquiry but by fighting it out. Neither side emerges from the settlement with a new sense of the nature of the conflict, of its causes and consequences, or of its meaning for organizational theory-in-use.

On the other hand, parties to the conflict may engage the conflict through inquiry of the following kinds:

- They may invent new strategies of performance which circumvent the perceived incompatibility of requirements. They may, for example, succeed in defining a kind of research and development addressed solely to the existing pattern of business, which offers the likelihood of achieving existing norms for growth. They will then have succeeded in finding a single-loop solution to what at first appeared as a double-loop problem.

- They may carry out a "trade-off analysis" which enables them to conclude jointly that so many units of achievement of one norm are balanced by so many units of achievement of another. On this basis, they may decide that the prospects for R & D payoff are so slim that the R & D option should be abandoned, and with that abandonment there should be a lowering of corporate expectations for growth. Or they may decide to limit R & D targets so that the disruptions of patterns of business operation generated by R & D are limited to particular segments of the corporation.

Here there is a compromise among competing requirements, but it is achieved through inquiry into the probabilities and values associated with the options for action.

• In the context of the conflict, the incompatible requirements may not lend themselves to trade-off analysis. They may be perceived as incommensurable. In such a case, the conflict may still be resolved through inquiry which gets underneath the members' starting perceptions of the incompatible requirements. Participants must then ask why they hold the positions they do, and what they mean by them. They may ask, what factors have led them to adopt these particular standards for growth in sales and earnings, what their rationale is, and what are likely to be the consequences of attempting to achieve them, through any means whatever? Similarly, they may ask what kinds of predictability in operations are of greatest importance, to whom they are most important, and what conditions make them important.

Such inquiry may lead to a significant restructuring of the configuration of corporate norms. Or it may lead to the invention of new patterns of incentives, budgeting, and control which take greater account of requirements for both growth and predictability.

We will give the name "double-loop learning" to those sorts of organizational inquiry which resolve imcompatible organizational norms by setting new priorities and weightings of norms, or by restructuring the norms themselves together with associated strategies and assumptions.

In these cases, individual members resolve the interpersonal and intergroup conflicts which express incompatible requirements by creating new understandings of the conflicting requirements, their sources, conditions, and consequences—understandings which then become embedded in the images and maps of organization. By doing so, they make the new, more nearly compatible requirements susceptible to effective realization.

There are three observations we wish to make about distinction between single- and double-loop organizational learning. They will become clearer through our discussion of examples in later chapters but need brief mention here.

First, it is often impossible, in the real-world context of organizational life, to find inquiry cleanly separated from the uses of power.

Inquiry and power-play are often combined. Some of the ways in which they are combined, and some of the ways in which power-play inhibits inquiry, we will consider at length in Part II. Given such mixtures, we will want to differentiate the two kinds of processes which are often mixed in practice so that we may speak of those aspects of interpersonal and intergroup conflict which involve organizational learning and those which do not.

Second, while we have described the *kinds* of inquiry which are essential to single- and double-loop learning, we have not yet dwelt on the *quality* of inquiry. Two different examples of double-loop learning, both of which exhibit detection of error and correction of error through the restructuring of organizational norms, may be of unequal quality. The same is true of single-loop learning. Organizations may learn more or less well, yet their inquiries may still qualify as learning of the single- or double-loop kind. The standards we mean to apply to such judgments of quality will occupy us in later chapters, particularly in Chapter 6.

Finally, we must point out that the distinction between single- and double-loop learning is less a binary one than might first appear. Organizational theories-in-use are systemic structures composed of many interconnected parts. We can examine these structures from the point of view of a particular, local theory of action, such as the industrial firm's theory of action for quality control, or we can attend to more global aspects of the structure, such as the firm's theory of action for achieving targeted return on investment. Furthermore, certain elements are more fundamental to the structure and others are more peripheral. For example, the industrial firm's norms for growth and for predictability of management are fundamental to its theory of action—in the sense that if they were changed, a great deal of the rest of the theory of action would also have to change—and it is their fundamental status which gives a special poignancy to their conflict. On the other hand, a particular norm for product quality may be quite peripheral to the organization's theory of action; it could change without affecting much of the rest of the theory of action.

Now, an inquiry into a *strategy* fundamental to the firm's theory of action, such as the strategy of measuring divisional performance by monthly profit-and-loss statements, will be likely to involve much of the rest of the organization's theory of action, including its norms. But an inquiry into a *norm* peripheral to the organization's theory of action may involve very little of the rest of its theory of action. From this, two conclusions may be drawn. First, in judging whether learning is single- or double-loop, it is important to notice where inquiry goes as well as where it begins. Second, it is possible to speak of organizational learning as *more or less* double-loop. In place of the binary distinction we have a more continuous concept of depth of learning.

It is possible, we think, to make clear distinctions between relatively deep and relatively peripheral examples of organizational learning. We will continue to call the former double- and the latter, single-loop learning. Our examples of double-loop learning will involve norms fundamental to organizational theories of action, for these are the examples we believe to be of greatest importance. The reader should keep in mind, however, that we speak of these categories as discrete when they are actually parts of a continuum.

With these *caveats*, we can return to our main line of argument.

Deutero-learning

Since World War II, it has gradually become apparent not only to business firms but to all sorts of organizations that the requirements of organizational learning, especially for double-loop learning, are not one-shot but continuing. There has been a sequence of ideas in good currency—such as "creativity," "innovation," "the management of change"—which reflect this awareness.

In our earlier example, to take one instance, managers of the industrial firm might conclude that their organization needs to learn how to restructure itself, at regular intervals, so as to exploit the new technologies generated by research and development. That is, the organization needs to learn how to carry out single- and double-loop learning.

This sort of learning to learn Gregory Bateson has called *deutero-learning* (that is, second-order learning). Bateson illustrates the idea through the following story:

> A female porpoise . . . is trained to accept the sound of the trainer's whistle as a "secondary reinforcement." The whistle is expectably followed by food, and if she later repeats what she was doing when the whistle blew, she will expect again to hear the whistle and receive food.

> The porpoise is now used by the trainers to demonstrate "operant conditioning" to the public. When she enters the exihibition tank,

she raises her head above the surface, hears the whistle and is fed . . .

But this pattern is (suitable) only for a single episode in the exhibition tank. She must break that pattern to deal with the *class* of such episodes. There is a larger context of contexts which will put her in the wrong . . .

When the porpoise comes on stage, she again raises her head. But she gets no whistle. The trainer waits for the next piece of conspicuous behavior, likely a tail flip, which is a common expression of annoyance. This behavior is then reinforced and repeated (by giving her food).

But the tail flip was, of course, not rewarded in the third performance.

Finally the porpoise learned to deal with the context of contexts—by offering a different or new piece of conspicuous behavior whenever she came on stage.

Each time the porpoise learns to deal with a larger class of episodes, she learns *about* the previous contexts for learning. Her creativity reflects deutero-learning.

When an organization engages in deutero-learning, its members learn, too, about previous contexts for learning. They reflect on and inquire into previous contexts for learning. They reflect on and inquire into previous episodes of organizational learning, or failure to learn. They discover what they did that facilitated or inhibited learning, they invent new strategies for learning, they produce these strategies, and they evaluate and generalize what they have produced. The results become encoded in individual images and maps and are reflected in organizational learning practice.

The deutero-learning cycle is relatively familiar in the context of organizational learning curves. Aircraft manufacturers, for example, project the rate at which their organizations will learn to manufacture a new aircraft and base cost estimates on their projections of the rate of organizational learning. In the late 1950s, the Systems Development Corporation undertook the "Cogwheel" experiment, in which members of an aircraft-spotting team were invited to inquire into their own organizational learning and then to produce conditions which would enable them more effectively to learn to improve their performance (Chapman and Kennedy 1956).

In these examples, however, deutero-learning concentrates on single-loop learning; emphasis is on learning for effectiveness rather than on learning to resolve conflicting norms for performance. But the concept of deutero-learning is also relevant to double-loop learning. How, indeed, can organizations learn to become better at double-loop learning? How can members of an organization learn to carry out the kinds of inquiry essential to double-loop learning? What are the conditions which enable members to meet the tests of organizational learning? And how can they learn to produce those conditions?

Organizations are not only theories of action. They are also small societies composed of persons who occupy roles in the task system. What we have called the internal environment of an organization is the society of persons who make up the organization at any given time. These societies have their own characteristic behavioral worlds. These enable us to recognize a person as "an army man," "a government man," "a General Electric man." Within these societies, members tend to share characteristic languages, styles, and models of *individual* theory-in-use for interaction with others. In the light of these behavioral worlds, we can and do describe organizations as more or less "open," "experimental," "confronting," "demanding," or "defensive." These behavioral worlds, with their characteristic models of individual theory-in-use, may be more or less conducive to the kinds of collaborative inquiry required for organizational learning.

Hence, if we wish to learn more about the conditions that facilitate or inhibit organizational learning, we must explore the ways in which the behavioral worlds of organizations affect the capacity for inquiry into organizational theory-in-use.

SUMMARY

Organizational learning is a metaphor whose spelling out requires us to reexamine the very idea of organization. A collection of individuals organizes when its members develop rules for collective decision delegation and membership. In their rule-governed behavior, they act for the collectivity in ways that reflect a task system. Just as individual theories of action may be inferred from individual behavior, so organizational theories of action may be inferred from patterns of organizational action. As individuals have espoused theories which may

be incongruent with their (often tacit) theories-in-use, so with organizations.

Organizational learning occurs when members of the organization act as learning agents for the organization, responding to changes
in the internal and external environments of the organization by
detecting and correcting errors in organizational theory-in-use, and
embedding the results of their inquiry in private images and shared
maps of organization.

In organizational single-loop learning, the criterion for success is
effectiveness. Individuals respond to error by modifying strategies and
assumptions within constant organizational norms. In double-loop
learning, response to detected error takes the form of joint inquiry
into organizational norms themselves, so as to resolve their inconsistency and make the new norms more effectively realizable. In both
cases, organizational learning consists of restructuring organizational
theory of action.

When an organization engages in deutero-learning, its members
learn about organizational learning and encode their results in images
and maps. The quest for organizational learning capacity must take
the form of deutero-learning; most particularly about the interactions
between the organization's behavioral world and its ability to learn.

CHAPTER TWO

What facilitates or inhibits organizational learning?

THE MERCURY STORY

Let us consider the case of a corporation which we will call the Mercury Corporation.

It is a chemical company, initially formed in the 1920s around a single product line. It was among the first in its industry to set up a research and development division, and over the decades it has generated new businesses in many different fields. By the mid-1960s it had grown to over five billion dollars in sales. Management, preoccupied with maintaining the company's rate of growth, began to worry about signs of flagging vitality. They localized the source of the difficulty in the declining capacity of the research and development division to generate new products which could become the basis for new businesses.

They diagnosed the problem as "an entrepreneurial gap." Research, they thought, had the capacity to generate new technologies, but not to commercialize them. For this, Research depended on existing divisions of the company which were often reluctant to risk a very new product or process.

Given this diagnosis of the problem, management invented a solution that seemed appropriate. They would establish a New-Business Division which would be empowered not only to develop new technologies but to "incubate" them. The new division would be able to make and sell new products, turning them over to existing divisions only when they had already proved their worth. Existing divisions, freed from the need to shoulder the risks of the first reduction to practice, would no longer resist the new technologies generated by Research.

In the early 1970s Mercury experienced a different kind of crisis. The phenomenal growth of the corporation seemed now to go hand in hand with a declining rate of earnings. Management attributed this to the new scale of the business. The corporation's success in achieving its targets for growth had created an enterprise whose size and scope exceeded the capacity of the central administration. A business in excess of five billion dollars could not be run in the same old way. There was a decision to decentralize the management of the corporation, creating semiautonomous divisions, each with its own business charter and its own president. These presidents became known as the "barons."

By the mid-1970s the New-Business Division had accumulated 10 years of experience. It had accounted for some 20 million dollars in research and development expenditure without giving rise to a new business of any consequence. In spite of this record, the new Division remained in being. Indeed, top management had not directly criticized the Division. But members of the NBS staff were becoming uneasy, and they called in an outside consultant.

The consultant set out to map the problem. He found that various members of the organization held different and sometimes conflicting views of the problem, for example:

"It's a corporate weakness; we know how to manage capital better than we do technology."

"We're constrained by our charter; top management needs to free us up so that, if necessary, we can cut across the charters of existing divisions."

"We've taken the path of least resistance. We need to be more 'gutsy,' to take the business risks we were set up to take."

"We need to do much more of what we have been doing, only with more creativity. We need lots of balls in the air."

Individuals expressed such views in private but not in public. They had never confronted one another with their differences, nor had they pursued their disagreements to the point of asking what might test them.

The consultant proposed to get underneath these differences by asking his clients—the Vice President for Technology, the Director of Research, members of the NBD staff—to construct case histories of corporate development over the past decade, both the developments they saw as successes and those they saw as failures.

This turned out not to be an easy task. For one thing, the failures tended to remain buried; people were not eager to exhume them. For another, individuals who held parts of the stories in their own heads had never concerted or sought to reconcile their differing pictures of events. Knowledge of past efforts at development remained scattered among members of the corporation.

In consequence, the corporation had been able to create certain myths of development. These included, for example, the notions that "Good ideas come from the top," and "A good idea will find its own way." These myths were widely diffused throughout the organization, and they remained untested. Indeed, they became self-fulfilling prophecies. Successes were read, after the fact, as good ideas, and failures were read as bad ones. Because failures remained buried, the quality of their ideas was never compared with the quality of the successes. Moreover, success itself came to be accepted as the test of a good idea. Because (as we will see) top management support was essential to success, it was easy to believe that good ideas came from the top.

Nevertheless, with the consultant's urging and support, members of the corporation came together to construct case histories of new business development. The following, in brief, is the story of a "success":

> In the Resin Division, a new manufacturing process had been developed which the Resin Division itself could not use. But the process looked to the research director as though it might have potential for textile products, and there was a small Textiles Division. A task force was set up to conduct a feasibility study.
>
> At first, it was not evident to the Resin Division that they might *lose* market through the new development, as they lost old customers with whom the corporation would now be competing. So they contributed staff to the task force, as did the Textiles and Research Divisions. This was a drain on divisional resources, and

it hurt. But the chairman of the board was behind the effort. He made corporate funds available, and he smoothed the way. In addition, about midway through the study a big customer came along and said, "If you can make it, I'll buy it."

In the course of the construction of the story, the following dialogue occurred among the consultant, a vice-president, and a division manager:

C: Why hadn't they told the head of the Resin Division that he might actually lose market?

VP: If we'd told him, given our management policies, he would have been a fool to go along.

C: Did you test that assumption?

VP: No. You can't test something like that.

C: What happened when he found out?

VP: He blew his top, but he calmed down.

DM: And some of us wondered when someone was going to play that game on us.

C: Did this make you wary and mistrustful?

DM: You're right. You have to be that way if you're going to survive.

Other "successes" fell into a similar pattern. First, there was the perception of a business opportunity based on the development of a new technology. The technology usually grew out of an existing division; often, it was the unexpected consequence of planned R & D activity. The exploitation of the business opportunity required the recombination of existing businesses. Members of the corporation noticed, for example, that: "If we could only group these businesses together, we have a family of technologies that could help them all to take off," or "Here's a technology that would be good for fastening. We don't see ourselves now in the fastening business, but there are pieces of other divisions which have to do with fasteners. If we combined them in a new division, we'd have the marketing vehicle for our new technology."

Often, existing divisions resisted giving up a piece of themselves for the sake of creating a new business for the corporation. As one member said, "In every successful marriage, there's at least one unwilling partner!" As long as possible, promoters of the new business met that resistance by working around it and by withholding information. When those strategies were no longer feasible, there was recourse to top management. Top management would then make commitments to the new business, make corporate funds available for development, and talk one of the barons into going along.

Over the previous decade, three such successes had occurred, and they accounted for a major share of corporate growth.

"Failures" also fell into a pattern.

In these stories, too, technological opportunities had been detected. But here the technology was seen as "a way of entering a business we're not yet in." The new business had then to be described to top management. Typically, top management gave one of two responses. Sometimes they saw the new business as "too small" compared to the standard of size set by existing businesses; promoters of the new business found it difficult to make the case that a new and as yet untried business would meet those criteria. On the other hand, top management might see the new business as "too unfamiliar," "not our kind of thing." Even if the business seemed to promise a large enough volume of sales, the process of getting from here to there seemed too uncertain. When top management felt uncomfortable, they refused to make any commitment to the project.

Without top management commitment, even though some resources might be devoted to development, there was not enough energy to bring the project to fruition. The development would be dropped. Failure might then be attributed to "a bad idea" or to someone's "incompetence." As a consequence, the best technical people wanted to stay away from such developments, and those who had to stay with them acquired what someone called a "loser syndrome."

Taking the two kinds of story together, the consultant and the client group put together the following picture.

The imperative for increasing R & D productivity had led to the creation of the New-Business Division. The great increase in corporate size had led to decentralization of management. The new scale of corporate sales also set massive requirements for the volume of sales that would have to be delivered by a promising new business.

The divisions, with their semiautonomous status, operated under strict incentives to deliver profit. They held fiercely to their business charters, even when they were not fully exploiting them. They were reluctant to give up a piece of themselves for the sake of creating a new business for the corporation.

But given the standards for new businesses set by corporate scale, and the requirement for familiarity that made top management comfortable with a new business, promising new businesses were seen only in the recombination of pieces of the existing business. Only these were familiar enough to make top management comfortable, and big enough to make a still bigger business believable. Hence it was only the recombinations that could get enough support from top management to make the barons see themselves as pieces of the corporate puzzle.

Hence the pattern of the "successes."

But each such success left the barons more mistrustful of central administration, more wary of getting caught up in such losing games.

The New-Business Division was based on the theory that research would yield new technologies which had then to be combined with business opportunities. These "balls in the air" could then be screened according to corporate criteria, and the most promising of them selected for further investment.

However, NBD existed as an island surrounded by hostile divisional barons, every one of whom saw NBD as a threat to divisional integrity and a drain on divisional resources. NBD sought to avoid confrontation with the barons. They sought to protect themselves by going after new businesses which lay *outside* of divisional business charters. Hence, they spent their time exploring opportunities which lay outside the existing business. But NBD depended ultimately on top management for the support to carry a project forward, and top management saw these opportunities as either too small or too unfamiliar.

Hence the pattern of the "failures."

Moreover, the whole process remained undiscussable. For if it were to be discussed, it would have been necessary to bring out into the open the games played between central administration and the divisions, and the barons' competition with NBD. It would also have been necessary to face publicly the conflicting requirements of corporate development and of decentralized management. The first meant that each divisional manager must see himself, at least potentially, as a piece of the corporate puzzle, ready to give up resources and markets for the sake of a new corporate business. The second meant that each divisional manager must exploit and protect his business territory, and respond only to the demands, month by month and year by year, that he deliver expected earnings.

Hence the absence of direct criticism of NBD. No one was anxious to open that can of worms.

PERSPECTIVES ON ORGANIZATIONAL LEARNING

The Mercury story is both a story of organizational learning, and of organizational nonlearning. It illustrates concepts we have already introduced and others not yet defined which are important to the inquiry we intend to pursue.

At the heart of the story is an inconsistency in Mercury's corporate theory of action, an inconsistency generated by the company's very success in achieving corporate growth. In the early 1970s, that success had produced a situation which management had then defined as a problem of organizational structure: central administration overloaded by the task of managing the business. Management also found a structural solution to that problem: decentralization. And its theory-in-use for decentralization included the norm for central retention of control over corporate performance, even while divisional managers were being freed up to manage their own divisional businesses. The strategy of control was to set targets for divisional performance as measured by earnings, and to use the full array of corporate incentives and sanctions to reward the meeting of targets and to punish failure. Divisional managers' theory-in-use for responding to central control included self-protection by exercising their own unilateral control wherever they could do so, and by defending their charters and territories against all comers.

In the middle 1960s, however, management had constructed a different sort of problem: that of a decline in corporate rate of growth. In this case, the pattern of solution had taken more than one form. On the basis of its diagnosis of the "entrepreneurial gap," top management had again created a structural solution: the New-Business Division. This structural invention was based on an espoused theory for corporate development. New business opportunities were to be generated and screened; the most promising were to be incubated by New-Business Division, then passed on to existing divisions for management. To avoid conflict with existing divisions, the new Division developed a theory-in-use for its activities which included the strategy of seeking new opportunities outside the bounds of existing business. But at the same time the corporation manifested another kind of theory-in-use for the development of new businesses, one which employed the strategy of seeking new business opportunities from the recombination of pieces of the existing business, well within the zone that top management would find both credible and comfortable. But this theory-in-use carried with it the requirement that divisional managers, from time to time, give up parts of themselves to new corporate developments.

Thus the inconsistency in the requirements for decentralized management and for corporate development came to a head around the interaction of divisional with central management. Divisional managers were, as they saw it, subject to inconsistent corporate demands. The inconsistency in corporate theory-in-use manifested itself in conflicts between divisional managers and central administration. These conflicts might have been the occasion for organizational inquiry and hence for double-loop learning. The parties to the conflict might have reflected on the conflict and its sources. They might then have explored and restructured the corporate norms, strategies, and assumptions which generated the conflict. None of this happened. Instead, the organization responded to the conflict, and to the inconsistency which underlay it, through a kind of single-loop learning, peculiar in the sense that the learners were not the organization as a whole, but groups and components within the organization. Thus, existing divisions learned to protect their territories more effectively and to become more mistrustful of central. NBD learned to seek business opportunities outside the scope of existing business. Top management learned to criticize particular failures of NBD, but to avoid criticizing NBD itself.

In this, the organization functioned as a collection of subgroups, more accurately, as an ecology of subgroups, since each group functioned within the environment made up of other groups and functioned itself as a part of the other groups' environment. Each group then set and solved the problems presented to it by its environment, inquiring at the level of single-loop learning. The net effect of this pattern of single-loop learning (which we call *ecological adjustment*) was to maintain the constancy of organizational theory of action. Requirements for development and for decentralized management remained incompatible. Espoused theory and theory-in-use for corporate development remained incongruent.

It is not true, however, that organizational theory-in-use remained entirely constant. For each "success" in the realm of corporate development made divisional managers more mistrustful, more wary of central, more resistant to central's next incursion. It would be reasonable to predict that, in the future, such development successes would be few and far between.

The inconsistency in organizational theory-in-use had begun to take on the character of an organizational dilemma. That is, in the light of its conflicting requirements and its inability to resolve that conflict through inquiry, the organization had begun to find itself in situations of choice where all the options open to it appear equally bad.

What was it about the organization that created this dilemma?

One answer is that members of the organization had not reflected on and inquired into the issue. They had discovered neither the inconsistency in the requirements for development and decentralization nor the incongruity between espoused theory and theory-in-use for development. They had no map of the problem. In fact, they had treated the whole development process as undiscussable.

But this answer merely shifts the question. What prevented members of the organization from discussing the issue and mapping the problem? What prevented them, in short, from doing by themselves what the consultant enabled them to do?

Let us consider more carefully the consultant's process of intervention (we will be discussing it further in Chapter 9).

When the consultant found that different members of NBD held different and conflicting views of their problem, he brought them together to confront and discuss their differences.

Within the Mercury Corporation, the norms of the behavioral world induced members to express their diagnoses of sensitive issues in private, never in public. Public discussion of sensitive questions was considered inappropriate. It involved the risk of vulnerability to blame, and of interpersonal confrontation. Both were to be avoided.

As a consequence, the members of NBD did not know the extent to which they held different views of their own problem.

The consultant sought to test and explore the different diagnoses by collecting case histories of corporate development which were perceived as successes and failures—that is, by constructing an organizational history of development.

Perceptions and memories of the development stories were scattered among individuals who held their views private. No one, for example, held in their mind the whole story of the resin/textile "success" because no one had experienced that episode from many sides and from beginning to end. The story had to be constructed by piecing together many scattered perceptions, and the norms of the behavioral world militated against such an enterprise.

The consultant urged the various members of the organization to work together at interpreting the meaning of the stories.

As long as the stories remained scattered and uninterpreted, the map of the development process remained vague and the diagnoses of the development problem remained ambiguous. But such vagueness and ambiguity were considered normal and appropriate, given the shared wish to avoid exhuming corporate failures (which might give rise to blame) and to avoid raising in public features of organizational life that were consensually treated as undiscussable.

The consultant, then, undertook and supported others in undertaking the public confrontation of different and conflicting views of the problem, the testing and exploration of differences through the construction of organizational history, the concerting of scattered perception of organizational events, the shared interpretation of data pertaining to development, and the joint mapping of the corporate development process.

All of these interventions had the effect of reducing certain *conditions of error* (scattered perceptions, vague maps, ambiguous diagnoses) so that still other conditions for error (inconsistency and incongruity in corporate theory of action) might be surfaced and subjected to inquiry.

In the language of the previous chapter, the consultant sought to facilitate a process of organizational double-loop learning by reducing the conditions for error which prevented shared perception of inconsistency and incongruity in organizational theory of action. But these conditions for error were reinforced by certain prevailing features of the organization's behavioral world—shared strategies in individual theories-in-use—which included the following:

- Let buried failures lie.

- Keep your views of sensitive issues private; enforce the taboo against their public discussion.
- Do not surface and test differences in views of organizational problems.
- Avoid seeing the whole picture; allow maps of the problem to remain scattered, vague, ambiguous.

But these strategies reflect deeper and more fundamental norms, strategies, and assumptions:

- Protect yourself unilaterally—by avoiding both direct inter-personal confrontation and public discussion of sensitive issues which might expose you to blame.
- Protect others unilaterally—by avoiding the testing of assumptions where that testing might evoke negative feelings, and by keeping others from exposure to blame.
- Control the situation and the task—by making up your own mind about the problem and acting on your view, by keeping your view private, and by avoiding the public inquiry which might refute your view.

These features of the behavioral world, which the consultant sought to by-pass and counteract, constrain and guide the character and extent of organizational learning. They determine what will be discussed and what will be left undiscussable, which individual perceptions of organizational experience will be left scattered and which will be concerted. They limit the extent to which organizational maps will be constructed, shared, and tested. They determine whether and in what way conditions of error will be reduced so that inconsistencies and incongruities in organizational theory-in-use may be discovered.

But these features of the behavioral world which constrict the possibility for joint inquiry into the problems of corporate development also enter into the corporate development process itself. Thus central administrators protected themselves unilaterally and sought to control divisional managers (by withholding information from them, for example), and divisional managers protected themselves and sought to resist control (by their territoriality and by their wariness of central). And both groups sought to avoid confrontation and the evocation of negative feelings by avoiding the public testing of their assumptions about the other.

Thus features of the behavioral world which entered into the development process and helped to create its perceived difficulties also constrained inquiry into that process. One might say that the behavioral world protected itself from exposure.

The organization's theory of action is embedded in a behavioral world which shapes and constrains instrumental theory-in-use at the same time that it shapes and constrains organizational learning about theory-in-use. This is what we shall call the organization's *learning system*. Mercury's learning system limited organizational learning about corporate development to the process of ecological adjustment described above—that is, to a process in which each group carried out single-loop learning so as to cope, within unchanging norms, with the problems created for it by other groups in its environment. For a time, the consultant intervened so as to reduce conditions for error and to surface the central dilemma of development which the organization's learning had helped to create and preserve.

The Mercury story illustrates, then, some of the ways in which an organization's learning system may prevent double-loop learning, and it suggests a kind of limited intervention which by-passes features of the learning system so as to increase the likelihood of double-loop learning.

The Mercury story also suggests the dialectical nature of the larger process of organizational change within which we find episodes of learning or of failure to learn.

The organizational problems of corporate development arose and came to be perceived as a consequence of a dual process, each part of which took the form of the setting and solving an organizational problem. The phenomenal rate of corporate growth led to difficulties which were perceived as a problem of management overload, and were "solved" through decentralization. The wish to maintain that rate of growth, in the face of what was seen as declining R & D productivity, led to the creation of a New-Business Division. The working out of these two intertwined "solutions" led to the creation of a new inconsistency in organizational theory-in-use, an incompatibility between the requirements of decentralization and development which we have described as an organizational dilemma manifested in the conflict between central and divisional management.

We will use the term *"organizational dialectic"* to refer to such processes. In them, organizational situations give rise to organizational inquiry—to problem setting and problem solving—which, in turn, create new organizational situations within which new inconsistencies and incongruities in organizational theory of action come into play. These are characteristically manifested in organizational conflict. The organization's way of responding to that conflict yields still further transformations of the organizational situation.

We believe that organizational learning occurs within the frame of such dialectical processes, which stem from two conditions of organizational life: Organizations are necessarily involved in continual transaction with their internal and external environments (that is, in situations) which are continually changing both as a result of forces external to organizations, and as a result of organizational responses to their situations. Second, organizational objectives, purposes, and norms are always multiple and potentially conflicting.

As a consequence, it is no accident that organizational solutions give rise to further problems; they may be expected to do so, given the dialectic frame within which organizational inquiry occurs.

But this, then, raises sharply the problem of criteria for the evaluation of organizational change and learning. This problem is central to our inquiry, and will occupy us especially in Part III. At this point, however, we may note the following:

- The achievement of stable solutions is not an appropriate criterion for organizational learning; it is in the very nature of organizational problem solving to change situations in ways that create new problems.

- Organizational effectiveness—as measured by the achievement of espoused purposes and norms—is an incomplete criterion for organizational learning. It is appropriate in situations where error correction can occur through single-loop learning alone. It is insufficient where inconsistencies in organizational theory-in-use set requirements for double-loop learning.

"Good dialectic" is the term we will use to describe processes of organizational inquiry which take the form of single- and double-loop learning, as appropriate, and where (as we pointed out in the previous chapter) both single- and double-loop learning meet standards of high quality inquiry.

The achievement of good dialectic requires organizational deutero-learning. That is, it requires that the organization's members reflect on and inquire into their organizational learning system and its effect on organizational inquiry.

SUMMARY

The Mercury story illustrates some of the features of organizational learning systems which inhibit organizational double-loop and deutero-learning. The very features of Mercury's behavioral world which tended in the long run to make corporate development ineffective also worked to prevent members of the organization from collaboratively inquiring into the defects of the development process. The disposition to treat interpersonal and intergroup conflict as undiscussable, the *taboo* on public analysis of corporate failures, the wish to avoid direct interpersonal confrontation—all of these factors, and others related to them, contributed both to the ineffectiveness of the corporation's formal development agency and to the members' inability to diagnose and respond to patterns of ineffective development.

When, with the consultant's help, members of the corporation were able to piece together the stories of successful and unsuccessful development, their diagnosis revealed inconsistencies in organizational theory of action which had become organizational dilemmas. Imperatives of decentralized control led each baron to focus exclusively on the production of expected earnings and to cling to his own business territory; the imperatives of corporate development required the barons to view themselves as pieces of the corporate puzzle and to give up parts of their territories in the interest of the recombination and restructuring of existing business.

This dilemma expressed itself in a three-way conflict among the barons, central management, and the New-Business Division. Within the prevailing norms of the organization's behavioral world this conflict was undiscussable. Members of the organization could not, then, publicly reflect on the conflict in order to initiate a process of organizational double-loop learning. Instead, organizational learning took the form of ecological adjustment: Each unit of the organization learned (single-loop) to survive and to protect itself within the larger organizational context.

The organization had developed a pattern of intermittent corporate development which ran counter to its espoused theory of development and had little or nothing to do with the New-Business Division. But the organization had no map of this process; in a very real sense, it knew more than it could say. Moreover, the barons' increasing wariness of central management made this informal pattern of development less likely to succeed.

Within the prevailing learning system, members of the organization could not surface the underlying dilemmas which had arisen from the organization's earlier growth, nor could they surface the incongruity between their espoused theory and their theories-in-use for development. Mercury's learning system prevented its members from engaging in good organizational dialectic.

LIMITED LEARNING SYSTEMS

In Part II, we will examine in greater detail some of the processes sketched out in the previous chapter.

We will argue that most organizations have limited learning systems which are conducive only to single-loop learning. When their central norms and assumptions do change it is through eruption consequent on ecological adjustment, and not through organizational inquiry.

When individuals act as agents of organizational learning, they detect and correct errors in organizational theory of action. In order to do so, they must operate on information which is stored in maps and images. Certain features of this information—for example, inaccessibility, vagueness, and ambiguity—are conditions for uncorrectable error.

In Chapter 3, we will explore the ways in which individual theories-in-use reinforce conditions for error and are in turn reinforced by them. These characteristic interpersonal interactions, which radiate to create secondary interactions among larger units of the organizational ecology, we will call *primary inhibiting loops.*

In Chapter 4, we will consider examples in which these primary inhibiting loops constrict the organization's capacity to reflect on and change its own learning system—that is, to engage in organizational deutero-learning.

In Chapter 5, we will construct a model of limited learning systems, Model O-I, which displays the pattern of interactive processes which have limited organizational learning as a consequence.

CHAPTER THREE

Primary loops and limited learning

Each of the four cases to be discussed in this chapter will focus on a primary inhibitory loop, that is, on a self-reinforcing cycle in which conditions for error in organizational theory of action provoke individual members to behaviors which reinforce those conditions. So long as conditions for error remain in force, individuals are unable to function effectively as agents of organizational learning.

When maps and images of organizational theory-in-use remain scattered, ambiguous, and vague, individual members are unable to connect organizational errors to inconsistencies, incongruities, or mistakes in organizational theory of action. The work of error detection and error correction remains at the level of single-loop learning and, very often, at the level of ecological adjustment. Individuals then respond to detected error by functioning as learning agents for subgroups of the organization. Each subgroup learns, at the single-loop level, to cope with the problems created for it by the rest of the organizational environment, and inadequacies in organizational theory of action are protected from inquiry.

Primary inhibitory loops are the fundamental building blocks of limited-learning systems. Their operation must be clear if we are to understand how limited-learning systems work.

In Carlos's case (Case 1), vague task specifications and ambiguous role definition create for Carlos a set of dilemmas to which he responds by attempts at private analysis and unilateral control. In

Roberto's case (Case 2), an underlying conflict of organizational purposes generates an encounter in which each party emerges convinced of the other's untrustworthiness and unwillingness to listen. In the Principal's case (Case 3), mutual protectiveness of self and other prevents the surfacing of vague and perhaps conflicting criteria for organizational performance. In the case of the line and financial managers (Case 4), each group acts so as to maintain, unexamined, their conflicting interpretations of the ineffective intergroup relations to which they contribute.

In each case, the interaction takes on the character of a win/lose game. The parties involved experience dilemmas which they treat as undiscussable, and then act unilaterally so as to perpetuate them. In each case, the inaccessibility, obscurity, or inadequacy of organizational theory of action provokes the participants to interactions which then reinforce those conditions for error.

The materials for this chapter consist of cases of intervention prepared by managers and staff members of various organizations. The method is essentially the same as the one we employed for the research reported in *Theory in Practice* (Argyris and Schon 1974), except that in this research participants were requested to report difficult interventions they had undertaken in their own organizations. In each instance, we asked the participants to recollect and write a brief case describing an intervention they had found difficult to carry out in their own organization. The definition of "difficult" was left to the participants. Cases consist of a description of the background to the situation, the actual words of dialogue spoken in the course of the intervention as remembered by the person presenting the case, and, to their right, in italics, the thoughts and feelings which the person presenting the case experienced but did not state in the course of the dialogue.

The sample from which we have drawn consists of some 50 cases prepared by managers of research institutes, government agencies, and university departments in a developing country; 10 cases prepared by principals of schools; more than 50 cases prepared by members of various departments of business firms in the United States; and a small number of cases drawn from government agencies. There are some 150 cases in all.

Once the cases were prepared, we discussed them with small groups of participants. We asked the small groups to diagnose the theories-in-use manifested by individuals in the cases, and to comment on their effectiveness. The resulting discussions were tape-recorded and, in some instances, transcribed.

CASE 1: CARLOS

A man we will call Carlos, co-manager of a technical institute in a developing country, wrote the following case.

Carlos's organization carries out a program in food technology. The Institute's objective is to create capacity for solving technological problems in the production of tropical fruits and vegetables—training technical staff, constructing pilot plants, establishing laboratories, developing regional research programs, and providing technical assistance to local industry.

The program staff is made up of a group of international experts, drawn from an international organization, and a local team of counterpart technicians. The group is divided into several sections, such as horticultural production, post-harvest storage, processing, engineering, quality control, and marketing.

For each international expert in the program, there is at least one local counterpart. Carlos is the local counterpart of the Program Manager.

In this case, a local company wants to diversify its product line, and has requested the Institute's assistance.

(Carlos and Program Manager)	(Carlos's thoughts)
Carlos: How would you handle this one?	*He never makes quick decisions or gives his own opinion.*
PM: Well, I don't know. Maybe we should assign it to *A*, because he has been visiting that plant and is familiar with the equipment.	*As I expected.*
Carlos: Yes, but I think that in spite of *A*'s great experience, the others should be given a chance to express their opinions. The problem involves knowledge which *A* may not have.	*Before deciding what to do and whom to assign to the task, I will talk with the others.*

Carlos and B

Carlos: (Handing *B* a letter)
Any suggestions about this project?

B: I heard about this request.
I was wondering if you were
once again going to make a unilateral decision.

Carlos: I think we should give
the company a feasibility proposal to study any of the 20
products they consider potentially good.

B: We have to decide once and
for all on our priorities. Requests like this will happen more
often from now on, so we
should make up our minds
about the fruit products we
should advise. All of us, in a
meeting, should resolve this. I
think we should list the products
we prefer, for reasons each section will give, and then eliminate products on the original
list.

Carlos: What would you say
to brainstorming a list of products and a list of criteria, and
then judging the products on the
basis of some grading system?

(Carlos and A)

Carlos: Would you be in favor
of going through a brainstorming session to develop a list of

(Carlos's thoughts)

*Let me see what B thinks. He
makes his position very clear.*

*I don't like what he says or the
way he says it. This is not what
I asked.*

*Yes, he is right. And I share
part of the responsibility for not
having done this already. But
only I know how much work-
load I have, and how many
problems I have already solved.*

*I am supposed to be learning
how to lead this group with the
PM, yet all the initiative is left
to me.*

This is what I'm going to do.

(Carlos's thoughts)

*I already know what he is going
to say. He is the only one who
knows the truth.*

products and criteria, then judging the products according to
some grading system?

A: I am not familiar with the   *I know he is very experienced.*
technique. But why bother if I   *But why doesn't he consider the*
already know which products to   *experience of others?*
choose? There aren't too many
options.

Carlos: Yes, I agree that you
know. But how would the
others feel about that? Besides, I
think we should give them a
chance to contribute to the project. And I believe they will help
us.

A: Do as you wish. I am
ready to cooperate at any time.

Remarks: A decision was made to hold the meeting, as I proposed.
Much work was involved in the processing of the information. Some
people did not understand, or pretended not to understand, the assumptions used. It turned out to be as predicted, with little contribution from others. I consider it to have been a waste of time.

What makes the starting situation difficult for Carlos?
There is, first of all, the question of the best way of responding to
the local company's request, a question Carlos does not know how to
answer. The Program Manager suggests assigning the task to the more
experienced *A*. *B* proposes a general staff meeting in which all members of the Institute can work out a procedure. *A* shares the PM's view
that the task should be assigned to *A*.

In addition, Carlos is troubled by his relationship to the PM. He
asks the PM for advice, even though he does not expect it to be useful.
When the advice is given, Carlos disregards it. Later he complains to
himself that although the PM is supposed to be teaching him how to
lead the group, the initiative always devolves upon Carlos. Thus elements of the Institute's theory-in-use are both vague and ambiguous.
Neither Carlos nor the PM has a clear image of the procedures and cri-

teria to be used in assigning requests for service. Members of the organization hold conflicting views about the proper mode of response. Furthermore, there is ambiguity as to the division of responsibility between the counterpart managers. Apparently, both Carlos and PM believe that the other should take the initiative.

If Carlos goes along with the PM's suggestion to assign the project to A, he risks being perceived as making yet another unilateral decision. If he does not go along with it, he risks a failure which would confirm A (and the PM) in their assumption that A alone knows what products to choose.

If Carlos leaves the initiative to the PM, then the PM (Carlos believes) will not take a firm stand and nothing will get done. If Carlos makes the decision himself, all the initiative will be left to him, and he will be left holding the bag.

This dual dilemma, created by the vagueness of procedures for assigning tasks and the ambiguity of the design for management, contributes to the initial difficulty of Carlos's situation.

Carlos responds by firmly grasping one horn of each dilemma. Given his perception of the PM's unwillingness to make a decision, Carlos takes sole responsibility for the task. Given his wish to avoid being seen as unilateral, Carlos opts for a staff meeting to brainstorm the problem. The staff meeting fails, in Carlos's view, leaving the organization with nothing more than A already knew. A is presumably confirmed in his prior estimate of his own competence. Other staff members are presumably confirmed in their own lack of confidence in their ability to handle such a task.

The next time such a problem arises, Carlos will experience the first dilemma even more severely, for now all the staff share an experience in which A "knew the answer" and the other staff members did not. And the second dilemma will be exacerbated as well, for Carlos is left more angry at the PM's unwillingness to make quick decisions or to contribute his own opinion. And Carlos is frustrated at what happens when he takes matters into his own hands.

Thus the effect of the interactions presented in the case is to perpetuate the vagueness in criteria for task assignment and the ambiguity in division of responsibility between Carlos and the PM. Moreover, these interactions exacerbate the dilemmas which made the intervention a difficult one for Carlos.

The case describes a self-reinforcing process which we will call a *primary inhibitory loop*, and diagram as shown in Fig. 3.1. Within the system described by this loop, each side reinforces the other. Had there been clear criteria for task assignment, the ambiguous division of responsibility would not have been a problem in this instance; the task could have been assigned, even though the division of responsibility remained ambiguous. Had there been an unambiguous division of responsibility, it would have been clear who was charged with specifying criteria for task assignment. Given both the vagueness and the ambiguity, however, the business of the organization could not get done. The task could not be assigned.

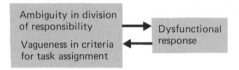

FIGURE 3.1

We look to the responses of Carlos, the PM, and the others, then, to specify the criteria or to remove the ambiguity in division of responsibility. But their responses have neither effect. And though Carlos takes the initiative, he feels he is made to do so unfairly; he continues to feel anger, which he does not voice, at the PM's refusal to take the initiative.

Carlos's dilemmas derive from both sides of Fig. 3.1. They are rooted partly in the vagueness of criteria for task assignment and the ambiguity in division of responsibility, and partly in certain assumptions which underlie Carlos's responses to vagueness and ambiguity.

Three of these assumptions are especially powerful:

1. *Either I control the process of deciding what to do, or I give up control of the process and leave it to others.* For Carlos, either he decides how to assign the task, or the PM does so. Once Carlos has determined that the PM will not decide, then Carlos must do so himself. This is a "law of excluded middle" for decision. It says that I must control the process of decision or abdicate; there can be no sharing of responsibility.

2. *People need a feeling of involvement, and in order to give it to them, you must put aside what you know.* Carlos does not want to "once again . . . make a unilateral decision," because he believes that "others should be given a chance to express their opinions," so he agrees with *B* that "all of us, in a meeting, should resolve this." But he does not bring into play his judgment about the competence of "all of us" to resolve the question or his belief in *A*'s greater experience.

3. *One must not confront others publicly with negative judgments about them, and one cannot surface the dilemmas that arise out of those negative judgments.* Carlos does not tell the PM that "he never makes quick decisions or gives his own opinion," and hence he cannot reveal to the PM the dilemma created by the PM's behavior. Carlos does not surface his anger over *B*'s attribution to him (Carlos) of unilateral decision making, nor does he confront *A* with his (Carlos's) perception that *A* values his own experience to the exclusion of others' experience.

But these assumptions appear to be shared by the PM. He also seems to believe that he must either control the decision or give it up. The PM does suggest that the project be assigned to *A*, but his, "Well, I don't know," leaves the door open to Carlos's assumption of initiative, which the PM then accepts without demurrer. The PM may wish to give Carlos a feeling of involvement, and apparently believes that he must therefore put aside what he knows.

It is quite likely, in short, that the PM is behaving toward Carlos much as Carlos is behaving toward the rest of the staff. It would not be surprising if other staff members felt toward Carlos as Carlos feels toward the PM—anger at his unwillingness to make a quick decision or express his opinion, frustration at being left to hold the bag. Carlos's comment about the brainstorming session, that "Some people did not understand, or pretended not to understand, the assumptions used," would be consistent with this surmise.

If the PM wishes to give Carlos a feeling of involvement, as he might well think his counterpart function requires; if he believes that he must then give up control of the decision and put aside what he knows; and if he believes that he cannot surface his own negative attributions to Carlos (for example, his doubts about Carlos's ability to handle the matter)—then the PM would be experiencing his own version of Carlos's dilemmas. And since both operate on the assumption that one cannot surface such dilemmas, their responses are based on private calculations. But their calculations are informed by the same assumptions: In order not to be unilateral, give up control. In order to give others a feeling of involvement, put aside what you know. Suppress your own negative judgments of others and your own negative feelings, and keep to yourself the dilemmas you seek privately to resolve. From these shared assumptions, the scenario of the case unfolds.

In a behavioral world informed by assumptions such as these, vagueness in criteria for task assignment and ambiguity in division of responsibility create dilemmas which, in turn, generate responses that perpetuate vagueness and ambiguity.

This primary inhibiting loop prevents Carlos and the PM from functioning as agents of organizational learning. The missed opportunity for organizational learning is that of restructuring, through joint inquiry, key elements of the Institute's instrumental theory-in-use, its criteria for task assignment, and its strategy for dividing management responsibility. But in order to restructure these elements, the participants would have to dispel the conditions for error, vagueness, and ambiguity which make error uncorrectable. That is, one cannot interpret and–correct an error in task assignment without specifying what the criteria for task assignment are and ought to be. One cannot interpret and correct an error in division of responsibility without clarifying what the division of responsibility is and ought to be.

The responses of Carlos and the PM are dysfunctional in the sense that they do not reduce ambiguity and vagueness but, on the contrary, perpetuate them. Moreover, it is highly unlikely that Carlos and the PM can learn from the events described in this case how not to replicate the scenario, in amplified form, the next time such an issue arises. The vagueness and ambiguity remain in force. The dilemmas remain private and undiscussable, and the assumptions underlying them remain tacit.

Conditions for error

Carlos's case helps us to understand a special kind of primary inhibiting loop; a more general understanding depends on a more comprehensive picture of both sides of the loop—that is, of conditions for error and of dysfunctional responses.

Conditions for error are those properties of organizational information which make error uncorrectable.

Organizational information is to be found in maps, formal and informal, and in the images of organization held by individual members. In organizational learning, members of the organization get information about some troubling, puzzling, or provocative feature of the organizational situation. The information may pertain to organizational environment, action, or theory of action. (Carlos's case involved information of all three kinds.) Characteristically, individuals get information about organizational error; that is, about a mismatch between actual and expected outcome of organizational action. They may also get information about an *anomaly*; that is, about an event which simply does not fit organizational theory of action and is not readily describable in the categories of prevailing maps and images.

In the first stage of an organizational learning cycle, error or anomaly is detected but undefined. Members of the organization are aware that something is troublesome but are not yet able to say what that something is. In the example of the previous chapter, members of the New-Business Division are uneasy because they have not generated the new businesses expected of them; but they are not at first able to account for this failure to meet expectations. They have detected error but have not interpreted it. Or to put the matter in somewhat different language, they have entered into a problematic situation, but have not yet set the problem.

Error or anomaly may be attributed to various features of organizational theory of action. To begin with, error may be attributed to a mistaken assumption. Suppose Carlos and the PM had organized the Institute into production, quality control, and marketing sections on the assumption that all requests for service would fall into one of these three categories. Then the request for help with new products would be anomalous in that it fell outside the organization's task system. And the design of the task system would have rested on a false assumption about the content of requests for service. Such a mistaken assumption in organizational theory of action may generate an entire class of errors.

Or the members of the organization might have attributed the error or anomaly to an incongruity between organizational espoused theory and theory-in-use. In Carlos's case, again, members of the

Institute might have found the request troublesome because espoused theory called for task assignment through staff meetings, whereas in theory-in-use such requests were funneled to persons the management thought most competent. The request would have been troublesome because it triggered awareness of this incongruity.

Or the members of the organization might have found the request troublesome because it revealed incompatible organizational norms —for example, the requirement that response to requests be quick and competent, *and* the requirement that such requests be used to extend the distribution of competence among the staff. The request would then have been troublesome because it revealed this incompatibility.

We will speak of mistaken assumptions, incongruities between espoused theory and theory-in-use, and incompatible norms as *inadequacies* in organizational theory of action. These are all conditions for error. So long as assumptions are false, expectations will be disappointed. So long as espoused theory and theory-in-use are incongrous there will be organizational actions in conformity with theory-in-use which violate expectations embedded in espoused theory. So long as norms for action are incompatible, actions which meet one set of expectations will violate another set.

When members of an organization detect a troublesome or puzzling feature of an organizational situation, they must then construct an interpretation of that feature which links it to an inadequacy in organizational theory of action; that is, to mistakes, incongruities, or incompatibilities. And they must try, subsequently, to remove that inadequacy. This pattern of inquiry, which is essential to the process we have described as good dialectic, depends on the recognition of inadequacies.

But certain features of organizational information which we group under the term "obscurity" make it difficult or impossible to recognize inadequacies.

In Carlos's case, we have already come upon two sorts of obscurity. The criteria for task assignment were so vague that they could not be applied, and the division of labor between Carlos and the PM was ambiguous in the sense that organizational images contained two different representations of this division of labor with no means for choosing between them. So long as the criteria for task assignment were vague, and the division of labor was ambiguous, it would not be possible to discover that they were mistaken.

There are other kinds of obscurity. For example, information about an organizational situation may be excessively rich. Members of the organization may find there is more information than they can handle, which is another way of saying that they lack a theory of the situation. The task of organizational inquiry would then be to get rid of excess information, to select the information which would allow interpretation of error or anomaly.

Conversely, organizational information may be too sparse. There may be too little information about the situation to allow members of the organization to link the troublesome features to inadequacies in theory of action.

Or the organizational information may be in other ways untestable. There may be propositions in espoused theory which are formulated so globally, for example, that it is impossible to apply them to a particular case.

Vagueness, ambiguity, excess, sparsity, and untestability are features of organizational information which are often associated with uncertainty. The task of organizational inquiry is then to specify vague information, to clarify ambiguity, to prune excessive information, to enrich sparse information, to make untestable propositions testable, so that error or anomaly can be linked to inadequacies in organizational theory of action. The work of organizational inquiry at this stage is to convert uncertainty to correctable error.

But from the perspective of organizational learning, the shared awareness of obscure information is already an achievement. For members of an organization cannot share awareness of obscure information until that information becomes *accessible* to them.

Inaccessibility is a property of the way members of an organization hold information, and it may take several forms. Information may be scattered. In the Mercury case, for example, each of several members of the company had a small piece of the development story. Because they had not shared and assembled their several pieces, the full story was known to no one. There was no accessible map of the story. Or, to put it differently, the organizational map was scattered among individual images. Indeed, there was a two-fold scattering: Organizational memory of the development process was scattered among individuals, and these individual recollections referred to events which, at the time of their occurrence, were also known to the organization only through the scattered images of individuals.

On the other hand, some members of the organization may possess organizational information which they withhold from others. A member of Carlos's Institute may know what factors prompted a particular request for service and may withhold that knowledge from others, perhaps because he or she is afraid to reveal it, or has repressed it, or wishes to protect or damage the organization by withholding it. Suppression by others, suppression by self, and repression, may all enter into the process by which an individual withholds his or her knowledge from the organization. Whatever the cause, he or she then knows something the organization does not know.

Finally, organizational information known to everyone may still remain inaccessible to organizational inquiry. There may be a *taboo*, an open secret, which everyone tacitly agrees to withhold from public discussion. In Carlos's Institute, the very existence of the conflict between Carlos and the PM might be treated in this way. Or the information may remain inaccessible to organizational inquiry because it includes ideas which are not among the limited set of ideas in good currency that are powerful for action in the organization. In every organization, ideas tied to theory of action occupy limited space; ideas compete, as it were, for entry into that space. If certain principles of management are in good currency—"one man, one boss" to take one instance—then competing notions may be inaccessible to organizational inquiry just because they are not in good currency.

Information must be made organizationally accessible before it can enter into the subsequent phases of organizational inquiry. Just as individual reflection depends on the surfacing of unconscious material, so organizational inquiry depends on bringing into public discussion what has been scattered, withheld, or kept powerless for action.

The several kinds of conditions for error correspond to somewhat idealized stages of organizational learning. Organizational learning is a process in which members of an organization detect error or anomaly and correct it by restructuring organizational theory of action, embedding the results of their inquiry in organizational maps and images. This process, enacted by individuals who function as learning agents for the organization, may be divided into stages which

Table 3.1

Conditions for error	Corrective responses*
Mistaken assumption	Reformulate
Incongruity	Reconcile
Incompatibility	Resolve
Vagueness	Specify
Ambiguity	Clarify
Excess/sparseness	Prune/enrich
Untestability	Make testable
Scatter	Concert
Information withheld	Surface
Information kept important for action	Bring into good currency

*Corrective responses to conditions for error may be inhibited by the behavioral world of the organization.

in Chapter 1 we named discovery, invention, production, and generalization.

At each stage, inquiry operates on organizational information. At each stage, the properties of organizational information, which we have called conditions for error, set criteria for the work of inquiry. In good organizational dialectic, members of the organization respond to conditions for error by transforming them so as to set in motion the next phase of inquiry. Thus information must be made organizationally accessible before it can be found to be obscure. Information that is vague or ambiguous must be clarified before it is possible to discover inadequacies in organizational theory of action. Inadequacies—mistaken assumptions, incongruities, incompatibilities— must be resolved in order to correct the errors they generate. Their resolution is central to the restructuring of organizational theory of action.

In an idealized organizational learning process these stages are sequential. But in reality, conditions for error and their corrective responses (shown schematically in Table 3.1) are intertwined. In Carlos's case, for example, vague criteria for task assignment go hand in hand with the inaccessibility of individual views about those criteria. Indeed, vagueness is reinforced by individual decisions to withhold private views in order to avoid the interpersonal conflict which would accompany the surfacing of incompatible criteria.

It is useful, nevertheless, to keep in mind an idealized version of the organizational learning process as a schema for the study of real-world processes which, because they are real, are also less tidy. But in doing so, it is important that we should not isolate a full cycle of organizational learning from the larger organizational dialectic in which it is embedded. In good organizational dialectic, new conditions for error typically emerge *as a result of* organizational learning. Good dialectic is not a steady state free from conditions for error, but an open-ended process in which cycles of organizational learning create new conditions for error to which members of the organization respond by transforming them so as to set in motion the next phase of inquiry.

Dysfunctional responses

In primary inhibitory loops, members of an organization respond to conditions for error in ways that reinforce conditions for error. In our analysis of Carlos's case, we pointed out that Carlos and the PM both shared, in their individual theories-in-use, assumptions that prevented them from jointly specifying the criteria for task assignment or from clarifying their own division of labor. Both acted from the following assumptions:

"Either he decides, or I decide; there can be no middle ground."

"People need a feeling of involvement, and in order to give it to them you must put aside what you know."

"One must not confront others publicly with negative judgments about them, and one cannot surface the dilemmas that arise out of those negative judgments."

These assumptions are instances of a larger model of theories-in-use, a constellation of assumptions, strategies, norms, and expectations which is by no means peculiar to Carlos and the PM.

In *Theory in Practice*, we examined many cases of individual efforts at intervention, and we found that they all conformed to this model, which we called Model I. Model I, we argued, reduces long-term effectiveness and capacity for double-loop learning. Moreover, we showed that Model I theories-in-use held by individuals both create and are reinforced by the Model I features of the behavioral worlds in which those individuals live. Here, we want to show that these same Model I features of the behavioral world produce the responses that reinforce organizational conditions for error.

In Table 3.2 we present a schema of Model I.

The first column lists governing variables of norms:

1. *Define goals and try to achieve them.* Participants rarely tried to develop with others a mutual definition of purposes; nor did they seem open to being influenced to alter their perception of the task.

2. *Maximize winning and minimize losing.* Participants felt that once they had decided on their goals, changing them would be a sign of weakness. Thus Carlos privately decided that "success," for him, would consist in unilaterally managing the task assignment. And in doing so, he engaged in a win/lose game with the PM. Within this context, we can understand Carlos's feeling that either the PM must decide what to do, or he, Carlos, would decide.

3. *Minimize generating or expressing negative feelings.* Participants almost unanimously declared that generating negative feelings showed ineptness, incompetence, or lack of diplomacy. Permitting or helping others to express their feelings tended to be seen as poor strategy. Neither Carlos nor the PM surfaced negative feelings about the other, nor did either encourage the other to express his feelings.

4. *Be rational.* This is the counterpart to (3). It is an injunction to be objective, intellectual, and to suppress feelings. Interactions should be construed as objective discussions of the issues, whatever feelings may underlie them.

The second column identifies action strategies that participants adopted to achieve governing variables.

1. *Design and manage the environment unilaterally.* Plan actions secretly, and persuade or cajole others to agree with one's definition of the situation.

2. *Own and control the task.* Carlos privately decides to resolve the task assignment through a full staff meeting, and tries to get others to see it his way. Carlos then owns and controls the meeting, and when he perceives the meeting as having failed, he also sees it as his failure.

3. *Unilaterally protect yourself.* Keep yourself from being vulnerable by speaking in abstractions, avoiding reference to directly ob-

Table 3.2
Model I Theory-in-Use

Governing variables	Action strategies	Consequences for behavioral world	Consequences for learning	Effectiveness
Define goals and try to achieve them.	Design and manage the environment unilaterally. (Be persuasive, appeal to larger goals, etc.)	Actor seen as defensive, inconsistent, incongruent, controlling, fearful of being vulnerable, withholding of feelings, overly concerned about self and others or underconcerned about others.	Self-sealing.	Decreased long-term effectiveness.
Maximize winning and minimize losing.	Own and control the task. (Claim ownership of the task, be guardian of the definition and execution of the task.)	Defensive interpersonal and group relationship (dependence on actor, little helping of others).	Single-loop learning.	

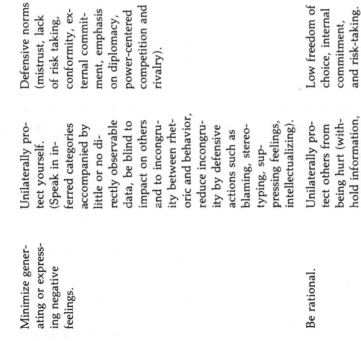

Minimize generating or expressing negative feelings.	Unilaterally protect yourself. (Speak in inferred categories accompanied by little or no directly observable data, be blind to impact on others and to incongruity between rhetoric and behavior, reduce incongruity by defensive actions such as blaming, stereotyping, suppressing feelings, intellectualizing).	Defensive norms (mistrust, lack of risk taking, conformity, external commitment, emphasis on diplomacy, power-centered competition and rivalry).	Little testing of theories publicly. Much testing of theories privately.
Be rational.	Unilaterally protect others from being hurt (withhold information, create rules to censor information and behavior, hold private meetings).	Low freedom of choice, internal commitment, and risk-taking.	

served events, and by withholding the thoughts and feelings that lead you to do what you do. In order to achieve mastery of the situation, keep your own thoughts and feelings a mystery.

4. *Unilaterally protect others from being hurt.* Withholding valuable and important information, telling white lies, suppressing feelings, and offering false sympathy are examples of this strategy. The speaker assumes that the other person needs to be protected, and that this strategy should be kept secret; neither assumption is tested. Thus Carlos protects both the PM and A from his feelings about them. In doing so, he also protects himself from their negative reactions to his feelings.

To the extent that one behaves according to any of the four action strategies, one will tend to behave unilaterally toward others and protectively toward oneself. If successful, such behavior controls others and prevents one from being influenced by them. But as a consequence, the actor tends to be seen as defensive (since he or she is defending); interpersonal and intergroup relations tend to become more defensive than facilitative, more a matter of win/lose than of collaboration. This tends to generate mistrust and rigidity.

Given these governing variables and strategies, there is likely to be little public testing of the assumptions embedded in theories-in-use. For such testing would require confronting one's own defensiveness and the defensiveness of others. Carlos could not test his assumptions about the PM, for example, without confronting his own defensiveness and without risking the PM's negative reactions to Carlos's negative feelings.

If there is little genuine public testing of one's theory-in-use, and if one must nevertheless act, then one will act on an untested theory-in-use. Since behaving according to one's theory-in-use will influence the behavioral world, self-sealing will probably occur. Thus, Carlos begins by believing that the PM will not take a firm stand and "give his own opinion." Carlos then disregards the PM's expression of opinion and goes on to decide, privately and unilaterally, what is to be done. The PM may then very well conclude that Carlos wishes to disregard the PM's opinion and to own the task himself. Carlos will then be locked into his assumption about the PM, who will continue to do what Carlos expects of him, though for reasons that Carlos is unlikely to discover.

In *Theory in Practice,* we describe the resulting situation as follows:

> . . . lack of such public testing risks creating self-sealing processes . . . the individual not only helps to create behavioral worlds that are artifacts of his theory-in-use but also cuts himself off from the possibility of disconfirming assumptions in his theory-in-use and thereby cuts himself off from the possibility of helping to create behavioral worlds that disconfirm his starting assumptions about them.

> However, public testing of theories-in-use must be accompanied by an openness to change behavior as a function of learning. The actor needs minimally distorted feedback from others. If others provide such feedback—especially if they do so with some risk—and if they experience that the actor is not open to change, they may believe that they have placed themselves in a difficult situation. Their mistrust of the actor will probably increase, but this fact will be suppressed. The result will be the creation of another series of self-sealing processes that again make the actor less likely to receive valid information the next time he tries to test an assumption publicly . . . (p. 78)

Because double-loop learning depends on the exchange of valid information and public testing, Model I tends to discourage it. And because long-term effectiveness depends on the possibility of such learning, Model I leads to long-term ineffectiveness.

This brief sketch of Model I will be illustrated and extended in the cases that follow. The elements of Model I interact in ways that are far more complex than we have so far described, and similarly there are many ways in which the behavioral world created by Model I behavior feeds back to reinforce that behavior.

Our main interest here is the function of Model I within the primary inhibiting loops. In organizational settings, conditions for error trigger Model I reactions. Vagueness and ambiguity in organizational theory-in-use yield organizational situations that individual members, programmed with Model I theories-in-use, find threatening. Uncertainty over the nature of troublesome situations, over what is to be done and by whom, or over criteria for performance, increase individual feelings of defensiveness and mistrust. Incompatibilities in organizational theory-in-use tend to be expressed in interpersonal conflicts, which individuals then live out in terms of win/lose games.

When individuals make Model I responses to conditions for error, they reinforce those conditions for error. Carlos and the PM reinforce the vagueness and ambiguity that gave rise to their inter-action. Model I interferes with the concerting of scattered information, the specifying of vague information, the resolution of incompatible norms, and, in general, with all of the remedial responses to conditions for error that are required for good organizational dialectic.

CASE 2: ROBERTO

Roberto is the director of a Centre for engineering research in a developing country. Roberto's Centre is located in a larger institution which also contains a School of Engineering. The School's director is interested in having his faculty work in the Centre, so that they may be more firmly established in their profession. He is against the Centre's entering into contracts with outside specialists in areas of his faculty's competence. On the other hand, Roberto knows, as a result of prior experience, that he cannot count on the majority of the faculty, either because they are insufficiently experienced in work on industrial problems or because they have too little time to make a real contribution to the Centre's projects. Many of the faculty lecture at several schools.

Roberto's case concerns a specific request for service. A company that manufactured bus bodies needed to make dynamic tests on a prototype in order to start a production line within 30 days. In the School of Engineering, the teacher in this field had all the necessary equipment, but he had neither the time nor the experience to work on the problem.

Roberto defined his problem, therefore, as one of persuading the Director of the School to allow Roberto to use the School's equipment even though he would be contracting with an outside specialist.

(Roberto and Director)	*(Roberto's thoughts)*
Roberto: I have a specific problem and would like to ask your help.	*I want to feel out his point of views, and gain his good will to solve the problem.*
Director: Of course, I am at your entire disposal.	

Roberto: We have a job to do for firm X, with a time limit for delivery of 25 days. It will take about 80 hours of work by a specialist, and the use of a strain gauge.

Director: Fine! We have all the equipment and also a teacher who is a specialist in the subject.

Roberto: Well, but do you believe the teacher can do the work in time?

This could be a problem, but I'll try to make the best of it.

Director: We can study the possibility that an assistant could give classes so the teacher could have the necessary time.

Roberto: But do you believe that the teacher could do this work within the deadline? What about the time he spends teaching in other schools?

I doubt that the teacher has the necessary experience.

Director: I believe so. He can arrange his time schedule so that he can do the work.

Roberto: But does he have the necessary experience to undertake such a responsible task?

I know I'm forcing the situation, but I must present my point of view.

Director: I want to inform you that this teacher has been qualified in his field for 10 years and therefore has great experience in the use of the equipment.

Roberto: I would like to know he can interpret the data properly to solve the problems.

This is very exasperating. I've got to be sure.

Director: I do not accept your
doubting the ability of my staff.
I also want to inform you that
you can use the equipment only
if you hire the teacher!

Roberto: I thank you for your *I had better not aggravate the*
attention. I am going to study *situation further.*
the matter and will speak to you
again.

What makes this situation difficult for Roberto?

To begin with, the institution has multiple objectives. The School seeks to establish and promote its teachers and the Centre tries to get research contracts which it can perform competently and quickly. These objectives might be mutually compatible, or even initially supporting, were it not for certain other features of the institution's theory-in-use. There is a strong bond connecting teachers to their equipment. It is the School's policy to allow use of the equipment only if a faculty member supervises the work. Faculty members are supposed to be full-time, and in fact spend a good deal of time lecturing at other schools. In Roberto's opinion, some teachers whose credentials indicate competence in the use of their equipment actually lack that competence. And the Centre depends upon its ability to use the School's equipment.

At the level of espoused theory, teachers are competent and full-time. In practice, teachers are often part-time and lack the competence their credentials would suggest. Given this incongruity, the "strong bond" between faculty members and equipment, and the Centre's dependence on the School's equipment, the objectives of the School and Centre become incompatible. Promotion and establishment of faculty interferes with the competent performance of research contracts, and conversely.

Roberto is aware of these features of the situation from the very outset, but his awareness does not help him, for the process of resolving conflicting objectives is itself unclear. Roberto and the Director apparently depend on one another for the means to achieve their objectives—Roberto, for the use of equipment; the Director, for the Centre's access to outside projects which could be used to build the faculty. Each can effectively either block or support the other. In order to resolve the conflicting objectives, in order to realize the potential for organizational double-loop learning which is inherent in the situation, the two men would have to engage in joint inquiry. They would have to reflect on their conflict and on its sources in the conflicting requirements of their two institutions. They would have to identify and explore those features of the organizational context which make these requirements incompatible.

But organizational theory of action does not tell the two men how to carry out such an inquiry. The program for their interaction is largely unspecified. It is left to be completed by the participants themselves through interchanges like the one just reported.

What, then, is Roberto's theory-in-use for the interaction?

First, he conceals his knowledge of the conflicting objectives and his own negative assessment of the competence and availability of the Director's faculty. Instead, he tries at the beginning to frame the interaction as a request for help—"I have a specific problem . . . ," saying to himself that he wants to "feel out (the Director's) point of view and gain his good will." Here, Roberto is being incongruent, since he already knows what he wants and that the "help" will be incompatible with the Director's policy. The Director responds in kind, "Of course, I am at your entire disposal."

Once Roberto has described the problem, the Director responds predictably by offering the faculty/equipment combination.

Roberto does not then surface his own position, but proceeds to ask a series of questions, each of which is designed to strengthen the argument for his own position. Thus, he questions first the time available to the teacher, then the teacher's ability to work to a deadline, then the teacher's experience, and finally the teacher's ability to interpret the data. At each point, the Director answers either by giving information or by stating his willingness to make new arrangements. And after each such intervention, Roberto ignores the preceding response and goes on to his next argument.

This strategy Roberto describes as designed to "feel out" the Director—a form of self-protection, since Roberto wants to learn where the Director is before he reveals his own position.

There is also unilateral protection of self and other in Roberto's withholding of his negative judgment of the teacher's competence. Presumably, he hopes that he may be able to avoid revealing this judgment, which he believes likely to make the Director angry and perhaps also to provoke retaliation.

But in the process of following this strategy of gradual revelation, Roberto succeeds in ignoring each of the Director's responses. The Director would be justified, given this data, in believing that Roberto will stick to his (hidden) view no matter what the Director says. Each of Roberto's responses simply triggers the next layer of the Director's defenses; each of the Director's responses simply triggers the next layer of Roberto's defenses. With the final revelation of what Roberto had initially sought to conceal—his judgment of the teacher as incompetent—the Director reacts with eruptive anger. Roberto can read this anger as a confirmation of his strategy, since he had taken his probing line in order to avoid this revelation. But Roberto can also be read as having produced, or at any rate amplified, the Director's angry response, by designing a series of questions each of which *looked* as though it were answerable but was actually unanswerable, since it masked a deeper and unstated concern.

In short, by being blind to the provocation inherent in his own behavior, Roberto can read the Director's final response as a confirmation of his strategy of intervention. But the Director, attentive to Roberto's behavior, can read Roberto as having led him through a series of deceptions—presenting himself as asking for help when he was not, asking questions and then ignoring the responses, holding a firm position when he appeared to be inquiring.

When the Director's anger finally erupts, Roberto retreats into a diplomatic position, reestablishing his incongruity with: "I thank you for your attention. I am going to study the matter and will speak to you again."

At the end of the case, Roberto and the Director are more firmly polarized than ever around their respective policies and goals. From the organizational point of view, the internal incompatibility of policies and goals is more firmly established. Roberto leaves more firmly convinced of the Director's defensiveness and the Director may well leave more firmly convinced of Roberto's incongruity.

In a postscript, Roberto tells us of a subsequent interaction in which a "solution" emerged. It was agreed that a new man would be hired to work on the project. He would be hired because of his competence to use the equipment, but he would report formally to the teacher and would be presented to the outside world as an assistant to the teacher.

That is, at the level of espoused policy the new man would report to the teacher, and the teacher (whom Roberto believes incompetent) would have final responsibility for the project. Informally, and at the level of theory-in-use, the new man would have responsibility for the project and the teacher would be window-dressing. The "solution" consists of creating a new incongruity between organizational espoused theory and theory-in-use. Moreover, both the teacher and the new man would be aware of this incongruity. Roberto would tell the new man of the arrangement when he hired him; otherwise, the arrangement would not be a solution from Roberto's point of view. And the teacher would discover the arrangement, if he did not know of it from the outset, as soon as he sought to act on his formal authority.

The solution is face-saving for the Director, humiliating for the teacher, and temporarily useful for Roberto. Imagine what would happen, however, if something went wrong with the project and the client complained to the person formally in charge of the project. The nominal project director would be faced with the choice of disclaiming responsibility, or of accepting responsibility for decisions he did not make. The actual project director would be similarly caught; how could he accept responsibility without revealing the hidden arrangement?

Roberto's case does illustrate a kind of single-loop learning. The two directors adopt a strategy which allows each of them to get something he wants in the short term. The strategy for the arrangement enters into the store of organizational devices for coping with conflicting requirements. But the new arrangement perpetuates a pattern of incongruity, wherein organizational arrangements are not what they seem to be, and it creates a potential for future dilemmas.

Faced with a situation created by incongruity and incompatibility in organizational theory of action, Roberto and the Director enter into a Model I interaction which yields a single-loop invention that is likely to create more such situations.

CASE 3:   THE PRINCIPAL

A woman newly promoted to the position of school Principal, wrote a case about her interaction with a male third-grade teacher who had previously taught and served as acting head master on a high school level.

The teacher is in his second year of teaching third grade. He runs what the Principal feels is a sloppy open classroom—children running about and playing in a cluttered room, some working. The Principal, in her first year, wanted to find out what the third-grade teacher was actually doing. She visited his classroom several times in a week, and she questioned whether the children are learning. She called the teacher into her office in order to inquire what his program was and to voice her concerns about the learning in his class.

(Principal and Teacher)

(Principal's thoughts)

Principal: I have enjoyed visiting your classroom the last few weeks. The kids really seem to be fond of you.

Only half true. The kids do genuinely like him, but I did not enjoy the visit.

Teacher: Yes, well come in anytime. We're always glad to see you.

Principal: I noticed it was a bit noisy—some of the kids were pretty wound up yesterday.

Teacher: Yes, well when you came in we had just broken from Reading. I give them a chance to release their energies —after all, they're young kids.

I was there nearly half an hour. They never went into anything. How much release time? Didn't say this.

Principal: Do you work in groups, or what?

Teacher: We do both; usually the kids read independently, but sometimes I read with them in groups.

Principal: Well, how do you help the child who is having difficulty in reading?

Answers are so vague. I don't feel I know anymore than when I started.

Teacher: Well, while the rest of the class is busy, I work with him on his problems.

Principal: How?

Teacher: Well, he'll read to me and I listen. I'll help him with words and we talk about it.

What books? What materials? How do you help with words? Worksheets?

Principal: How effective do you feel your reading program is?

Check out how he feels about the program.

Teacher: Oh, I'm quite satisfied. The kids seem to enjoy the books. I love reading myself.

Principal: The reason I ask is when I was up in your classroom during the Reading the other day, there were a number of kids not reading, some were playing board games on the floor, some kids were laying on the rug, I thought looking kind of bored, not doing anything.

Actually, I don't think you're providing the kids with good reading experiences.

Teacher: Really! I don't think so. I didn't see that. Maybe it was just that morning. I think it was near the end of the period. You should come up more often.

Just what I was afraid of. Thought I was good to get up as much as I did.

(*Note:* We proceeded in similar fashion through Language Arts, Math and Social Studies. Same kinds of questions, same kinds of answers. Nothing!)

Principal: Well, I feel I have a better understanding of what is going on up there. They cer-

Not at all true, but I have to say something pleasant to close.

tainly are a nice group of children.

Teacher: Thanks, yeah, they're good kids. Come up anytime, glad to see you.	*Again, I don't feel the invitation is sincere.*

Remarks: What I really wanted to do is find out what he thought he was doing; help him see the need for improvement; and explore ways of helping. He seemed to feel he was in one place, and I didn't see him as being there. Where he saw himself in the classroom was wrapped up in his whole perception of himself. I could not bring myself to confront (destroy) what I felt to be an illusion.

The Principal begins by seeing the teacher as ineffective, vulnerable, potentially dangerous to the Principal's position, and unconfrontable. The Principal seeks to discover what the teacher is really doing (i.e., to confirm her own view of it), to get the teacher to change, and in the process to maintain both the relationship and her edge in the situation.

There *may* be an inconsistency between her criteria for classroom effectiveness and his. The Principal says he "tends to run what I feel is a sloppy open classroom." She asks questions about the content of activities. How does he help the child who has difficulty with reading. How does he promote reading effectiveness? He answers in terms of "release of energy," and "enjoyment." As far as the case informs us, the School's theory of action does not specify the criteria for teacher effectiveness in the classroom. This is left to the members to complete, at the informal level. Incompatibilities in criteria for classroom effectiveness may arise in the course of gap-filling. In this interaction, however, we must guess at the existence of incompatible criteria, for they are never made explicit. Indeed, the Principal and teacher must also guess at their existence.

The Principal and teacher may also hold incompatible criteria for the Principal's proper role in relation to the teacher. In the background statement, the Principal indicates that she wants to find out what the teacher is doing in the classroom, to inquire into his program, to voice her concerns regarding learning in his class. Her questions do suggest a cross-examination. But, at the espoused level, she presents herself as a visitor who enjoys getting a better understanding of what is going on. The teacher, in turn, expresses gratification with the visit but answers the questions defensively and in a way that seems designed to cut off inquiry (" . . . after all, they're young kids"; "Oh, I'm quite satisfied . . . I love reading myself"; "Really! I don't think so. I didn't see that . . . "). It seems plausible to infer from her behavior that the Principal sees herself as a legitimate evaluator and monitor of the teacher's classroom work on the basis of *her* criteria for effectiveness, and that the teacher either believes she ought to leave him alone or believes she has a right to be there and wants to counter her implicit judgments. But at the level of espoused theory, both present compatible views of the interaction as one of enjoyable visiting and exchange of information.

Thus there is perhaps an incompatibility in the criteria for classroom effectiveness held by Principal and teacher. And there is perhaps an incompatibility in the images held by each concerning their proper division of labor and responsibility. But the answer to the first depends on the answer to the second, for there will be incompatibility in criteria for classroom effectiveness only if one person takes his or her criteria to be binding on the other. Otherwise one could imagine a school which allows each teacher to formulate and live out his or her own criterion of effectiveness.

Apparently the school's theory of action is unspecified in both respects. Its specification would occur through interactions of the sort reported in this case.

In short, our difficulty in specifying these features of the school's theory of action is also the difficulty experienced by the participants. The vagueness of criteria for classroom effectiveness and for principal/teacher interactions, corresponds to the inaccessibility of the criteria held by the two individuals.

What, then, is the Principal's theory-in-use for the interaction, and what are its effects?

The Principal seeks to inquire what the teacher's program is and voice her concerns regarding learning in his class, but she senses his vulnerability and his incongruence: "He seemed to feel he was in one place, and I didn't see him as being there. Where he saw himself in the classroom was wrapped up in his whole perception of himself." And she does not want to hurt him. "I could not bring myself to confront (destroy) what I felt to be an illusion."

Her strategy is to cover the field with a series of objective questions designed, indirectly, to reveal what is going on and what is wrong.

Both parties seem to be engaged in a game in which "winning" has two meanings. In the first sense, "winning" means, for the Principal, achieving her objective by finding out what is going on in the classroom and getting the teacher to see that there is something wrong; for the teacher, "winning" means defending his performance and neutralizing the Principal's negative evaluation. But in a second sense, each is also trying to follow certain rules: never asking one's real questions, never alluding directly to differences in criteria for classroom performance, never revealing feelings or confronting the other, and always giving lip-service to the illusion of a friendly, welcoming interaction. These rules serve to keep the interaction from penetrating to the potentially dangerous ground below the surface.

Within this game the Principal seeks to control the interaction and achieve her goals by keeping the focus on the teacher and asking leading questions under the rules. The teacher seeks to control the interaction and achieve his goals by keeping the focus on the material and on the kids, by denying what the Principal says she sees, and by tracking the Principal's questions with his answers in such a way as to obey the rules and still defend his own performance.

The competition results in a stand-off. The Principal does not get the teacher to see that there is something wrong, or to see the need for help. The teacher does not change the Principal's negative evaluation of his performance. The Principal's governing variables and strategies play into the teacher's game. Her unilateral efforts to protect the teacher (from what might "destroy" him) support his efforts to protect himself. His "diplomacy" and "tact" support her efforts to protect herself.

The Principal does ask the teacher what sort of things are done in Reading—"Do you work in groups, or what? . . . Well, how do you help the child who is having difficulty in reading?" but she never confronts him directly, reveals her underlying questions, or follows up on his answers. Hence, when she thinks, "I was there nearly half an hour. They never went into anything," she keeps that thought to herself. The objective questions are designed to uncover what is going on, but the lack of confrontation, follow-up, and revelation of her private judgments are designed to protect the teacher and maintain the relationship. Unilateral protection of other may also be combined here with unilateral protection of self. The Principal may well be assuming—as she indicated in discussion of the case—that if she withholds her real questions and feelings, the teacher will do the same, and will not respond with counterconfrontation and anger, which she may not be able to handle.

The Principal seeks to keep control of the interaction by keeping it rational and cool, through this series of objective, information-seeking questions focused on the teacher. This strategy is plausible as a means of satisfying the governing variable, "keep control," if she assumes something like, "If the interaction gets 'hot' or loses its focus on him, it may get out of control."

But the strategy proves ineffective as a means of discovering what is going on. For the teacher tracks the Principal's questions with his answers, each of which just meets the formal requirements of answer, yet without giving the Principal the information she seeks. When the Principal asks, "How effective do you feel your reading program is?" the teacher gives an answer that contains no information about the program: "Oh, I'm quite satisfied. The kids seem to enjoy the books. I love reading myself."

What is learned that may influence the pattern of future interactions?

The teacher learns that the Principal will not confront him with her negative evaluation of his performance or surface their perhaps conflicting criteria for performance. The Principal learns that the teacher is prepared to play the game and can play it to a stand-off. Each learns that the other is, and is prepared to be, incongruent. Each, therefore, learns to mistrust what the other says as a signal of what the other believes. Each learns that the other will not take responsibility for initiating a departure from the game. Neither can test with the other his or her assumptions about the other's beliefs and feelings. Each has a theory-in-use, therefore, which is self-sealing with respect to these assumptions.

And the interaction of these self-sealing theories-in-use makes it unlikely that the inaccessible, potentially incompatible criteria for classroom performance and for principal/teacher interaction will become accessible. Vagueness of these criteria in the school's theory of action, and inaccessibility of individual images of these criteria, characterize the end as well as the beginning of the case. The behavioral world created by the participants is likely to perpetuate both the vagueness and the inaccessibility, hence to impede the joint inquiry, into criteria of performance and division of responsibility, which would be necessary for organizational double-loop learning.

CASE 4: LINE AND FINANCIAL EXECUTIVES

We have drawn the last of this chapter's cases from a large American corporation. It is actually a combination of several individual cases. It illustrates the ways in which primary inhibitory loops ramify to encompass the interactions of whole departments within an organization.

Company K had reorganized itself into a holding company with numerous relatively autonomous divisions, each having a president. Corporate headquarters contained, among other members, the chief executive officer and the senior financial officer. Each subunit contained a president and a chief financial officer.

All agreed that the decentralization was a key factor in the company's ability to grow and to manage the increasing complexity of their organization. Also, they agreed that financial information systems were crucial in making decentralization possible.

When one of the authors met with the group, the new organization had been in operation for about five years. The fears on the part of the line executives regarding the "financial types" were surfaced during a meeting led by the faculty advisor. It was discussed for an hour. Everybody agreed that it was a problem, that it could get worse, and that it should be resolved. The financial people denied they were trying to get control; the line people denied that they were acting in a paranoid fashion.

As the first step to resolving the problems, each individual was asked to imagine a meeting with a financial officer (or, if a financial officer, a meeting with a line officer). The purpose of the meeting would be to resolve the issue that all had just acknowledged existed. The participants were asked to write a scenario of: (1) what each would say; (2) what each believed the other would say, and; (3) any thoughts and feelings each might have that they would not say. Sixteen line executives and eight financial executives (almost a 100-percent sample of the people at the top) generated such cases. The following two examples present viewpoints of both the factions.

A meeting designed by a line executive

(Line and financial executives)	*(Line executive's thoughts)*

L: Jones, it appears to me that your office requires reports and info on an increasing scale.

I feel Finance is making it difficult to operate the business. Not only are they asking for info they already have, they quarrel with the info when received.

F: Any figures we ask for are necessary for our reporting.

L: We are spending more and more time on these reports and usually on a rush-rush basis.

It appears they are trying to run the business center rather than let me operate as I have been.

F: Sometimes it's necessary for IRS, or governmental agency. Your accounting people know this.

L: We can live with normal input and we give you our info but you question our input more often than not.

F: Hopefully, we can work more closely and communicate better.

L: If we are going to run our business effectively, we need to know what actually happened, not only the net periodic financial consequences. We need to know which sales are reflected in the numbers, what the physical units were, which deductions and expenses have been recognized, and which specific transactions each applies to.

Why don't you give some thought to the preparation of information which will help us, rather than strictly financial data, which is often meaningless and seems to be generated only for the purpose of helping our superiors critique our performance? Why can't you work for and with us, at least part of the time, instead of for the accounting profession and for our superiors?

A meeting designed by a financial executive

(Financial and line executives)	(Financial executive's thoughts)
F: You know I am having an awful time trying to get numbers out of your department. Is there some way you can help me?	
L: Well, could you be a little more specific?	*Here comes the run-around again.*
F: I feel that perhaps we are not communicating as well as we could. I sometimes receive inputs which answer my questions, but feel as if you are holding something back. What can I say to make you understand that this is important?	*He always has something more important.*
L: I'm sorry, but it is a low priority as far as I am concerned.	*Help... I am trying to help you. It's always a low priority with him; that's why he's in trouble.*
F: Look, Smith, I am really here to help you, and this is only logical since we have these divisional companies. Each company is supposed to be more or less on its own in the decision-making process. Therefore, to round out the management team you can use a financial man loyal to you.	*I must convince him that I am not an auditor or a policeman, nor am I a spy in his organization for upper management. I must show him by actions that I am part of his team and his team only. I am here to help him to better his company. I must show him that through my experience everyone will benefit.*
L: But you are getting more information that I get.	
F: But a lot of the material I get is passed on for governmen-	

tal or stockholder purposes and has no value for our own internal purposes of managing our business. The better and more useful information stays right here and helps us, and especially you, to manage the business more effectively.

A content analysis was made of the 24 scenarios to ascertain the strategies used by the participants. Line management attempted to solve the problem by emphasizing points such as these:

1. There's not enough time to prepare the reports.
2. The number of reports required constantly increases.
3. Finance questions and mistrusts the figures we give them.
4. Finance doesn't have the people needed to handle the paperwork they create.
5. Finance is not trained, or is too busy, to provide management with the information needed.

Yet, at the same time, Line held the following thoughts and feelings but did not express them:

1. Finance is interested in empire-building and power creation.
2. Finance is insecure.
3. Finance people are mistrustful of Line.
4. Too much of the information collected is meaningless.
5. Finance information systems create climates that stifle initiative and creativity. They reduce the freedom of management to make its own judgments.

Note that the material which was not communicated represented the important factors that were causing the problem described above (which Line and Finance had agreed existed). The material that was communicated dealt with the more mechanical aspects of the problem (e.g., too many reports, not enough time to fill them out, asking unnecessary questions).

Thus we see line people programmed with Model I theories-in-use holding back the important information because it could be upsetting to the financial people. The causes of the problem, as the line people experienced them, were taboo areas of discussion. How can problems be solved genuinely if the key factors are undiscussable?

Financial managers used the following strategies to influence line executives:

1. You need loyal financial people.
2. Our task is to help you.
3. We understand that you feel accountable, but we are responsible for informing the top.
4. If you had to deal with bankers, it would be worse.
5. It is the line people who are running the company.
6. The ladder to the top is Finance.

At the same time, the financial people were having thoughts and feelings that they were *not* expressing. For example:

1. Here comes the run-around.
2. Why don't line executives say what they think?
3. We are low priority on his list and that is one reason why he is in trouble.
4. We must convince the line people that we are not policemen or spies.
5. Our job is not to make decisions, but to avoid surprises.

Again we see that the important causal factors were not surfaced by the finance people. They chose to communicate assurances that they were there to help line personnel, not to take power; they asserted that banks were worse; and they lamented the fact that the real power for promotion was held by the line people.

But how will this persuasion be heard by the line executives who believe (but do not say openly) the opposite of what the financial people say? Also, how will the financial people hear the line people accurately if they believe that line people are hiding information and giving them the run-around?

Company K's instrumental theory of action includes a financial information system which requires the regular interaction of line and financial executives. It is, and is perceived to be, essential to decentralized divisional management. But its actual implementation is perceived by line and financial executives alike as ineffective.

The sources of ineffectiveness are given conflicting interpretations by line executives and by financial managers. Each has his or her own interpretation of past problems, and each has an espoused theory for the generation and use of financial information. Moreover, these conflicting views are not peculiar to individuals; they are shared among members of the two departments. The conflicting interpretations and espoused theories enter into an intergroup conflict. The interactions between the two groups illustrate the same self-reinforcing relationship between conditions for error and dysfunctional theories-in-use that are to be found in the interactions of individual line and financial people.

The two examples given above illustrate the imagined efforts of line and financial managers to inquire into their conflicting views of the sources of their ineffective interaction. The result is a set of inhibitory loops in which acknowledged and known issues are circumvented, feelings are suppressed, and thoughts about the key causal variables are withheld. Also, there are the implicit messages that: (a) the other side never had it so good, and (b) the other side is requiring them to do things that they wish they did not have to do. For example, Finance wished it did not have to ask for or continually correct management reports. Line wished that it did not have to spend time on the reports.

The systematic distortion described above was produced under conditions where the predisposition for such distortion should be low. The line and financial people were at a seminar away from the office; the chief operating officer was absent (although he had completed a comparable scenario-case); both sides had generated and agreed on an analysis of the factors (but disagreed somewhat on the potency of the factors); and both sides agreed that the present situation was better than before. One can imagine that the defensiveness might have increased if the participants found themselves asked to hold actual problem-solving sessions on this issue with the chief executive officer in attendance, under conditions where the problem has aged and festered for several years.

The scenarios also illustrate the phenomenon of open-secret, or deception. The line people, for example, knew that they were hiding important thoughts and feelings, and given the discussion held previous to writing the scenarios, they also knew that the financial people knew that they were hiding these thoughts and feelings. The same was true for what the financial people were doing in their scenarios. Both knew they were deceiving and the game of deception was understandably suppressed. It is not being unfair to predict that the problem will not be solved effectively. Indeed, if every meeting held to discuss the problem contains dialogue as described above, it would be safe to predict that the situation will get worse. However, since deception and open secrets dominate, one can also predict that increasingly each side will doubt the openness and credibility of the other side. We would predict that as these feelings mount, the members of both sides will conclude that the problem is unsolvable except by a major crisis, or a new top management, or the loss of the chief financial officers.

We would also predict that if these individuals attempted to discuss the subject in small groups (or remain as one large group), the win/lose competitiveness, the low trust, the low risk taking, the deception, etc. would tend to lead to second-order inhibitory loops such as highly defensive group dynamics which, in turn, would lead to a low degree of cumulative progress in the discussion with an increasing degree of frustration with group meetings.

The same prediction would be made if the groups attempted to resolve the issues in an intergroup discussion. The phenomena frequently reported in the literature of groups generating high internal cohesiveness to protect themselves against the "enemy" and of developing traitor/hero phenomena would all interact to make it difficult to resolve the issues. Indeed, one may predict an increasing probability of the polarization of issues, irritation of nerves, frustration, and conflict. As the intensity of these factors increased, they would have to be dealt with by the individuals. But the reader may recall, the individuals are programmed with the theories-in-use that produce the inhibitory loops in the first place.

SUMMARY

The four cases presented in this chapter represent variations on the theme of primary inhibiting loops, in which members of an organization interact with one another according to theories-in-use which reinforce and are reinforced by conditions for error.

In the real world of organizations, individuals can act as agents of organizational learning only by operating on information which is initially inaccessible or obscure. Organizational inquiry can proceed only by concerting inaccessible information, by clarifying obscure information, and by resolving the inadequacies in organizational theory of action (the mistakes, incongruities, and inconsistencies) which clarification reveals.

But members of organizations typically live in behavioral worlds that are characterized by Model I theories-in-use. Hence individuals respond to problematic or troublesome encounters with one another in Model I ways, withholding negative information, avoiding direct confrontation, seeking unilaterally to control the situation and to protect both self and other. These Model I behaviors, triggered by underlying inadequacies in organizational theory-in-use and by organizational information that is inaccessible or obscure, reinforce the very conditions for error which give rise to them. Inaccessible information tends to remain inaccessible. Obscure information tends to remain obscure. Underlying inadequacies in organizational theory of action tend to remain unexamined, and individuals are unable to function as agents of good organizational dialectic.

CHAPTER FOUR

Primary loops that inhibit deutero-learning

INTRODUCTION

In Part I we defined deutero-learning as learning about the detection and correction of errors in first-order performance. When organizations engage in deutero-learning, they inquire into previous learning contexts and, like Gregory Bateson's porpoise, they evolve new ways of seeing that enhance their capability for learning across a range of situations. Deutero-learning is organizational when it is embedded in maps and images which guide organizational decision, control, and instruction.

Since World War II, some of the most prominent ideas in good currency in American organizations have been those like research and development, organizational innovation, planning and evaluation, and the management of change, all of which have to do with deutero-learning. Awareness of these ideas has passed beyond rhetoric. Most organizations, public and private, now have individual roles and even whole departments whose functions are intended to promote what we would call deutero-learning. Managers recognize that they must not only respond to particular changes in the corporate environment, but must also build organizational competence for responding continually to such changes, foreseeable and unforeseeable.

Their efforts have often been disappointing, however. Departments of planning often turn out to be merely decorative. Relations between research and development and line management are frequently troubled. Concerns for innovation and the management of change often receive little more than lip service. Such disappointments tend, in our opinion, to reflect models of organizational practice which ignore inhibitory features of learning systems.

A most important kind of organizational deutero-learning consists precisely of reflection on the processes by which the learning system inhibits inquiry; for example, on the ways in which the mutual defensiveness of the line and financial managers mentioned in Chapter 3 induced them to withhold the information that might have helped them to resolve their conflicts and improve their joint performance.

Good organizational dialectic depends on deutero-learning. What happens, then, when members of an organization seek to inquire into their own learning systems?

CASE 1:   THE NARROW FUNNEL

A government agency had received a substantial increase in its budget so that it might fund a new set of educational programs. A new director came on board, hired new staff, and began to generate proposals.

One year into this process, a member of the staff called one of the authors in as a consultant to discuss a proposed institute for continuing education. The consultant's meeting with staff began in the evening and continued, with interruptions, throughout the next day.

On the first evening, the consultant began by talking about the problems of organizations which try to foster learning for others. The staff quickly saw themselves in the consultant's examples, and as the evening progressed, they began to talk about their own processes over the eight-month period in which they had been attempting to create their new institute. They expressed a great deal of frustration. The consultant asked them why this was so.

One of the staff members objected to the consultant's use of the term "frustration." He said that they had funded a number of small-scale projects and had made a good beginning.

An Associate Director of the agency, the highest-ranking official present, offered the opinion that in a short time they had actually made a great deal of progress.

Consultant: I find this puzzling. Up to this point, we have all been asking why it has taken so long to establish the institute.

AD: (With great authority) We have taken so long because we want to produce a very good product, and every member of the staff has a great many other things to do besides this.

Consultant: Would you be willing to test that view against the perceptions of others in the room?

The Associate Director paused, and while he did so, others appeared hesitant to speak. Finally he smiled and said yes, he would be willing. Then various staff members offered comments:

SM1:   Perhaps we have been simply inept. We have explored proposals with five organizations and we have not followed up on any one of them. We found something wrong with each one. One was too theoretical, another too long-range, another failed because it didn't come from a local source, and another focused on target groups that were not of primary interest.

SM2:   Our difficulty has been that the responsibility for this effort has been too diffuse. We should follow here a model we followed in another area where we gave responsibility to one person. He then takes the ball, brings together a group of experts in one room, hashes out a program, and brings it back to the offices of the Agency.

Consultant: What would happen if this suggestion were followed?

SM1:   We feel comfortable going to our Review Board only if we have consensus on a program. If we followed this suggestion, we'd be right back in the glue, because we would still have the problem of building consensus.

SM3:   We have agreed, haven't we, to bring in a new man to take on this job? (Some tentative nodding of heads and an exchange of glances.)

Consultant: If I were a member of the group working on the project, I would find it very hard to know where I stood. How many people feel some responsibility for this venture? (Three or four persons raised their hands. Several others seemed undecided whether to raise their hands or not.)

SM1:   What is the purpose of this meeting?

Consultant: Well, I had no explicit contract for the process in which we are now engaged. But it seems to me that we are exploring how decisions about the new Institute are being arrived at. I think this process reveals some of the critical issues that any competent manager, who wishes to increase his organization's capacity to learn, will have to confront.

SM1:   I think we have to look at the double problem of our own management processes and the kind of management we would like to train others to carry out.

SM2:   I know how I want to begin but I'm not sure where the rest of you are.

AD: We've done a few things, but we haven't attacked the problem.

Consultant: It seems that one of the difficulties is that it is extraordinarily difficult to arrive at a commitment to a proposal.

SM1:   Yes, commitment is the central question.

Consultant: Would you be willing to give some examples about the problems of trying to generate commitment?

SM1:   No, I don't think so.

Consultant: Then we shouldn't pursue that issue here. It's very important that members of this group feel free to accept or reject further exploration.

AD: I don't see why we can't talk about this.

SM1:   I don't want to hold up the conversation.

The consultant said that it was important to preserve freedom of choice about the deeper exploration of interpersonal and organizational problems. It had by now gotten very late. The sentiment of the group was that the discussion should be continued in the morning, even though most of those attending the evening meeting had not originally planned to be present in the morning.

Following the session, several of the staff members said how helpful they had found the meeting. One said, "This ambiguity in the way things are, although it can be seen as a problem, may be very necessary. If you knew clearly where you were, you might discover that you were in trouble."

The consultant had drinks with a few members of the group, following the meeting. Then it immediately came out that "the central and overriding problem" was that all decisions for all expenditures of $25,000 or more had to be cleared with the chairman of the Review Board, Mr. Harrison. The process was for the Director to review every such proposal with Mr. Harrison, who spent most of his time in Florida and came up to the Agency only one or two days a month. Mr. Harrison and the Director were a "narrow funnel" through which all proposals had to pass.

Staff members often got no feedback about the reasons for rejection of proposals and frequently were in doubt on where such decisions stood. In a recent example, one staff member made a proposal to the Board for which he was allowed 10 minutes. The Board then discussed the matter for 20 minutes, during which the staff member was asked to step outside. He was not told what the substance of the discussion was, although his proposal was rejected. Such an instance was not atypical. Nevertheless, someone said, "We have a very good track record with the Board." All of those present felt that the processes focusing on Mr. Harrison were central to the agency's ineffectiveness, but that this problem could not possibly come to public discussion.

The following morning, most of the evening group returned and, in addition, the Agency Director put in an appearance. Several persons thought it would be productive to pursue the question, "What holds us back?" The consultant asked a staff member if he would repeat his formulation of the state of the Continuing Education Institute. The staff member then gave a concise summary of his comments of the evening before, and the Director offered the following diagnosis:

Director: We have really made a great deal of progress in a short time, but we are pressured with a great avalanche of proposals to which we must respond. The problem is how to sustain activity in the face of all of this initiative in the field. Perhaps we should allow staff members to be free of the need to respond to the proposals, or perhaps we should set aside a day or so a week free of this requirement.

Consultant: The avalanche theme had been present in last evening's discussion. But there were other themes as well.

At this point, many of those present, picking up the Director's tone, reaffirmed that much progress had been made. The Consultant asked, "Then what is the problem?" and the Director indicated that perhaps there really was no problem.

A staff member then began a long discourse, in the middle of which the Director left the meeting. The staff member said, "I've been sitting here waiting for the new man. I don't know if his coming is a fantasy or a reality. We really have no way of knowing who is going to be here next. In the midst of all this ambiguity, it is very hard to know what to do."

The Associate Director then introduced the problem of Mr. Harrison. Contrary to staff expectations, he confirmed the post-meeting description of the process that usually takes place between Mr. Harrison and the Director. It turns out, he said, that the process works not only for projects but for personnel decisions as well. He added, "Not only do we not know whether the new man will be coming, but we also don't know whether the Board will make the commitment of roughly half a million dollars which is our estimate of the money required for the program."

In the subsequent discussion of the new man, the following questions were raised:

- Who needs to know, and do they really?
- It is very difficult in meetings such as these to get sustained attention to our problems rather than our progress.
- There is a narrow and distant funnel (Mr. Harrison) through which all decisions must pass.
- We are in a vicious circle with the Board. We cannot put salable projects together unless we have a sense of their commitment, and yet we cannot get this sense of commitment without salable projects.

Some examples of agency effectiveness were offered. For instance, they had been able to put together a program for inner-city children. But they had known that inner-city children were of special interest to a very powerful member of the Board.

There was consensus that the group could pursue projects effectively where they had a strong sense of the Review Board's commitment; where they lacked that sense, they were unable to do so. One of the major difficulties was that of distinguishing the situations in which the Board was committed from those in which it was not.

One of the younger staff members said, "It is very difficult here to distinguish between a decision and a discussion. You never know. I have decided that I'm always in discussions."

Consultant: The officers of the Agency seem to be in a relation to the Board where they do not know the basis on which ideas will be accepted or rejected. They must wait, item by item, for Board decisions, before they know where they stand. The same is true of junior staff members in relation to senior ones. And the same is true of outside proposers in relation to the Agency. It is a kind of mirror effect.

AD: Are there things we can do to improve the staff's effectiveness, apart from the question of Board/staff interaction?

Consultant: I find it very hard to separate these questions.

One of the staff members present was a woman who had been with the Agency for a long time. When she told the Associate Director, "The Board/staff question is now in your hands," there was a flurry of confirming statements.

Consultant: In the context of uncertainty and ambiguity you have described, the Associate Director's role becomes a very sensitive one. Everyone looks to him as a source of feedback to the staff group about the Board's actions and attitudes.

AD: There's a staff meeting every week, but it's mostly taken up with the work we need to do in order to "prep" for the Board meetings.

Consultant: We have raised a number of important issues in the last 24 hours. I think it's very important that there be some clearly perceptible action in response to them. Otherwise, the learning is likely to be that when one talks

> openly about problems they are only vented, but not
> further explored.

AD: I hope that when you come back next, there will be
considerable progress on these matters.

After the consultant's earlier intervention ("Would you be willing
to test your view against the perceptions of others?"), staff members
and the Associate Director had begun to contribute pieces of information that combined to form a fuller picture of the organization's learning system, a picture that went well beyond the continuing-education
project.

Some of the elements of that picture were as follows:

- It is extraordinarily difficult to arrive at commitment to a project.
  The problem of obtaining commitment is the central problem of
  organizational effectiveness.

- We feel compelled to arrive at consensus before presenting a project to the Board. It would not help to assign a project to one
  man, because we would still be "back in the glue" of the consen-
  sus-building process.

- Although the staff feels the need for consensus, it is hard to get
  and keep consensus.

- One of the reasons it is hard to get and keep consensus is because
  of several kinds of ambiguity. For one thing, it is ambiguous who
  is responsible for the project. Some people see themselves as
  responsible, but others are unsure, or present themselves as being
  unsure. It is also ambiguous whether steps have been taken to respond to first-order error. Will a new man be coming in or not,
  and, if so, when will he come? And it is ambiguous whether we
  have made a decision or not and, if so, what decision we have
  made. Some members, at least, have learned to assume that we
  are always involved in discussion rather than decision.

- The staff's feeling of need to achieve consensus before going to
  the Board comes in part from their perception that Board commitment is very difficult to achieve. There is a very narrow funnel through which all projects must pass. And it is difficult or impossible to get feedback about the basis on which this funnel
  operates. The decision process appears to staff members as a
  black box. They must guess at "what will fly."

- This is in part responsible for the difficulty in achieving consensus, for staff members feel a high stake in being right about Board decisions; they want their track record to be good. Projects are "safe" if there is reason to believe ahead of time that Mr. Harrison, or other powerful members of the Board, approve of them. Hence there is a disposition to limit proposals to "safe projects." But about many kinds of projects, the staff feel there is no way of knowing ahead of time whether Board members will approve them or not. Staff members tend to be unwilling to commit themselves to projects in the absence of this knowledge. Hence, the difficulty in achieving staff consensus.

- There is a vicious circle with the Board. Staff feel that they cannot put salable projects together unless they have a sense of Board commitment, yet they cannot get this commitment without salable projects.

Some of these interactions are displayed in Fig. 4.1. Clearly, the interactions are more complex than have been indicated here, and there are factors at work other than those named. At least in two cases (Board responses to staff proposals), the relationships are highly speculative, as yet unsupported by data. Nevertheless, what begins to emerge is a map of a part of the Agency's learning system which affects first-order performance. The map may be consulted in the effort to answer questions such as: "Why is it so difficult to gain staff commitment to projects?" "Why do we not follow up on proposals?" "Why does it take so long to bring projects to fruition?"

Prior to the two-day meeting reported in this case, no one had formulated such a map; nevertheless, many individuals held the perceptions which provided the information for it. Small groups were in the habit of discussing some of these matters in private meetings. Their perceptions had never been concerted, however; that is, they had never been broadly shared and pieced together so that they could be tested ("Do you feel, as I do, an unwillingness to commit to a project before knowing what the Board will do?"). And they had never been laid out together so that their interrelationships could be explored. Knowledge of the pieces of essential information had been scattered throughout the organization. Once the pieces were brought together in a map, the Associate Director and members of the staff confirmed it.

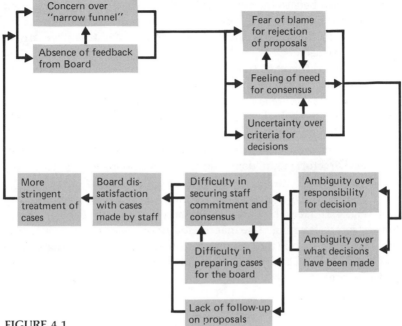

FIGURE 4.1

What had prevented members of the organization from constructing such a map of the learning system prior to the consultant's
intervention?

Central issues, such as the narrow funnel, remained inaccessible
to public inquiry because they were held to be undiscussable, and the
shared behavioral world supported their undiscussability. The Director and Associate Director (at first) conformed to a norm of denying
the problems revealed by the map, and other staff members kept to a
norm of accepting such denials.

Other parts of the learning system depicted in the map also
worked against the construction of the map. For example, staff meetings were not used to explore problems in performance because "We
were too concerned with the need to 'prep' for the next Board
meeting." In the face of continuing ambiguity over whether and what
decisions had been made, individuals privately decided that "We are
always involved in discussion, never in decision." If this position were
extended to the consideration of the learning system itself, it would

lead staff members to the conclusion that there is no use talking about these things, since they will never be able to come to a decision about them. And in the light of the pervasive knowledge that "We are all keeping open secrets," and "We are all incongruent," individuals may have found it difficult to trust one another sufficiently to initiate public discussion of problems in the learning system.

The whole picture is one that would tend to make members of the organization, those high in authority as well as those in subordinate roles, feel that the system is fragile and brittle and cannot stand much scrutiny. This would help to make it understandable, for example, that the Director might deny the problem and promptly leave the meeting.

What we have described is familiar. It is a primary inhibitory loop (Fig. 4.2). Here, however, the primary loop inhibits the organization's deutero-learning. The inaccessibility of open secrets assures the organization's inability to inquire into features of its learning system which are, in turn, sources of continuing ineffectiveness in first-order performance.

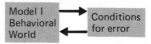

FIGURE 4.2

From the point of view of those features of the organization's learning system which prevent the detection and correction of first-order errors, the loops that inhibit deutero-learning make the organization's learning system into a disease that prevents its own cure.

The very features of the learning system which create conditions for first-order error also undermine the organization's capacity to detect and inquire into the learning system. Deutero-learning is the one route to a restructuring of the learning system. But the learning system prevents deutero-learning.

CASE 2: DILEMMAS OF REDESIGN

This case is drawn from the involvement of one of the authors in a two-year study of a State system of higher education.

When legislation was drawn up in the middle 1960s establishing a new structure of governance for public higher education, the Board of Higher Education was created. Some of its functions were clearly set forth, but in one crucial respect its functions were left ambiguous. Was the Board to govern the weak confederacy of public institutions only, or was it to represent the State as a whole with respect to all sectors of higher education?

At that time, when both sectors were growing rapidly, this ambiguity received little attention. The Board was entirely taken up with public-sector questions, and the private institutions had little occasion to think in terms of State support. In the early 70's, however, both sectors began to feel budgetary pressure. When the pressure increased—as a result of inflationary costs, shrinking endowments, and declining rates of growth in enrollment—people began to speak of a "crisis" in higher education. It was this crisis that led some people associated with higher education to the view that representatives of public and private education must begin together to confront issues facing the entire system. And it was this crisis which led the Chairman and Chancellor to make a bid for system-wide leadership.

Each of them had only recently attained his position with the Board. The Chairman had just been appointed by the Governor. He was a businessman eager to bring a manager's skills to the business of higher education. The Chancellor was a planner, for some time in a subordinate role with the Board, who had just been promoted. The two quickly made common cause. What was needed, they argued, was a new mechanism through which public and private institutions of higher education in the State could meet together to work out their differences, discover their shared interests, and shape mutually beneficial policy proposals. If public and private sectors were to begin to work as a single pluralistic system, there would have to be an organizational mechanism for doing so. They set about the creation of a public/private Forum for Higher Education.

The Chairman and Chancellor had worked out a theory of the redesign they wished to achieve. They knew, to begin with, that a pattern of public/private cooperation could not be established in one fell swoop. There were too many sources of mutual hostility and misunderstanding. For example, presidents of private colleges complained that the "publics" were "down the street giving away what we're trying to sell." They tended to see the publics as pale, low-cost imitations of themselves. On the other hand, the presidents of the public institutions tended to see the "privates" as "fat." Why should the private institutions receive State support unless they were willing to trim their costs? Moreover, they argued that it had been the public institutions, not the private ones, that had responded to the needs of the State's poor and minority students. The private institutions had not come forward when they were needed; they were late-comers to the bandwagon, driven only by their own financial needs.

The Chairman and Chancellor believed these obstacles to cooperation could be overcome if only the representatives of public and private institutions could be induced to sit down and talk together. Then they might find a policy issue on which the various institutions could work cooperatively. As they established a pattern of working together, the systems connections could gradually be solidified. In the meanwhile, their increasing familiarity with one another, their fear of the changing climate which affected them all, and their anxiety over unknown alternatives to the Forum would hold them together.

Redesign of the public/private system depended on the creation of a temporary system. The Forum was to be a vehicle for inquiry into the problems of higher education in the State and for the design of new policies and structures. Its status, at the outset, was to be informal. There was no legislative basis for the creation of a new system-wide agency. The existing Board of Higher Education, with its ambiguous scope, was an impediment to the creation of any new formal institution.

At the initiative of the Chairman and Chancellor, some 20 heads of public and private institutions began to meet together. Early meetings were uncomfortable and confusing; many policy questions arose, and they all seemed to be interconnected. There were, for example, the questions of tuition levels, educational costs, state scholarship policies, differentiation of educational programs, and transfers of students. Norms of gentility and politeness barely concealed the feelings of distrust and hostility which some of the presidents felt toward one another.

Gradually, however, attention began to focus on the issues uppermost in the minds of all: the financial squeeze being experienced in different ways by each institution, declining rates of growth in enrollment and support, and a climate of opinion that seemed to be increasingly skeptical of the claims of higher education.

The Chairman and the Chancellor argued that the Forum's effectiveness would depend on the ability of the various institutional representatives to inquire effectively together. Each had more to gain by joining with the others than by going his separate way. Each brought to the discussions assumptions about the others which had to be confronted and tested publicly. The members had no difficulty in giving allegiance to the Chairman's call for openness, trust, and concerted inquiry.

The Chairman and Chancellor devised a policy proposal designed to respond to the interests and fears of both sectors and to strike a balance of conflicting requirements. It was in essence a plan for funneling State funds to private as well as to public institutions. Moneys would flow with students, who could use them in either sector. Private institutions could participate if they would establish quotas for low-income students. The program would be used to induce the Governor and the legislature to increase the total resource available to higher education in the State.

Over a period of months, public and private representatives agreed to the plan, providing certain conditions were met. The publics insisted on a uniform system of cost accounting under which all institutions would open their books to one another. This was to make sure that the "fat" private institutions did not maintain their fat at public expenses. The private representatives insisted that the publics institute a freeze on new capital budgeting. This was to assure that public institutions did not continue their incursions into private sector enrollment while negotiations were under way.

Each side agreed to these conditions, but certain difficulties began to appear. The opening of the account books was acceptable in theory, but in practice each side found it troublesome. The public presidents argued that because the private institutions did not know their costs, the books would not tell the full story. The private presidents argued that the publics understated their estimates of cost-per-student. Neither side was prepared to open its books unless these issues were first resolved, and there was no obvious way to resolve them without first inspecting the books.

The President of the State University submitted his budget request for the year. That request, it turned out, contained several large items for new capital facilities. The heads of the private institutions were shocked. Their representatives declared that they felt betrayed. The State University President pointed out, however, that these new requests had been in the pipeline for many months. He had not intended to include *them* in his agreement to the freeze. Nevertheless, the private presidents resented his unilateral behavior. In private caucus, they decided to oppose his request to the legislature.

In retaliation, the State University President held a press conference. He defended his budget request and reiterated his old criticisms of the private institutions.

At a subsequent meeting of the Forum, both parties made formal statements. Each argued that he had been illegitimately constrained and then betrayed by the other. Each called for trust, open deliberation, and the honoring of public commitments. Each asserted that the Forum could not work unless these conditions were met.

The Chairman and Chancellor of the Board of Higher Education, recognizing that their enterprise was now in jeopardy, sought to heal the wounds by holding a series of private meetings. The President of the State University and the chief representative of the private group were convened. They were friends and could talk easily together. They agreed on a strategy for recementing the Forum.

At the next meeting of the Forum, they read a joint statement of cooperative intent. Nevertheless, several of the private presidents who had not been a party to the earlier meeting demanded that a new condition be met. The public institutions must agree to seek no new capital appropriations, and they must support a constitutional amendment which would allow the State to support private institutions directly. Otherwise, the private representatives would leave the Forum.

Some of the public representatives, who were in any case skeptical of the new proposals, now expressed more rigorously their doubts about the new policies. Their earlier statements, they said, had reflected only their willingness to explore new ideas. Their actual commitment would depend on what the private institutions actually did.

The Chairman and Chancellor attempted to mollify both sides. They played for time while they sought, through private discussions, to work out the conditions for continued cooperation. In the meantime, however, the Forum was gaining in visibility. Its policy proposals were receiving wide discussion. There was coverage in the press. At this point, the ambiguous status of the Board of Higher Education began to surface as a problem.

Members of the Board wondered why the Board itself should not be carrying out the Forum's function. Privately, they said they felt the Chairman had kept them in the dark, that he and the Chancellor had been high-handed. They were not pacified by the Chairman and Chancellor's assurances that the Board had been kept informed of the Forum's progress. Members of the Board felt their functions were being usurped by the Forum. The issue came to a head over the Chairman's effort to get the Board to provide funding for the Forum.

The Chairman called a meeting of the Board so as to give them a history of the Forum. He felt that an "objective presentation would be helpful." After the presentation, however, the following discussion ensued:

Mr. T: If the Forum wants money from us, they should be accountable to us. The Chairman of the Board also serves as Chairman of the Forum. Why shouldn't the Forum be reconstituted as an advisory committee to the Board?

Mrs. A: The Forum has managed to continue as an amorphous mass, with no linkage to any other institution. How have they been able to sustain this condition?

Mr. T: Why has the Forum not taken seriously the structuring of its relations with the Board?

Mrs. B: I am not uncomfortable, as I used to be, over the Forum's informal status. It needs that informality in order to permit free discussion. But I can understand how others might be uneasy over their lack of structured relations to the Board.

Mrs. C: The Forum wanted to move too quickly toward implementation. They should have stuck to their discussion function.

The Chairman explained that private members of the Forum felt uncomfortable with the Board, which they saw as a dominantly public institution. He went on to say, "You can't mandate compliance in the public sector. People have to understand and come aboard." But several of the Board members were unwilling to come aboard. They felt resentful of the Chairman's actions and fearful of the Forum. Now they saw that they had regained some control of the Forum through the request for funds, and they were unwilling to let go of that control.

Subsequently, the Chairman's "highhandedness" in the matter of the Forum became one of the issues used by his opponents on the

Board to depose him. With the Chairman gone, the Chancellor felt powerless to continue his efforts on behalf of the Forum. In any case, the Board saw him as the old chairman's boy and was reluctant to see him continue in office.

The Forum, however, did not at once dissolve. Neither did it prove itself effective in working toward a new public/private system of higher education. Public and private representatives had, indeed, become familiar with one another and were used to meeting together. Although they were unable to agree on new policy positions, they were also unwilling to disband.

The Chairman and Chancellor had wanted to create a new vehicle through which representatives of public and private sectors of higher education could inquire into their shared crisis. Their starting points were these assumptions:

- Higher education in the State was in trouble, and the trouble was of a sort that required closer and continuing cooperation between public and private sectors. The diagnosis was that educational institutions could best respond to the crisis in higher education by learning to function as a unified, albeit "pluralistic," system. The present nonsystem of higher education would have to take on some of the properties of an organization.

- There was a need for the creation of a mechanism for inquiring into the problems of public/private interaction in higher education. The existing Board could not do this, because of its ambiguous scope, and because it was seen by private institutions as a vehicle for public education. But the existence of the Board precluded the creation of a new formal structure. Hence, the new mechanism would have to have informal status.

In our language, the Chairman and Chancellor wanted to launch a process of deutero-learning. They wanted the members of a system, which did not yet quite see itself as a system, to begin to reflect on their own interactions. They attempted to create a temporary system within which this inquiry could take place.

As they sought to act on these assumptions, the Chairman and Chancellor found themselves caught in a set of interconnected difficulties which gradually revealed themselves as dilemmas.

The Chairman and Chancellor recognized that the Forum's effectiveness depended on the creation of a climate of mutual openness and trust. Public and private representatives could discover their mutual interests if they inquired jointly into the problems each experienced separately, and that inquiry could take place only if the two sides suspended their mutual distrust sufficiently to let it happen. The members of the Forum shared this recognition, at the level of espoused theory. But they could not behave in accordance with their espoused theory.

There was, after all, a risk in providing valid information about one's costs. There was a risk in surfacing one's full intentions for strategies of growth and survival. There was a risk in suspending one's private plans while joint inquiry proceeded. How could one take such risks before the other had demonstrated good faith? But the other, operating on the same theory-in-use, held the same cautious position. Each side wanted the common venture to succeed, provided it did not have to take risks in order to make it succeed. But what each party perceived as an intolerable risk, the other perceived as a necessary condition for commitment to the joint inquiry. Hence the members of the Forum drove themselves round in a vicious circle of distrust which prevented them from undertaking the joint inquiry which held the promise of revealing the shared interests and policies which might have brought them together.

The Chairman and Chancellor had a theory of action for responding to this impasse. On the one hand, it consisted of exhortations toward trust, openness, and cooperation; on the other hand, it consisted of resort to private meetings and agreements. But exhortations were ineffective. It was not the espoused theory of mutual trust which was troublesome to the participants, but rather the perceived risks involved in carrying it out. The participants could and did accept the espoused theory, but they continued to violate it whenever they perceived congruent behavior as risky. Private meetings were also ineffective. In the context of the impasse, private meetings and agreements were themselves a source of suspicion.

Within the group, the norms for behavior were toward politeness, humor, generality in discussion, and avoidance of conflict. Only when crises arose, such as were generated by feelings of betrayal, was there expression of negative feeling. Then anger was eruptive and discussion was in the form of parallel proclamation. The pattern was one of oscillation between pleasant, diplomatic discussion and open, eruptive conflict. Neither state was conducive to the establishment of mutual trust.

The issue of trust also entered into the Chairman's relation to his Board.

The Chairman and Chancellor had wanted to create a new vehicle through which representatives of public and private sectors could inquire into their shared crisis. They believed the Board had come to be seen as ineffective, weak, captured by the public institutions and mistrusted by the private ones. But the move to create a new vehicle triggered the fears of some members of the Board, for they could see the Board as mandated under its legislative authority to carry out such functions.

Moreover, the Chairman had found that the Forum's effectiveness would depend on its credibility as a vehicle for action. It had to be shown, he thought, that representatives of public and private sectors could, through this new vehicle, *do* something. But as the Forum moved away from the "discussion function" and toward "implementation," it became more threatening to the Board. The more visible and apparently effective the Forum, the more it came to be seen by Board members as an intrusion into their territory. And the "informality" necessary to "free discussion," which the Chairman and Chancellor had sought to assure, appeared to some Board members as an "amorphous mass" through which the Forum sought to escape legitimate accountability.

The Chairman had tried to maneuver in the space between his ineffective Board and the initially unwilling public and private participants in the Forum. Now he found himself confronted with serious dilemmas. The more he worked toward goals—such as informality and credibility—which he thought would make the Forum effective, the more he seemed to be infringing on the authority and territory of the Board, on which the Forum would be dependent for funds. And, in the process, the Chairman himself came to be seen by his Board as unilateral and high-handed, undermining his effectiveness with them.

These dilemmas arose in the very process of attempting to create a new vehicle for inquiry into the first-order problems of the higher education system. The new vehicle was to have been a first step toward solving those problems. But the design for inquiry turned out to be embedded in a learning system which undermined it.

The story of this process reveals a complex of primary loops that inhibit deutero-learning. To begin with, we will display the loop specifically related to institutional structure (Fig. 4.3).

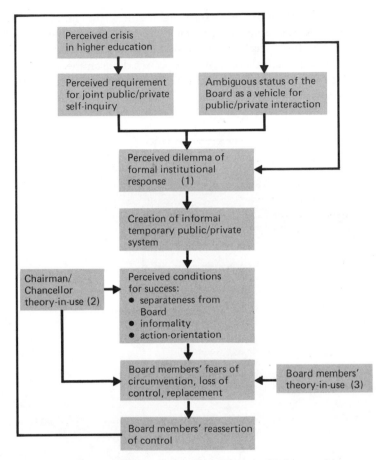

(1) Board seen as ineffective, distrusted by private institutions, unable
     to function as vehicle for public/private inquiry. Formal
     alternative institution seen as threatening to Board members, in
     violation of Board's ambiguous charter, uninteresting to Chairman
     and Chancellor of *this* Board; also, as unacceptable to public and
     private participants.

(2) Make private plans. Seek to "bring others aboard" once plans have
     been made. Control the task. Do not invite confrontation.

(3) Seek to control the task. Try to win. Form private attributions
     about others; do not make them testable.

FIGURE 4.3

The creation of a new, informal vehicle for inquiry was a response to the dilemmas of a formal solution to the problem, dilemmas which had their origins in the ambiguous status of the Board. The effect of the responses and counter-responses diagrammed in Fig. 4.3, given the behavioral world of the participants, was to sustain both the Board's ambiguous status and the dilemmas inherent in a formal institutional solution.

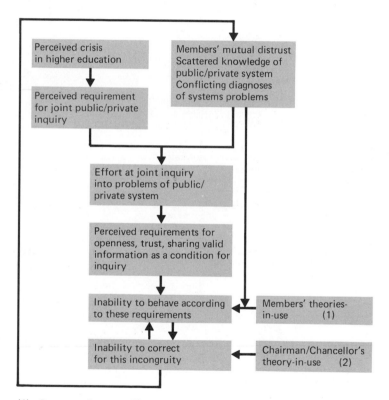

(1)   Do not make yourself vulnerable by initiating risk-taking. Demand of others risk-taking of the sort that you will not engage in. Do not observe this inconsistency.

(2)   Exhort others to be open, trusting, and to share valid information. Resort to private meetings and agreements. Control the task: make private decisions about the dilemmas in which you are caught.

FIGURE 4.4

There is also a loop peculiar to the operation of the Forum (Fig. 4.4). The effect of this loop is to reinforce the scattered knowledge of the system's problems and the conflicting diagnoses of them which first triggered the effort at joint inquiry.

The two loops interact in several ways. There is a significant overlap in the theories-in-use which characterize the behavioral world in both cases. Some of the responses in the second loop (Fig. 4.4) —notably, the effort to engage in action in order to build credibility and to hold private meetings in order to keep the Forum going—contribute to the first loop (Fig. 4.3).

Together, the two loops sustain both the institutional, intergroup, and interpersonal conditions for ineffective inquiry into the system. They sustain, as well, the scattered map of the system and the inconsistent diagnoses of its problems.

SUMMARY

In both cases, members sense the ineffective performance of their own organization. In the first case, they are aware of unexpected delays and of an inability to carry out intentions. In the second, they sense that symptoms such as declining enrollment and financial squeeze indicate fundamental mistakes in organizational theory of action. In both cases, members are aware of their inability to correct organizational error. Hence, they seek to inquire into their own organizational performance. But they find themselves prevented from doing so by the very same features of their learning systems that caused their organizations to be ineffective in the first place.

In the case of the new government Agency, members are able with a consultant's help to generate a map of the learning system which accounts for their first-order errors. But, left to their own devices, they could not generate such a map. Their mutual protectiveness, their unwillingness to discuss issues that may trigger conflicts, their keeping of open secrets, prevent them from concerting the data which each one holds about the learning system that all find ineffective.

In the case of higher education, the Chairman and Chancellor attempt to create a temporary system for inquiry into the interaction of institutions of higher education. But the Model I behavioral world of the system prevents them from surfacing and sharing the information on which such inquiry would depend. And the very effort to do so triggers reactions which paralyze the effort.

In the first case, attempts at deutero-learning are foiled by the inhibitory loops which might have been eliminated by that learning. In the second, efforts at organizational dialetic lead to an awareness of need for organizational self-inquiry which, when it is attempted, the organization's learning system undermines. The organizations remain limited-learning systems.

CHAPTER FIVE

A model of limited-learning systems

INTRODUCTION

We can now present a model of organizations whose learning systems are conducive to limited learning—a model of organizations which are unlikely either to correct first-order error by double-loop learning or to inquire into their own learning systems.

The model set out in Fig. 5.1 is a systems model which incorporates, in summary fashion, the information presented in the last two chapters. Beginning with primary inhibitory loops, the model traces their rings of consequences.

Primary inhibiting loops lead to secondary inhibiting loops—that is, to group and intergroup dynamics which reinforce conditions for error. Within such processes, some kinds of error remain correctable, while others do not.

Correctable errors enter into a learning cycle which eventuates in action which, in turn, yields new error or appropriate response (a match of outcome to expectation).

Uncorrectable error tends to be camouflaged (that is, to be hidden, denied, or disguised). The camouflage of uncorrectable error leads to new primary loops which make organizational double-loop and deutero-learning unlikely and, for individuals, make double binds likely.

Figure 5.2 (pages 112, 113) displays a more complex version of this model. Reverse arrows along the bottom of the figure indicate feedback loops that close the system. The order of columns, from left

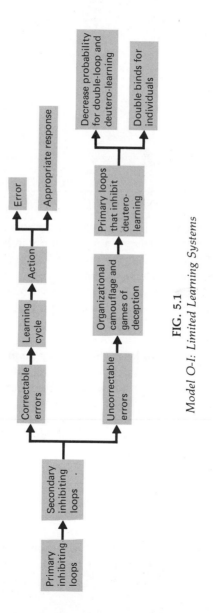

FIG. 5.1
Model O-I: Limited Learning Systems

to right, and the numbered arrows in the reverse direction, show the interaction effects which seem to us to be most important. Complex as it is, the model is still oversimplified in a number of ways. For example, arrows along the top might also have been numbered; secondary loops, to take one instance, lead not only to correctable and uncorrectable errors (Col. 7) but also to camouflage of error (Col. 8). Each column has its effect not only on the one immediately following but on others further down the line. However, we have tried to arrange the columns so that left-to-right order is a pretty good representation of direct effects.

The model does not describe the etiology of limited-learning systems. Its meaning is *not*, for example, that primary inhibitory loops came first in the evolution of organizations and that they led later on to dysfunctional group and intergroup dynamics, which still later led to deutero-learning loops. We think it more likely that a limited-learning organization, at any period of its evolution, displays at least embryonically the full configuration of the system.

What the model does reveal is the set of direct and indirect effects and feedback loops which interconnect with the principal elements of a limited learning system. Given any column, such as Col. 8 (camouflage), one can look to the left to find its immediate and less immediate conditions, and to the right to find its immediate and less immediate consequences.

We have begun with primary inhibitory loops because they seem to us the best starting point in order to explain a limited-learning system. In addition, as we will argue in Part III, they seem to us the best starting point for intervention. They are "primary" not in the sense of temporal order, but in the sense of their primary importance among the processes which make up the system.

The model, then, has the principal function of guiding the mapping and diagnosis of limited-learning systems. Because such mapping is essential to effective intervention, as we understand it, the model will reappear in that context, as well.

We will proceed through the model, from left to right, taking up each column and its interactions with others.

COLUMN 4: PRIMARY INHIBITORY LOOPS

These are the loops described in Chapter 3, and illustrated in the cases of Carlos, Roberto, the Principal, and the Finance/Line officers.

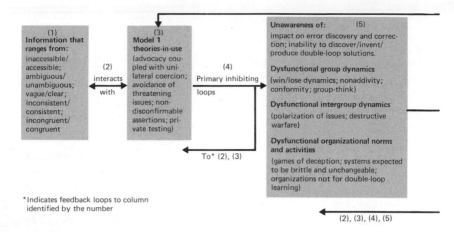

FIG. 5.2
Model O-I: Limited Learning Systems

Elements of an organization's instrumental theory of action are inaccessible, unclear, or inadequate. One or more of these features of organizational theory of action gives rise to error (Col. 1). In a good dialectic, such conditions of error would be confronted and reduced through organizational inquiry. In a Model I behavioral world, however, such conditions trigger Model I interactions (Col. 3) which reinforce those conditions for error, or create new ones.*

In the case of the government agency, for example, ambiguity over decisions which may or may not have been made induces some staff members to decide privately that "I am always involved in a discussion, never a decision," which further contributes to the ambiguity over decisions.

Within such loops, conditions for error become uncorrectable and trigger the very responses which make them so.

COLUMN 5: UNAWARENESS; DYSFUNCTIONAL DYNAMICS

Primary inhibitory loops reinforce unawareness of their effects on organizational learning.

Carlos, for example, is aware that he has failed to find a good solution to the problem of project assignment. He is unaware, how-

---

* "Model I" refers to *personal* theories of action and to a behavioral world made up of interpersonal interactions. "Model O-I" refers to an organizational learning system.

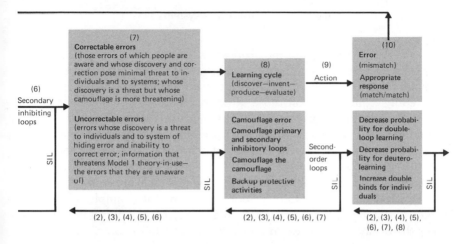

(6) Secondary inhibiting loops	(7) Correctable errors (those errors of which people are aware and whose discovery and correction pose minimal threat to individuals and to systems; whose discovery is a threat but whose camouflage is more threatening)	(8) Learning cycle (discover—invent—produce—evaluate)	(9) Action	(10) Error (mismatch) Appropriate response (match/match)
	Uncorrectable errors (errors whose discovery is a threat to individuals and to system of hiding error and inability to correct error; information that threatens Model 1 theory-in-use—the errors that they are unaware of)	Camouflage error Camouflage primary and secondary inhibitory loops Camouflage the camouflage Backup protective activities	Second-order loops	Decrease probability for double-loop learning Decrease probability for deutero-learning Increase double binds for individuals
	(2), (3), (4), (5), (6)	(2), (3), (4), (5), (6), (7)		(2), (3), (4), (5), (6), (7), (8)

ever, how he has contributed to interactions which perpetuate the vagueness of criteria for project assignment, thereby increasing the likelihood of continued failure. Nor is he aware of his inability to design and contribute to interactions which would surface and confront both conditions for error (such as vagueness) and the Model I behaviors (including his own) which reinforce those conditions.

Given such awareness, Carlos would be more likely to seek to reduce his own contribution to the primary loops. Without such awareness, he is unlikely to do so. Hence his unawareness helps to preserve the primary loops. But the primary loops tend to reinforce his unawareness. Within the loop described in his case, for example, Carlos blames his failure on the Program Manager or on the unreasonable behavior of staff members. He sees the ambiguity of role definition, in which he and the Program Manager are both embroiled, as the latter's failure to take a firm stand. Such perceptions, sustained by the primary loop, are incompatible with awareness of the loop itself, Carlos's contribution to the loop, or the conditions for error reinforced by the loop.

Primary inhibitory loops yield intra- and intergroup dynamics which mirror and amplify the properties of primary loops. These secondary loops feed back, in turn, to sustain primary loops.

In the case of the government agency, a particular interaction between a staff member and members of the Board (Board refusal to allow a staff member to participate in discussion of the staff member's proposal, Board rejection of the proposal without feedback, the staff member's reluctance to confront Board behavior) leads staff members to make attributions about the Board ("they behave arbitrarily and unilaterally") and to act on those attributions in ways that prevent their further testing. Thus, staff members conclude: "We must second-guess the Board, we must submit safe proposals, we must establish consensus before we go to the Board, we must 'prep' so as to be well buttoned up." It becomes appropriate, then, to say that whole departments of an organization (Staff and Board, in this case) are engaged in an amplified primary inhibitory loop in which, for example, each makes untestable attributions about the other, each induces in the other the behavior most feared and disliked, and both contribute to the conditions of error (vague project criteria, ambiguity over decisions) which trigger such interactions.

Within such an intergroup context, small-scale interactions are still more likely to take on the properties of primary loops.

Sustained primary loops lead to the expectation that organizations are brittle and unchangeable. Where members learn to despair of double-loop learning, the stage is set for games of deception.

These are conditions for intergroup interactions of the sort described in the case of higher education. The presidents of public and private universities, having presented themselves to the public as engaged in an effort at cooperation, find themselves unable to cooperate. Their response is to engage in debate with one another, in private complaints, and (in this case) in leaks to the press, where each party accuses the other of betrayal and seeks to impose on the other the burden for failure of cooperation. The process takes on the character of a game in which winning consists of minimizing one's own risk, forcing the other to take risks, avoiding one's own responsibility for failure, and putting blame for failure on the other.

In Roberto's case, the conditions were created for another such game of deception. Roberto informs us that he and the Director eventually worked out a solution in which a new man would be hired, nominally reporting to the professor, but in fact taking sole responsibility for the use of the equipment. A necessary condition of the arrangement is that all parties agree to deny the arrangement. Now, if a client were to complain about performance on a project, the conditions would be set for the new man and the professor each to avoid for himself and relegate to the other the responsibility for poor performance, all the while refraining from public acknowledgment of the actual working relationships.

Games of deception, of gaining credit and avoiding blame, have a tendency to occupy the foreground of organizational attention. They loom large in each individual's universe of concerns, distracting him or her from awareness of the uncorrectable errors and the related processes which underlie it.

Moreover, such games create an impression of organizational fragility and rigidity. Polarization of groups and persons allows each person and group to feel that it is blocked by others. Each member of the organization, aware of the layers of potential vulnerability shared with others and of the games designed to protect against that vulnerability, experiences the organization as brittle. A false move, an unwitting disclosure, a direct confrontation, and the house of cards might come tumbling down. It is inherent in such judgments that they are unlikely to be put to the test.

COLUMN 7: CORRECTABLE AND UNCORRECTABLE ERRORS

None of the processes so far described prevents members of an organization from detecting and correcting errors in first-order performance, so long as the detection and correction do not require that the conditions for error be confronted in ways that threaten Model I governing variables.

Thus members of the Mercury Corporation, as described in Part I, could detect and respond to routine errors in production of quality control. It is also entirely plausible that the Principal and the third-grade teacher could jointly detect and correct errors in the assignment of students to classrooms.

But Carlos and the PM could not correct errors in task-assignment. Members of the Agency could not correct for delays in proposal development. The Chairman and Chancellor of the Board of Higher Education could not remedy the failures of public/private cooperation.

Given the primary and secondary loops characteristic of these living systems, such errors become uncorrectable. Given the frame of conditions for error and Model I theories-in-use, efforts at error-correction tend, in fact, to amplify errors. In the government Agency, the act of "putting one man in charge of a project" would simply "put us right back in the glue." The Chairman and Chancellor's resort to private meetings simply exacerbated the Forum's climate of distrust.

The constraints imposed on organizational learning by limited-learning systems depend on the scope of uncorrectable error. We have argued that errors tend to be uncorrectable when their correction would entail double-loop learning for the organization; that is, when norms central to organizational theory-in-use would have to be questioned and changed. We have also argued that errors tend to be uncorrectable when their correction would threaten Model I governing variables; that is, when it would require double-loop learning at the level of the behavioral world. Within the range defined by these criteria, however, there is room for great variation. And organizations vary greatly along these lines, as we will see in the chapters that follow.

COLUMN 8: CAMOUFLAGE

In a Model I behavioral world, the discovery of uncorrectable errors is a source of personal and organizational vulnerability. The response to vulnerability is unilateral self-protection, which can take several forms. Uncorrectable errors, and the processes that lead to them, can be hidden, disguised, or denied (all of which we call "camouflage"); and individuals and groups can protect themselves further by sealing themselves off from blame, should camouflage fail.

Camouflage may take the form of resort to espoused theory ("We are open, trusting, and cooperative with one another"), where everyone makes an open secret of the incongruity. Or the uncorrectable error may be attributed to external factors, over which members of the organization have no control. Members of the organization may make a public show of attack on the problem while sharing an understanding of the ritual nature of that attack.

Protection often takes the form of anticipation of the consequences of uncorrectable error so as to give the anticipator a margin for acceptable performance. Staff members in the agency, for example, might deliberately overestimate the time required to bring a proposal to fruition in order to compensate for the delays they have learned to expect. Or one might cover oneself by documenting his or her own performance in such a way as to throw the blame for delay upon others. These are phenomena familiar to all members and students of organizations.

What is often less familiar are the consequences of camouflage and protection. Camouflage is a response to uncorrectable error which draws off energy which might be used to engage such error. The hiding, disguising, and denying of uncorrectable error tend further to protect it from inquiry and thereby to reinforce second-order loops.

Moreover, when camouflage and protection are broadly practiced, they set the conditions for a second layer of camouflage. The hiding, denial, or disguising of uncorrectable error cannot come to light without actualizing this double layer of vulnerability. Hence, *these* processes must be hidden, denied, or disguised.

In the case of the agency, there is as much of a taboo against public discussion of the fact that we are making the "narrow funnel" an open secret as there is on discussion of the "narrow funnel" itself. In effect, we must tacitly agree not to discuss our denials and disguises if they are to do their job. This, then, represents a further impediment to deutero-learning. The very allusion to such defenses may create a sense of intolerable risk.

COLUMN 9: PRIMARY LOOPS THAT INHIBIT DEUTERO-LEARNING

These are primary loops which arise in the course of attempts to inquire into an organization's first-order activities. They are generated by the same kinds of factors—conditions for error, Model I behavioral world—which create first-order primary loops. But they are also reinforced by the secondary consequences of first-order loops. And they feed back to reinforce both of these.

In the case of the Agency, the very existence of a problem in first-order performance is ambiguous. ("Do the delays in launching the new Institute constitute a problem, or do they not?") This ambiguity is sustained, in part, by the Associate Director's denial of the problem and by staff members' reluctance to confront that denial. But it is also sustained by the image each person holds of the prevailing norms for Staff/Board and Staff/Director interactions, norms which stress avoidance of confrontation, open secrets, and incongruity. In their collusion to maintain the ambiguity of the problem, members of the organization need have no sense of extraordinary experience; they are simply conforming to the norms for intra- and intergroup behavior.

When such normal behavior prevents inquiry into the learning system of the organization, however, it serves to maintain the prevailing patterns of the learning system. The primary loops that inhibit reflection on the learning system protect the complex of primary and secondary loops that make up the learning system.

COLUMN 10: DECREASE PROBABILITY FOR DOUBLE-LOOP AND DEUTERO-LEARNING; INCREASE DOUBLE BINDS FOR INDIVIDUALS

Double-loop learning depends on awareness of error, which primary- and deutero-learning loops prevent. When errors are uncorrectable, they cannot trigger double-loop learning.

Members of a limited-learning system might inquire into the features of their system which make errors uncorrectable. But deutero-learning loops prevent such inquiry. Hence, in limited-learning systems, double-loop and deutero-learning are unlikely.

From the viewpoint of an individual living in such a system, the organizational world is apt to be peculiarly frustrating and constraining. Such a person is apt to find himself or herself in lose/lose situations which present intractible dilemmas. A staff member of the government agency, for example, is likely to experience a world of ambiguity in which he fears punishment for delays he does not see as his responsibility; fears the consensus-seeking process and fears to avoid it; feels he does not understand the problem; and believes he cannot raise with others the issue of the factors that have put him in this situation. The school principal finds herself ineffective in her efforts to get the teacher to recognize his poor performance, and feels vulnerable as a consequence; but the prospect of a more direct confrontation with the teacher makes her feel equally vulnerable. The resulting dilemma is one that she also feels unwilling to surface, since it could be taken as a sign of poor performance which would bring with it still further vulnerability.

These are situations that meet the conditions Gregory Bateson has laid down for "double binds" (Bateson, Gregory, 1972)—namely, one is caught in a no-win game and the rules of the game are undiscussable.

Limited learning systems are predictable generators of situations such as these. They require, as a condition of membership, that individuals assume the double layers of vulnerability inherent in camouflage and games of deception. They then put a taboo on discussion of these conditions and on the processes by which one has gotten caught in them.

Bateson advances his theory of the double bind to account for the etiology of schizophrenia. Double binds often reinforce features of limited learning systems by intensifying Model I behavior, by generating internal stresses conducive to deteriorating performance or to sporadic eruption, and by creating double-binds for others.

SOURCES OF THE O-I MODEL OF ORGANIZATIONS

The O-I model of organizations—the model of limited-learning systems—is so awe inspiring in its apparent irrationality that one is moved to ask how it can possibly result from apparently rational processes of organizational design. After all, formal organizations are consciously designed; they are calculated to achieve intended objectives. But when we look at what actually goes on in organizations, as we have been doing throughout Part II, we find much that is counterproductive to the original design. Moreover, the counterproductive activities are just as obvious and commonplace as the ones that are more nearly congruent with the original designs. How is it that people design organizations in ways that eventually allow or induce these organizations to take on the characteristics of limited-learning systems?

In order to answer these questions, we should remind ourselves that to design an organization is to calculate ahead of time what the organization needs to accomplish its tasks. In order to make these calculations, the designers must have some model of where they are, where they are going, and how they are to get from where they are to their destination. Obvious as this statement may be, we know very little about these calculated design or map-making processes. As we shall see, one of the great gaps in our knowledge is in understanding the causality of the obvious.

When people begin to design an organization, they are usually aware of some objectives for the organization and the resources that will be available to it. They also know something about what they can or cannot do with these resources. For example, they know something about how money may and may not be used, policies that are legal or illegal, time perspectives that are realistic and unrealistic. The constraints embedded in these resources are relatively clearly defined and rigid. This is true for human beings as resources. We know very little about their potential limits, and what we do know suggests that, for a fair reimbursement, human beings are willing to be quite flexible and work under less than optimal conditions.

There is one quality about human beings, however, that is crucial and not as flexible as many other human qualities. We are speaking of the way human beings process information and think; the way they deal with complex problems. It appears that people think hierarchically when they deal with complexity (Miller 1956; Simon 1968 [as already noted]). For example, a person may have some experience with and remember different automobiles. As the number becomes large, there is a need to store the information effectively so that it can be retrieved efficiently. One device is to create higher order constructs which permit the individual to subsume many of the individual cars. The constructs may be in terms of color, size, or any other attribute. But whatever attribute has been selected, it becomes the key to dealing with the cars. If the numbers continue to expand, the individual may invent new and even more abstract categories. Again the invention means that some new attribute has been selected in order to remember and to form the basis of action. The basic assumption is that whatever the attribute, it is adequate for storing and retrieving that information.

We suggest that these basic thought processes are also used in the design of organizations. Organization designers begin with people who are to act as agents for the organization. To be an agent of an organization means to produce that behavior which the organization is thought to require. And this behavior, under prevailing organizational paradigms, is usually conceived as a patterning of components that looks like Fig. 5.3. The pyramidal pattern, which is so invariant that people often define organizations as pyramidal structures, derives from the principles of specialization of work and of hierarchical control.

Designers think hierarchically about organizations, just as they think hierarchically about complex problems in general. Complex tasks are to be broken down into relatively simple ones and grouped

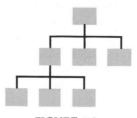

FIGURE 5.3

for ease of recognition and control. This strategy, which suits the pattern of hierarchical thinking, also suits the designers' wish to mini-max, that is, to devise task systems which minimize the organization's loss and maximize its gains. For designers tend to mini-max by defining roles that almost anyone can fulfill. The resultant specialization of work, with its associated pyramid, appears to the designers to make it easier to find people, educate them to the requirements of the organization, and manage them.

But in using this strategy the designers have created two major new problems. The first is an organizational problem. If people specialize, then their efforts must be coordinated and controlled in order to achieve the desired goals. In order to coordinate and control, there is a need for people to perform these functions. Since these people, who are assigned the roles of superiors, are human beings, there are limits to how much information they can process; and so there are limits to the number of people who may report to them.

Also, the designers are aware that people are organisms with their own motivations, theories of action, and goals. Therefore, they try to give the superiors the resources they need to minimize complexity and noise. For example, the superiors are given power to control and coordinate; to reward and penalize; to evaluate performances, etc.

The combination of specialization of work and centralization of power and information (which when diagrammed is the pyramidal structure) has the advantage of making organization activity manageable. However, built into this design are some contradictions that create tensions and discontinuities that must be dealt with.

Let us begin with the inner contradictions that arise from the fact that this mini-max strategy is being used on individuals. They may be summarized as follows.

1. People in our society are programmed with Model I theories-in-use. The bases for competence and a sense of effectiveness are behavioral strategies of advocacy coupled with unilateral control over others, over the immediate environment, and over the task to be accomplished. But these are the very conditions that are taken away from them by the organizational designers in order to mini-max. More accurately, the lower one goes down the organization, the less it is possible for the people to have these conditions.

2. People in our society are educated to develop many and complex abilities. Yet, the lower they go down the organization, the less it is likely that they can use these abilities.

Until recently, the most frequent strategy for reducing these inner contradictions was for organizations to pay as fair wages as they could, to guarantee (with the influence of the unions and the government) as much job security as they could, and to strive to educate superiors so that they did not use leadership styles (e.g., authoritarian, unilateral) that compounded the problem.

These strategies have probably worked as effectively as was possible, given the constraints imposed by human beings. For example, a worker may be willing to be paid off to forget that he is composed of more than the hand the company wishes to hire, but to do so he will have to learn to deal with boredom. One can suppress feelings of boredom only to a certain limit, so employees create all sorts of informal activities that liven up their world, especially such activities as breaking rules.

Workers may also be willing to give up much of their control over their work world if they can trust their management to be fair and not take advantage of them in their dependent, submissive position. But the trust between management and the worker is difficult to develop and even more difficult to maintain. The same inquiry suggests that both employees and management may be responsible for these difficulties.

3. People in our society are programmed with Model I theories-in-use that predispose them toward single-loop learning rather than double-loop learning. The result of this is a paradox. On the one hand, organizations prefer people who remain at the single-loop level of learning, especially if they accept the game plan of the organization. This makes it possible for organizations to accomplish some of their

most important functions; i.e. to create continuity, consistency, and stability, and to maintain the status quo in order to achieve objectives within desired costs.

On the other hand, organizational designs are imperfect and incomplete. They require continual reflection and monitoring to meet challenges from the changing external environment as well as from the counterproductive activities of the internal environment. Organizations must be concerned with discontinuity, inconsistency, instability, and changes in the status quo. Otherwise, they take on the quality of dynamic conservatism, a quality that may threaten long-range survival. These conditions require double-loop learning, a competency that we have just said people do not tend to develop in our society.

The problem becomes even more complex because people with Model I theories-in-use will not only tend to create ineffective problem solving, they will tend to create defensive group dynamics. For example, group processes tend to become highly competitive, rarely additive, low in openness, trust, and risk-taking, high in closedness, mistrust, and emphasis on not rocking the boat. Group-think, identified by Janis (1972), is a natural consequence. Organizations are therefore full of intergroup warfare and rivalries.

To compound the problem even further, since most of these consequences are inimical to the organization's effectiveness, those that carry them out expose themselves to potential punishment. Organizations are full of rules and policies that caution people against violating regulations and identify penalties for costly errors.

The difficulty, however, is not that policies exist and penalties are known. The difficulty is that to overcome these consequences requires reflection and learning of the double-loop variety—and that, we suggest, is inhibited by individual lack of competence reinforced by defensive group and intergroup dynamics. The problem is not that these conflicts and rivalries exist; it is that they are not discussable. It is not possible to manage effectively events that are not discussable.

Moreover, the fact that everyone knows that these counterproductive activities exist and are not discussable means that people are, in effect, in collusion to deceive the organization and each other.

How do people cope with deception that appears to them to be inevitable and necessary? One way is to develop games which are played in order to maintain open secrets, avoid punishment for error, and camouflage uncorrectable error.

One consequence of gamesmanship and mistrust is that executives place greater emphasis on the use of rationality, direction, control, rewards, and penalties. In practice, this tends to mean that they begin to check on other people's work, not only to see if it is done, but also to see how it was accomplished. They also operate by asking detailed questions about issues and problems that may exist at levels lower than that of the person being questioned, but for which he or she is responsible. For example, they may ask a personnel vice president for the capacity of a parking lot in a plant away from the home office.

The result of such action by the superior is to create defensiveness in the subordinate. The subordinate now checks constantly on all details so that he or she will not be caught by the superior. However, the activity of the organization is not carried forward by such behavior. The result is simply to make the subordinate (and usually his or her subordinate) more defensive. Their response is to build up organizational defenses to protect themselves.

Organizational defenses may therefore be developed to protect various individuals and groups. These defenses can be used to needle . people, which tends to occur when the rational methods seem to fail. But since the use of feelings is deviant behavior, and since neither the superiors nor their subordinates have much experience in their use, the tendency may be to create feelings that are much stronger than the situation warrants.

Executives may speak of "needling" the boys, or "raising a little hell to keep them on their toes," and so on. But if these conditions continue, it is not long before the "hot" decisions of the organization are administered by using emotions. This is commonly known in industry as management by crisis.

As management by crisis increases, the subordinates' defensive reactions to the crises will tend to increase. One way for subordinates to protect themselves is to make certain that their areas of responsibility are administered competently and that no other peer executive "throws a dead cat into their yard." Thus each subordinate's attention will become centered on the interests of his or her own department—and as department-centeredness increases, interdepartmental rivalries will tend to increase. The result is to decrease the organization's flexibility for change and the cooperation among departments. In turn, top management will tend to adapt to this decrease by increasing directives, which again begin to recentralize the organization.

The external commitment, conformity, interpersonal mistrust, ineffective decision making, management by crisis, and organizational rigidity will tend to feed back to reinforce each other and to decrease interpersonal competence. Moreover, each will feed on all the others to reinforce itself. We would conclude that, under these conditions, the tendency will be to increase the energy required to produce the same input, or someday it may decrease the output, even though the input remains constant. When this state of affairs occurs, it may be said the organization's effectiveness has begun to deteriorate.

As the level of problem-solving effectiveness goes down, confidence in the processes also goes down. Feedback from a decrease in confidence will make future problem solving less effective, and this will require further counterproductive activities, which in turn will require more games. Thus we have several levels of circular processes serving not simply to maintain the counterproductiveness of the status quo, but actually to increase it.

So much for the inner contradictions caused by using human beings as agents. We now return to the inner contradictions created by the very nature of organization. As we have suggested, the basic purpose of organization is to maintain stability in order to achieve its goals and to survive. But in social organizations the requirement of double-loop learning and change becomes especially important, because the external environment tends to be dynamic and changing and because the internal environment is also basically unstable.

Thus social organizations have some built-in contradictions that arise from the paradoxical requirement of maintaining yet changing the steady state. The result is that agents are required to think and behave in contradictory manners. For example, agents may be told:

1. Take initiative.	1. Don't violate rules.
2. Sound alarms early for errors.	2. You will be penalized if errors are made.
3. Think beyond the present.	3. It is the present performance that is the basis for rewards and penalties.

4. Think of the organization as a whole.	4. Don't cross into others' areas of responsibility.
5. Cooperate with others.	5. Compete with others.

Again, the troublesome fact is not that these inconsistencies exist, but that they are not discussable. The personnel involved are not competent to discuss the undiscussable, nor do group processes and intergroup norms encourage them to develop that competence. Again, these conditions will lead to a set of games to protect people who must behave in counterproductive ways if they are to survive—or indeed, if the organization is to survive.

Earlier we noted that many of the activities "tacked on" to the original organizational design were counterproductive. Now we realize that they may be counterproductive but rational, given the fact that designers seek to minimize costs and maximize gains by using the behavioral strategies embedded in the pyramidal structure.

Participants involved in organizations, and scientists trying to comprehend them, cannot ignore these "added" activities. Both the original design and the added parts, within the context of the behavioral world, make up the larger, more comprehensive whole that we have called the learning system. For example, quality-control departments and budgeting departments may be added to control for the counterproductive tendencies of employees at the lower levels. Management information-systems departments may be created to control for possible counterproductive activities at all levels of the organizations.

The most important and least consciously and calculatedly recognized parts of the learning system are the "informal" systemic activities, such as rate-setting through group pressure, distortion of reality so as not to upset top management, intergroup administrative warfare, norms of psychological withdrawal, competitive win/lose dynamics, etc. Assuming that the original system was competently designed, if that system does not work effectively it would be because (1) parts of the learning system have evolved *and* (2) most of these parts are publicly known yet covertly maintained; they are omnipresent in everyday problem solving yet consciously not discussed with the upper levels of power.

The reason that we give great emphasis to these parts is that they are typically underemphasized. Indeed, they are suppressed, yet they are critical for helping an organization to move toward double-loop learning. No matter how complete it may be, a diagnosis that is limited to the formal organization will not help the people to understand what the undiscussable subjects are, why they are undiscussable, or how to learn to discuss them.

One cannot understand the present state of an organization merely by knowing its original state. The parts of an organization are multilevel and more complex than the original design. To understand their existence and their interrelationship one must first observe the inner contradictions of formal organizational design. Then one must recognize that, while human beings may be willing to fulfill the organization's initial demands, they must also come to grips with the problems that they and their groups and intergroups create for the organization and for one another.

People who live in the learning systems of most organizations come to conceive of the factors that inhibit double-loop learning as natural and expectable. They do this for sound reasons. In a world where double-loop learning is not sanctioned, it *is* natural to expect double-loop learning to be unlikely. Similarly, people come to believe that organizations are brittle and hopelessly unchangeable. People become upset, for example, if they are asked to focus on deception and mistrust. They do not know how to deal with such feelings. Hence, the feeling of brittleness.

Undiscussability, rigidity, and emphasis on the status quo come to be seen as part of common sense, and, as Geertz (1975) has shown, thereby acquire additional qualities of naturalness, practicality and embeddedness. Through processes such as these, the "rational" patterns of organizational designers come to resemble limited-learning systems.

INTERVENTION TOWARD O-II ORGANIZATIONAL LEARNING

In Part III we present a model of an organization learning system (O-II) that can be used to decrease the inhibitions to double-loop learning embedded in Model O-I. We also include several probable scenarios of how organizations would go about double-loop learning.

Next, we address the question, how do we get from here to there? How do we help organizations move toward Model O-II learning systems? The answer to this question is, in effect, our model of intervention. We differentiate between limited and comprehensive intervention and note the conditions under which each may be utilized.

CHAPTER SIX

O-II learning systems

An O-I learning system cannot learn to alter its governing variables, norms, and assumptions because it does not permit double-loop learning to take place. If we are interested in overcoming the forces that inhibit double-loop learning, we must seek another learning system. But if our assertion that most organizations contain O-I learning systems is valid, and if Model O-I systems deter the creation of new learning systems that run counter to their basic structure, then the new learning system we seek is not likely to be found by looking at the world as it presently exists. The creation of Model O-II will therefore have to be a rare event.

Rare events cannot be created without a map that describes the new territory. A map is needed of a new learning system that provides us with a picture of the probable end state. Our candidate for this new learning system is Model O-II. But if O-II learning systems can not evolve from O-I, then we need a map of how to move Model O-I toward O-II. Such a map should inform us of the conditions that, if violated, would take us off our course. For example, if we make non-disconfirmable statements, or if we unilaterally control others in order to win, then such behavior will inhibit the likelihood of achieving Model O-II. Models II and O-II can be used as guides to the conditions that should not be violated during the transition.

However, these models are not sufficient for the guidance needed. Rules, maxims, heuristics are needed to guide people in advocating a position and coupling it with inquiry. Also rules are needed to inform the individuals how to make disconfirmable statements. These rules are the operational definitions for action without which the guideposts provided by Models II and O-II cannot be achieved.

One other caution. When we speak of Models II and O-II as being end states there is the risk of implying that there are final states which, when reached, are fixed and unchangeable. There are at least two reasons why they are not. The first is that Models II and O-II represent ideal states that may never be achieved but only approximated. Such maps are valuable to have because they provide models for creating a good organizational dialectic. This leads to the second and more important reason. Models II and O-II will not tend to become fixed and rigid because of their built-in capacity for double-loop learning. Such learning continually questions the status quo.

Since O-II learning systems are rare phenomena, it will not be possible to provide as rich descriptions of actual examples as was possible for O-I learning systems. Neither of us knows, for example, of an organization that has a fully developed Model O-II learning system, nor are we aware of any such O-II learning system described in the literature. Indeed, we believe that the intervention theory needed to transform organizations to include O-II learning systems is also extremely primitive. The best that we are able to do is present cases of the beginnings of Model O-II learning systems in various settings in which we have worked.

CARLOS AND THE PM: A NEW SCENARIO

A key component of an O-II learning system is the theory-in-use which people use to deal with the conditions of error (i.e., scatteredness, ambiguity, vagueness, etc.). O-II learning systems require conditions (Chapter 3) under which mistaken assumptions can be reformulated, incongruities reconciled, incompatibilities resolved, vagueness specified, untestable notions made testable, scattered information brought together into meaningful patterns, and previously withheld information surfaced. As we have suggested, these conditions are highly unlikely when people utilize Model I theories-in-use because they create primary inhibiting loops. What would an individual theory-in-use look like that helped people to confront conditions of error in ways that led to the conditions being reduced and the error corrected?

Let us return to the case of Carlos. Let us suppose, contrary to fact, that he and the PM set about trying to confront and remedy the first-order errors in organizational theory-in-use that gave rise to their uncomfortable interaction. What would their inquiry have been like? What tasks would they have had to perform, and what difficulties would they have encountered?

Carlos might have begun by saying: "We have a request from Company X to carry out an audit of new product possibilities, and I am unsure how best to assign the task. But you know, I sense an additional difficulty. It is not clear to me how you and I should be working out problems such as these."

Carlos might then have said that he had wanted the PM to suggest a way of proceeding in the Y case—but he wanted also to be able to question suggestions of that kind so as to be able to understand the reasoning behind them. Perhaps the PM had interpreted his questioning as a rejection of advice, but this was not what Carlos had intended. And Carlos, feeling that the PM would not come forward with a proposal, had assumed that *he* must take initiative. This he had done. He had been unhappy with the results. But he had assumed, on the basis of his earlier attribution to the PM, that the PM did not want to take responsibility for engaging matters of this kind, and so Carlos had kept his unhappiness to himself. As a result of the Y incident, he had wondered what the original intentions had been in setting up counterpart managers. If there were policies for the interaction, Carlos did not know what they were. But Carlos had not felt free then to raise this question with the PM; after all, the PM had given no sign that he thought the relationship needed discussion.

In such a discussion, Carlos and the PM would be attempting to discover the nature of their situation. They would be examining their respective pictures of the policies that governed their relationship and of the events that had actually transpired. As each revealed his interpretations of those events, the assumptions he had made, and the ways in which interpretations and assumptions determined his subsequent behavior, he would be providing data against which the other could test his interpretations and assumptions. In such an inquiry, each would depend on data provided by the other. Together, they might then be able to construct a picture of the pattern of interaction into which they had fallen. They would be mapping the small-scale learning system they had been in process of creating with and for each other.

PM: What do you mean?

Carlos: How should we be dividing up the responsibility for making this kind of decision? In past cases, like the Company Y request, I felt you were giving the ball to me. I acccpted it then, even though I felt unsure how to proceed and would have welcomed advice from you.

If the PM had felt nondefensive and free to enter into this inquiry, he and Carlos might then have reflected on the case of Company Y. How did each of them perceive what went on in that case? What did the PM assume about Carlos, and Carlos about the PM, and how did each behave on his assumptions? And how was that behavior then perceived by the other? The PM, for example, might say that he saw himself primarily in a teaching role here; Carlos was, after all, his counterpart and would eventually take on the program management job. He (the PM) was unsure how best to do this teaching. And there were, so far as he knew, no policies for it. He had at first tried to offer advice, but had found that Carlos, in the Y case, rejected advice and went on to do it his own way. Though offended by this at first, the PM had decided that it might be best, after all, to let Carlos try his own approaches and make his own mistakes. Perhaps he could teach best by giving Carlos a free hand and by remaining available for consultation if Carlos wished it.

Carlos might have been surprised at the PM's perception that his advice had been rejected. He might ask the PM for his memory of the events that led him to this interpretation. The two men would then compare their memories of events, and test their differing interpretations against those events. They might or might not be able to resolve that difference. They might, in any case, notice that their differing, private interpretations had gone unexpressed and untested.

They might then realize that, together, they had generated a behavioral world, self-sealing up to that point, in which each had been responding privately to the uneasiness generated by the ambiguity in their relationship. Carlos had expected and wanted initiative and advice from the PM and had been blind to the ways in which he

(Carlos) showed himself unwilling to accept such advice. The PM had privately interpreted Carlos's behavior as a sign that Carlos wanted to be left alone, and, again privately, had revised his interpretation of his own teaching role according to this assumption. Each privately attributed to the other the responsibility for initiating the present pattern of their interaction.

Such a picture is at once a map and a diagnosis. It draws on remembered history to construct a model of existing patterns of interaction which, in turn, account for what each finds troublesome in the situation.

But the use of such a map/diagnosis is that it gives Carlos and the PM a way of thinking about how they might now redesign their pattern of interaction, on the occasion of the present incident, the Company X request. This requires invention. What is to be invented is a new pattern of interaction for dividing up and sharing responsibility for decisions like the present one. Not only "new" but "better"; "better" in terms of their respective expectations for the relationship, and their respective images of the kind of interaction that will be organizationally effective. But then, the meaning of "better" will have to become a part of their shared inquiry, for up to this point neither has made public his expectations and images of effectiveness. Their joint invention will have to include a reference to the inquiry itself—to the ways in which they might set criteria for and test their own inquiry as it proceeds.

The PM might suggest, for example, that he does have a notion about the way in which the request from Company X ought to be handled. Perhaps Carlos has one as well. The PM will present his initial idea and the thinking that lies behind it. Carlos might agree but add that he will want to be able to take exception and to suggest alternatives without feeling that the PM will interpret this behavior as a wish on Carlos's part to take sole charge of the business. They ought then to settle on a joint approach. Or, if they find that they cannot do so, to get the further information they will need (including, perhaps, the opinions of other staff) and feed that back into their deliberations. They will want, then, to test out an approach to assigning the task, reflecting ahead of time on the data they will consider in its evaluation.

Such an invention will be a new espoused theory of action for assigning projects like the Company X request. It will not be clear at the outset just how broad the class of "decisions like X" is to be; the generality of the invention remains to be defined. However, there will still be a considerable gap between the invention and behavior required to carry it out. The invention must still be produced.

A great deal more information will be involved in production than was contained in the brief description of the invention. Like all descriptions of designs, the description of this invention does not take account of the theories-in-use that Carlos and the PM will bring to the tasks called "presenting," "taking exception," "settling on a joint approach," "seeking information," and the like. Nor does the description specify the design for interaction—the timing, density, and rhythm of their meetings. Nor does it specify what is to be done when unexpected information is forthcoming or when unexpected consequences ensue.

The invention, in short, is an incomplete program for action which Carlos and the PM must, in the fine-grained structure of their further behavior, complete. In the nature of things, such a program cannot be specified completely ahead of time.

Given the content of their invention, Carlos and the PM will be engaged in testing both a specific approach to the assignment of Company X's request and an approach to the making of further decisions like that one. They will be engaged, then, in learning what to make of the task-assignment process they devise and what to make of the decision process itself. In both senses, they will be involved in evaluation and generalization. Was the method of assignment effective? And on what criteria were they making this judgment? Did things work out as expected? And what were their respective expectations? If there are discrepancies between expectation and outcome, to what do they attribute these discrepancies?

If they discover that they see the events differently, they will need, once again, to produce the data that led to these perceptions, and to state the assumptions on which their different interpretations were derived from the data. Whatever their learning from the process, they will—tacitly or explicitly, privately or publicly—assign a certain generality to the learning. Do they infer from the experience a program to be followed in assigning further requests from Company X; from all such companies; from all clients? Or are only certain features of the method applicable to future instances? With respect to the decision process, the same sorts of questions will also be pertinent.

In effect, Carlos and the PM (and others, depending on the process they adopt) will again be engaged in a process of mapping and diagnosis. This time they will be mapping and diagnosing the new situation that has resulted from their efforts to produce their invention. Again, they will be dependent on one another for the surfacing of attributions and the generation of data. Again, they will be confronted with the shared task of constructing a picture of the situation their several, interactive behaviors have created.

In this scenario we have described a learning cycle, highlighting the phases of discovery, invention production, and generalization which for clarity's sake we have kept separate from one another. (In real-world processes, these phases would blur into one another; discovery and invention, invention and production, production and generalization, would take the form of interactive loops.) The context of this learning cycle is a small-scale interaction between Carlos and the PM, during which each of them learns. But through their joint inquiry, the two individuals serve as agents of organizational learning. They detect and correct errors in the organizational theory-in-use for task assignment. They also reflect on their earlier attempts to learn about problems of task assignment, drawing from that reflection a new approach to the setting and solving of such problems. They function as agents both for first-order organizational learning and for organizational deutero-learning.

MODEL II THEORY-IN-USE

The scenario of behavioral strategies and consequences that we have just presented is informed by a model for *individual* theory-in-use which we call Model II (Argyris and Schon 1974, pp. 85–93).

Briefly, the governing variables or values of Model II are not the opposite of Model I. The governing variables are valid information, free and informed choice, and internal commitment (Fig. 6.1). The behavior required to fulfill these values also is not the opposite of Model I. For example, Model I emphasizes that the individuals be as articulate as they can be about their purposes and simultaneously control the others and the environment in order to assure that their purposes are achieved. Model II does not reject the skill or competence to be articulate and precise about one's purposes. It does reject the unilateral control that usually accompanies advocacy because the typical

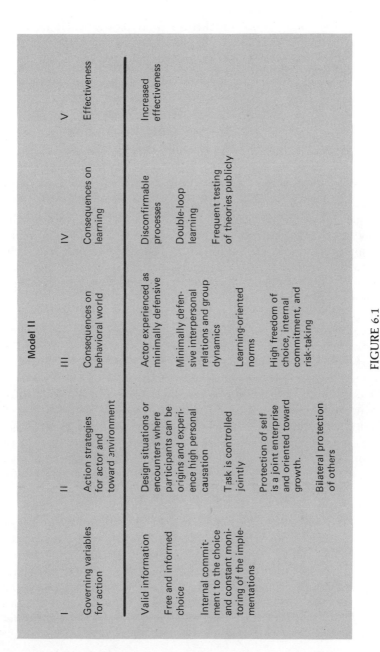

Model II

I	II	III	IV	V
Governing variables for action	Action strategies for actor and toward environment	Consequences on behavioral world	Consequences on learning	Effectiveness
Valid information	Design situations or encounters where participants can be origins and experience high personal causation	Actor experienced as minimally defensive	Disconfirmable processes	Increased effectiveness
Free and informed choice		Minimally defensive interpersonal relations and group dynamics	Double-loop learning	
Internal commitment to the choice and constant monitoring of the implementations	Task is controlled jointly	Learning-oriented norms	Frequent testing of theories publicly	
	Protection of self is a joint enterprise and oriented toward growth.	High freedom of choice, internal commitment, and risk-taking		
	Bilateral protection of others			

FIGURE 6.1

purpose of advocacy is to win. Model II couples articulateness and advocacy with an invitation to others to confront one's views; to alter them in order to produce the position that is based on the most complete valid information possible and to which people involved can become internally committed. This means the actor (in Model II) is skilled at inviting double-loop learning on the part of other individuals.

Every significant Model II action is evaluated in terms of the degree to which it helps the individuals involved generate valid and useful information (including relevant feelings), solve the problem in such a way that it remains solved, and do so without reducing the present level of problem-solving effectiveness.

The behavioral strategies of Model II involve sharing power with anyone who has competence and who is relevant to deciding or implementing the action. The definition of the task and the control over the environment are now shared with all the relevant actors. Saving one's own face or that of others is resisted because it is seen as a defensive nonlearning activity. If face-saving actions must be taken, they are planned jointly with the people involved. The exception would be with individuals who can be shown to be vulnerable to such candid and joint solutions to face-saving yet who need to be protected from others (and since it is done unilaterally) from themselves.

Under these conditions individuals will not tend to compete to make decisions for others, to one-up others, or to outshine others for the purposes of self-gratification. Individuals in a Model II world seek to find the most competent people for the decision to be made. They seek to build viable decision-making networks in which the major function of the group is to maximize the contributions of each member so that when a synthesis is developed, the widest possible exploration of views has occurred.

Finally, if new concepts are created under Model II conditions, the meaning given to them by the creator and the inference processes used to develop them are open to scrutiny by those who are expected to use them. Evaluations and attributions are minimized. However, when they are used, they are coupled with the directly observable data which lead to the formation of the evaluation or attribution. Also, the creator feels responsible for presenting the evaluations and attributions in ways that encourage their open and constructive confrontation.

If the governing values and behavioral strategies just outlined are used, then the degree of defensiveness in individuals, within groups, and between and among groups, will tend to decrease. Free choice will tend to increase as will feelings of internal commitment and essentiality.

The consequence of learning should be an emphasis on double-loop learning, by means of which individuals confront the basic assumptions behind the present views of others and invite confrontation of their own basic assumptions, and by which where underlying hypotheses are tested publicly and are made disconfirmable, not self-sealing. Where individuals function as agents of organizational learning, the consequences of Model II should be an enhancement of the conditions for *organizational* double-loop learning, where assumptions and norms central to organizational theory-in-use are surfaced, publicly confronted, tested, and restructured.

UNAWARENESS OF THE INABILITY TO DOUBLE-LOOP LEARN

The description of Model II appears to us and most of our clients to date to be relatively straightforward. What we, and they, had misjudged was the degree to which they were unaware that they did not know how to behave in Model II ways. People have little difficulty in espousing and believing in Model II (indeed, some may rate it with motherhood and apple pie), but they do have enormous difficulties in making it their theory-in-use, *and* they tend to be unaware of this fact. We emphasize the word "and" because combining awareness of and the desire for Model II with the unawareness of the inability to produce it becomes a serious and unsettling prospect for people. This is especially true of adults who have rarely had to face the fact that they cannot discover-invent-produce-generalize double-loop solutions to organizational problems even after they wish to do so.

Elsewhere we have described in detail the reactions that people tend to have (Argyris 1976a, 1976b) under these conditions. Here, we will attempt to illustrate the point by referring to the case of Carlos. If double-loop learning is to occur, (1) the PM would have to feel less defensive, (2) Carlos would feel free to take risks, (3) each person would search for his inconsistencies and encourage the other to confront them, (4) both would be able to state their views in ways that are disconfirmable, and (5) both would believe that public testing would not be harmful.

Why didn't these conditions exist? The answer is that both people used Model I theories-in-use that were embedded in and nurtured by an O-I learning system. The idea of publicly testing one's views may appear acceptable at the espoused level, but in an O-I learning system such an act could lead to the other taking advantage of the openness and hence winning. The same would be true if they searched for inconsistencies and encouraged the confrontation of their ideas and feelings.

Under these conditions people do not learn the skills required for Model II even though they may espouse them. Since reflection on this incongruity or gap is unlikely under the conditions of Models I and O-I, individuals will not tend to be aware of their inabilities because they have had no reason to reflect on them. Moreover, even if they wished to reflect, it would be highly unlikely that they would find others who would provide them with the kind of feedback that would be required to detect and correct these types of errors. Hence the lack of ability to double-loop learn and the unawareness of this fact.

But if people do not know how to double-loop learn, then moving toward Model II means that they will have to learn to do so. This means that the learning processes which we have described as discovery-invention-production-generalization are much more complex. For example, if individuals do not know how to discover, then they will first have to discover how to discover, invent ways to discover, produce these ways, and learn and generalize. If they do not know how to invent, they will have to discover how to invent, invent how to invent, produce these inventions, and evaluate and generalize. In other words, double-loop learning requires that the learning process of discovery-invention-production-generalization be applied to each step of the larger learning process. Figure 6.2 shows these wheels within wheels.

For example, President A told five presidents (together forming a learning group) that he had serious doubts about his subordinate B's ability eventually to become the president. As A described the difficulties, the five presidents began to infer that A may manage B in ways that coerce B to take less initiative and be more conforming than A says he wants. President A was surprised to learn this, but through

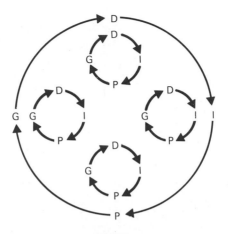

FIGURE 6.2

several hours of discussion, he concluded that he probably was over-controlling B. The point being made is that A thought that he knew how to discover problems (e.g., B was too passive and dependent), yet the discussion helped him to see that for such problems, he did not know how to discover.

President A then invented a solution. Put simply, it was that if he were overcontrolling, he would become undercontrolling—he would leave B alone. After a lengthy discussion with his peers, A realized that the invention could be counterproductive. For example, B might interpret A's sudden withdrawal differently than A intended. Again, the point is that A soon learned that he did not know how to invent. The same was true for producing and generalizing, not only for A and his group (Argyris 1976a), but also for other groups that we have tested (Argyris 1976b).

MODEL O-II LEARNING SYSTEM

As in the case of Model O-I, we begin the description of Model O-II (Fig. 6.3) with the conditions of error shown in Col. 1. They now interact with Model II theories-in-use (Col. 3) that couple advocacy with inquiry, encourage the surfacing of threatening issues, sanction the making of disconfirmable statements and the testing of these statements publicly.

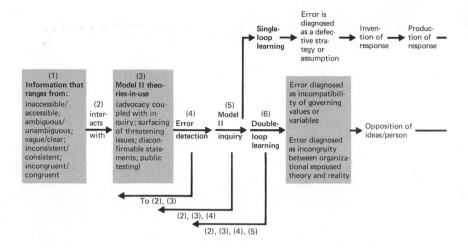

Error is detected and Model II inquiry is begun. Model II inquiry (Col. 5) increases the probability that a corrective response will be made to the conditions for error. As pointed out earlier, this means that mistaken assumptions will tend to be reformulated, incongruities will tend to be specified, ambiguity will tend to be clarified, testability will tend to be substituted for untestability, scattered information will tend to be brought together in concert, information withheld will be surfaced, and information kept impotent for action will be brought into good currency.

The result will be that the conditions of error that were met with dysfunctional responses in Model O-I now will tend to be met with functional responses. Instead of the reaction maintaining or magnifying the errors, errors will now tend to be corrected. The feedback is negative in the sense that it is corrective.

Two kinds of learning are possible in an O-II learning system. The first kind that would be encouraged is single-loop learning. This is relatively straightforward learning because the errors are usually attributable to defective strategies or actions. Consequently, with Model II inquiry it is not too difficult to invent-produce-evaluate effective actions to correct errors. As Fig. 6.3 indicates, inventions are produced to correct the error in strategy or assumption. Since the behavior required fits within the existing theory-in-use, the task of producing it is relatively straightforward. Evaluation then follows: If

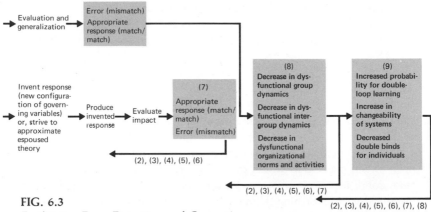

FIG. 6.3
Facilitating Error Detection and Correction

the response corrects the error, the learning is terminated; if the response is a mismatch, the actor returns to diagnosing the error.

The second type of learning is double-loop learning. Here the error is diagnosed as incompatibility of governing values or as incongruity between organizational espoused theory and theory-in-use. The correction of such errors requires the conditions of the good dialectic, which begins with the development of a map that provides a different perspective on the problem (e.g., a different set of governing values or norms). The opposition of ideas and persons then makes it possible to invent responses that approximate the organization's espoused theory. Next, the inventions are produced and evaluated. If the error is corrected, and hence the response is appropriate, the learning cycle ends. If the response is a mismatch there is further inquiry (Col. 7).

Such a learning process should decrease dysfunctional group dynamics because the competitive, win/lose, low trust, low risk-taking processes are replaced by cooperative, inquiry-oriented, high trust and high risk-taking dynamics. Likewise for intergroup relations. Finally, dysfunctional norms and games of deception should decrease, as well as the need for camouflage, camouflage of the camouflage, and the defensive activities described in O-I (Fig. 5.2, Col. 8).

The result should be that the participants will tend to believe that double-loop learning for themselves and their organizations is possible, that organizations are for change, and that the double binds experienced by individuals should be decreased (Col. 9). Both Col. 8 and 9 reinforce the previous columns and hence we have a learning system that is simultaneously stable and subject to continual change.

One word of warning: As we pointed out in Chapter 3, it is important not to isolate a full cycle of organizational learning from the larger organizational dialectic in which the organization is embedded. In good dialectic, new conditions for error typically emerge as a result of organizational learning, hence the quality of stability combined with continual change. This means that the good dialectic is not a steady state free from conditions for error, but an open-ended process in which cycles of organizational learning create new conditions for error to which members of the organization respond by transforming them so as to set in motion the next phase of inquiry.

TESTS FOR EVALUATING GOOD DIALECTIC

As far as single-loop learning is concerned, we can evaluate good dialectic on a basis of effectiveness. Because norms for performance are given, we can ask whether single-loop learning yields a better or more probable match between expectation and outcome. Similarly, as far as deutro-learning is concerned, we can ask whether there is an increase in learning effectiveness from one learning episode to another. One can make such judgments absolutely, because one shares the organization's norms; or one can make them conditionally, saying, for example, "The organization learned effectively to realize norms of which I disapprove."

In the case of double-loop learning, however, norms are themselves in transition. They cannot be taken as given and used as criteria for learning. It is always possible to say about an organization, for example, "They (agents) learned the right thing," or "They learned the wrong thing." One might even say, "They drew the right (or wrong) lessons from their experience." But such judgments depend on whether or not one shares the values toward which the agents are moving. An outsider makes such a judgment much as a party to the inside conflict might make it, from the point of view of his or her own value stance. There is no Archimedean value-neutral point from which such an evaluation can be made.

Also, as discussed earlier, criteria for organizational inquiry may be defined which apply to each of the principal stages of organizational dialectic. Members of the organization must be able to detect mistakes in organizational theory-in-use, incompatibility in norms, and incongruity between espoused theory and theory-in-use. Hence, assumptions in organizational theory-in-use must be made testable. Members must have access to full and coherent maps of organization, organizational context, and organizational past. In the face of uncertainty, members must be able to restructure their picture of the organizational situation. Because incompatible norms are characteristically surfaced in the form of conflict, members must be able to resolve conflict through advocacy coupled with inquiry.

We can translate these general themes into more specific questions which illustrate features of good organizational dialectic:

- Do members of the organization treat organizational assumptions as testable? And do they search for disconfirming data?

- Are the members of the organization able to integrate, for example, the images of organizational theory-in-use held by employees at different levels and locations with those of management so as to make a single organizational map capable of revealing the interconnections of assumptions and values?

- Do the members of the organization share memories of the organization's past which provide them with a context for the interpretation of present error?

    If not, the organization may continue to respond in single-loop fashion to errors which can yield only to double-loop learning; or, without realizing that they are doing so, they may oscillate for a long time between incompatible values which are horns of a dilemma.

- Has the organization found that its expectations to achieve specified objectives are continually disappointed? If so, there may then be real uncertainty over the proper interpretation of this error. Are the members then able to respond to uncertainty by reflection and by efforts at restructuring their perception of the problem? Are they able to respond, for example, not only by altering work-methods and rates of production, but by reconsidering standards for freedom of work?

- Do the members test for congruence of organizational espoused theory with theory-in-use? Do they test for the compatibility of their norms?

- Do the individual members oppose one another without the awareness that their opposition represents a conflict of organizational values? If so, one side may win without recognizing the costs of victory, and without considering a restructuring of the problem which might allow both sets of values to be met.

- Or do members couple advocacy of their own positions with inquiry into the positions of others? Do they keep open the possibility that conflicting values could be internalized by the several members rather than distributed among them by polarization?

These questions point to features of inquiry which are interconnected. For example, the search for disconfirming data reveals errors which can require the restructuring of organizational assumptions. A coherent map of the organizational present, or the past, can reveal incompatible values which would otherwise be ignored.

THE DIALECTIC CONTRASTED WITH OTHER PERSPECTIVES OF ORGANIZATIONAL RATIONALITY AND CHANGE

The dialectical perspective differs significantly from prevailing schools of thought about organizational change and rationality. It does not agree with those who have written as though it were possible, through organizational development techniques of one kind or another, to reach an organizational stable state in which fundamental conflict or dysfunction would no longer arise. Good dialectic is not a matter of smoothness of operation or elimination of error. On the contrary, its goodness is inherent in the ways in which error is continually interpreted and corrected, incompatibility and incongruity are continually engaged, and conflict is continually confronted and resolved.

The dialectical perspective differs from approaches to organizational rationality which emphasize, as those of many management scientists do, the effective achievement of organizational objectives. From a dialectical perspective, we can recognize that there are zones of organizational experience in which objectives (and their associated norms) are stable, and where organizational rationality may be understood as the search for effective means. This is what we have called single-loop learning. But the dialectic perspective also focuses attention on incompatibility of norms and objectives which are not resolvable by a search for the most effective means. For norms set the criteria by which effectiveness may be judged.

Welfare economists and decision theorists usually take account of conflicting norms, but they tend to believe that such conflicts may be resolved rationally through trade-off analysis. The dialectical perspective recognizes that some conflicts of norms may be resolvable in this way, but that others may not. These intractable conflicts of norms are organizational dilemmas. Good dialectic entails their resolution through double-loop learning; that is, through organizational inquiry which leads to the restructuring of central elements of organizational theory of action.

Prevailing modes of thinking about organizational rationality tend to assume a framework of stable, compatible objectives for which rational inquiry consists of choosing the most effective means. Or, if such modes do accept the need and the feasibility of trade-off analysis among conflicting objectives, they tend not to recognize that conflicts of objectives may not be resolvable by trade-off analysis, or that such intractable conflicts (if they exist) may still be resolved through organizational inquiry, or that organizational inquiry is likely to lead to new organization/environment situations which give rise to new conflicts of objectives which, in turn, require organizational double-loop learning.

A SCENARIO OF ORGANIZATIONAL DOUBLE-LOOP LEARNING

As mentioned at the outset, we have not been able to find in our experience or to draw from the literature descriptions of O-II learning systems with the degree of concreteness that was possible for Model O-I. Nor can we depend on the reader to fill in our gaps with his or her own knowledge because we predict that few, if any, readers have observed organizations that double-loop learn.

Nevertheless, we thought it might be helpful to describe how such learning might go on in a particular case. In order to set the stage, we must describe an organization with a problem. Let us take, for example, the case of a well-known professional school that discovered that it was internally fractionated; that its students were not satisfied by their education; that the faculty had doubts about the school as a system; and that both had questions about the long-range viability of the school.

A new Dean was brought into the organization to clear up what most participants acknowledged was a mess. The Dean tried valiantly to produce responses from the faculty which were additive and could form the basis of a new charter for the school, but met with very little success. The faculty began to blame the Dean for the school's inability to change, yet whenever the Dean took initiatives, he was met with stiff resistance from segments of the faculty (depending on the action taken).

Part of the problem was that the faculty held Model I theories-in-use that led to primary and secondary inhibiting loops that prevented people from saying what was in their memories, and/or that led others to say what was in their memories in such a way that it produced defensiveness in others; and/or that led people to polarize issues, take sides, and cancel out the contributions being made. As a result, little progress was made, which acted to confirm in people's minds that the system was beyond change, and led them to place more of the responsibility on the Dean.

To illustrate, we draw heavily from parts of a report that one of us wrote describing important organizational games plus their consequences on the problem-solving activities. One of the most prominent self-protective (and organizationally destructive) devices may be called "distancing." For example, the stance of most of the senior faculty when the Dean first arrived was to distance themselves from any responsibility about the issues of planning and redesign. When the Dean asked for help and cooperation, the most frequent response he received was, "The task of redesigning the School is a Deanly decision." The Dean struggled several times to make such decisions at least a function of the senior faculty, but when he called meetings for that purpose the senior faculty operated beautifully to cancel each other out. They used such devices as polarizing issues, making assertions in ways that made the issues untestable, one-upping each other (for example, "The real problem is . . .," implying that the previous speaker was handling the issues at a skin-surface level), and so on.

What option did the Dean have? One was to confront the problem-solving dynamics and refuse to be caught up in them. The Dean believed that this alternative was dangerous and could lead to further difficulties. (Our analysis will confirm that fear.) He was soon to find himself in a double bind—damned if he took action, and damned if he did not.

The Dean finally chose the alternative of distancing himself from the faculty. This strategy fitted neatly into the living system. The faculty had a Dean who naturally defended himself the way they defended themselves; he too was now practicing the art of distancing. They could all live with each other now, but the solution would help to assure ineffective problem solving and planning in the future. Again the paradox: A helpful solution was also counterproductive.

There were several other very important consequences. The Dean had to find a group with whom he could talk candidly. He understandably selected the administrators that he had appointed plus a few junior faculty whom he had sponsored. This group became the "inner circle." But the creation of an inner circle divided the school into those who were in and those who were out. Since most of the faculty felt in the latter category, most of them also felt not valued. Being outsiders and feeling not valued gave the faculty structural reasons why distancing was no longer their personal responsibility, as well as rational reasons why they should continue their noninvolvement in such issues as planning. It also helped to produce an interesting reaction to the failure of the Dean's attempts to produce a plan for the school. On the one hand, there was genuine sorrow and dismay on the part of the faculty because they wanted to see the school progress. On the other hand, there was a sense of satisfaction because the failure of the plans "proved" to the faculty that the inner circle could not produce an effective plan, hence assuring that some day they would be needed.

The reader may wonder if the creation of an inner circle could not also lead to the administration becoming surrounded by yes-persons who could provide the top with information that was "shaped" and "managed," if for no other reason than out of concern for the already overpressured and overloaded Dean. Apparently this consequence has not tended to happen to the degree that it could. The people within the inner circle try hard not to distort reality even though it means that they must say things that may be difficult to communicate. But, neither is the administration trying to create the condition of "groupthink." It appears that the Dean's reaction is one of pride in the vitality of his group, but he wishes that they could come up with a structural solution that would not require that the organization's learning system be confronted.

Again a paradox: The members of the inner circle work hard to minimize the probability of group-think, which leads them to make life even more difficult for the Dean; and he, given his instinct, values their honesty even though it threatens his inner peace. The members are in a bind because either way they behave will make it difficult for the Dean. The Dean is in a double-bind because either way he reacts, he will create difficulties for himself.

During the past several years, the Dean has not been able to produce a plan that the faculty, administration, and other relevant people will accept and to which all would become committed. As a result, the school has continued on its path with little change in its intellectual thrust and structural incoherence. The Dean kept insisting there is a genius in the present organization which few insiders or outsiders could see. Perhaps he needed to see the coherence; otherwise, he would have to do the confronting of people, programs, and practices that were distasteful to all concerned, including himself.

According to this analysis, the Dean's assertion that the organization contains a hidden logic is valid in the sense that the organization's learning system is a creative response to the enormous multilayered defenses. However, his assertion is incomplete because the multilayered defenses prevent a cohesive system from developing that can double-loop learn, make decisions, and implement them with continual monitoring. Here we see another example of the paradox that is characteristic of the school: That which is valid is also dysfunctional.

This early period of distancing between the Dean and the faculty had one advantage: It gave the Dean's office time to straighten out the financial and many of the formal administrative problems. The disadvantage of this period was that it served as a continuous confirmation to the faculty that the school's learning system was brittle and unchangeable. That led them to continue their distancing, which led the Dean to continue his, which made it easier for the faculty to take pot shots at the Dean and vice versa. The faculty probably "knew" that time was on their side. If they waited long enough, the university administration would have to enter the picture.

And this is precisely what happened, because even though the waste and inefficiencies were reduced, the costs rose. The school some day would have to seek new money and/or cut its costs even further.

Both activities would require the kind of organizational learning and problem solving that was difficult to produce in this school.

Enter the President. He told the faculty that the destiny of the school was in their hands, and that to date the faculty was doing a questionable job of planning its future. The faculty responded that the school was financially disadvantaged and that the President did not understand how difficult it was to redesign the educational programs in their profession. No meetings were held by the faculty that would provide data to back up their assertions that the educational planning in their profession was uniquely difficult.

The President, in turn, showed little awareness of the complexities and defensiveness of the school's learning system. He appeared to act as if valid planning could occur if only the faculty wanted to do it and if the Dean were willing to take the initiative. Again, both of these conditions were valid, but the learning system made both highly unlikely.

The fact that the President showed little awareness does not mean that he was not aware. He knew about the school's difficulties, if from no other source than the letters received from the faculty in response to his request for their diagnosis of the school's problems. The probability is quite high, therefore, that the President was withholding this information because, like the Dean and the faculty, he could not see how bringing it up would help rational problem solving. But by not making these issues discussable, and by reinforcing these taboo areas, he (and all of the faculty) made truly effective and innovative planning even more difficult. And again, a valid course of action becomes dysfunctional.

The map presented to date is highly incomplete. Incidents could be presented which, if elaborated upon, would make the map more complex and the analysis more alarming. For example:

- Some senior faculty members voted against their will for appointments because the senior member of the involved field made the demand.
- Some senior faculty voted for a major senior appointment because they knew the individual would not accept it, while others refrained from making their abstention explicit.
- The Dean's office made decisions that had tenure implications

without discussing them with the senior faculty, and the faculty who were especially involved kept silent because they didn't want to lose their credits with the Dean.

• The Dean appointed a committee to create a policy that part-time study at the doctoral level was possible, partially to make legitimate a massive violation of the present policies.

Conditions such as these had an impact on the intellectual climate of the school. Most of the doctoral students worked part time in outside activities which made it difficult for them to do first-class work. Data indicate, for example, that the average of the grades of the students from the school in a large class of 100 students was one full grade below those of the other faculties, yet the students evaluated the grading system and the graders as being very fair (over 85 percent).

Interviews with the best students confirmed a lack of intellectual discussion and confrontation among the students, as well as the games students learn to play to keep the academic standards down so that they can hold outside jobs in order to live. These students found themselves in a race between classroom and office, between field work and consulting, and between pressures of term papers and pressures of reports. They left the world of action to reflect and they soon realized that they had probably jumped from the frying pan into the fire.

The students soon found themselves alone and distanced from each other. Like the Dean and the faculty, they too became full-fledged members of the learning system. For those who were lucky enough to attach themselves to a professor who had a grant or a contract, the isolation from each other remained but the pressures were somewhat reduced. Since these were usually the better students, the probability of their interacting with other students or faculty was reduced greatly. It is not difficult to imagine what happens when harried faculty, who protect themselves by "distancing," encounter harried students who do the same.

The faculty may seek a few dedicated students and work with them closely, leaving the others alone. After awhile, this appeals to those students who had returned to the school in order to do some thinking and reflecting about their practice. Many of these students were genuinely ambivalent about academic life and practice. They wanted both but they tired easily as soon as both academics and practice came in great amounts. Soon, if for no other reason than to live, their part-time work took on greater importance than their academic work.

One consequence can be seen in the results of an informal study which showed that an increasing number of students were not completing their doctorates. Another result was the accepted practice of openly asking a faculty member who had judged a thesis as inadequate to get off the committee in order for the student to pass. Still another result was that the faculty member passed a paper which, upon questioning, he concluded was not up to par with undergraduate honors theses that he had read in a fine university.

In Part I, we noted that organizations are in constant transaction with their internal and external environments. The transaction was described as a dialectic process, one that unfolded in a sequence of stages where each organizational response to perceived problems contributed to the reaction of a new organizational situation which was in its own way problematic. The examples we gave at that time to illustrate the dialectic began with changes in the environment, the creation of which was not discussed. We then pointed out that the dialectic was not necessarily good or bad; it was simply necessary. We defined good dialectic as that in which organizations take cognizance of their dilemmas and resolve them through double-loop learning.

To return to our example: If the school is to reorganize itself to meet the financial crunch, and if it is to do so in ways that reduce or eliminate the self-sealing, counter-productive problem-solving activities, it requires the creation of a good dialectic. The good dialectic, in turn, requires an O-II learning system.

What would the Dean and the faculty do to begin to move toward a good dialectic? What kinds of tasks would they have to perform to experience double-loop learning? (In the next chapter we will discuss what kinds of interventions may help them to achieve these tasks.)

Let us now suppose that the faculty of the school wanted to begin to alter their O-I learning system toward an O-II learning system in order to deal with the first-order problems like the financial squeeze and the development of a new identity.

In the discussion of the good dialectic, we stated that organizations always exist in an environment. The environment may have varying degrees of impact on the organization. One convenient place for the faculty to begin would be to explore the nature of their environment and its probable impact on the school. For example, faculty could inquire into the number and types of jobs that will be available in the future, and they could inquire into the financial support available to graduate students plus their attitudes toward that support. It may be, for example, that the major financial support for students is loans. But the more recent students may arrive already burdened with repaying loans for undergraduate or other graduate experiences. Such inquiry may lead to ascertaining how students survive in a high-cost area of the country. One answer may be that they must moonlight. Hence they may be unable to be full-time students even though the regulations require that they be. Such inquiry would naturally lead to inquiry into the admissions policies. For example, at the moment, the students who have been working in their profession for several years are favored over those who have not. But these students are older; they tend to be married and have children, hence they need more money to live. Assuming they are superior students with superior records, then they will be sought after by outside institutions for part-time work. The self-reinforcing cycle is closed.

This suggests another area of inquiry, namely the key organizational norms and policies that may be in conflict. For example, school policy is to require that most students be full-time, yet the students least likely to remain full-time are admitted to the school. Inquiry would also be conducted into the norms and policies about the expected contributions of faculty in teaching and research. For example, school policy is that senior professors are hired to study whatever interests them and to base their courses on these interests. Now, with the financial crunch, it may be necessary to ask senior faculty to teach some of the basic (large) courses. Pressure to get the senior faculty to teach other than their immediate research interests may also come from the students who chose the school primarily because of the reputation of the senior faculty. Also, given the financial crunch and the disappearance of new senior positions, the junior faculty may demand more opportunity to teach research seminars in order to enhance their research and increase the probability that they will find work when they must leave.

Another important conflict of organizational norms is represented by the fact that while the administrators are coerced by the faculty to worry about developing and managing new academic programs, no new academic programs can be actualized without the vote of the senior faculty. Another source of conflict is the fact that for professors to obtain and hold money for their teaching programs, they must have a political base; i.e., an organizational unit to which the school has committed financial resources. This means that teaching programs must be maintained over a period of time. And this means that the faculty of each program must focus on the differences among them so that the dean's office will have no rational reasons to combine and collapse the programs into fewer units. Each teaching program is therefore in a win/lose situation; if it cooperates or is willing to examine the degree of overlap, it may jeopardize its survival.

These conflicts are related primarily to the instrumental activities of the organization. Each is embedded in, or protected by, a set of norms (interpersonal, group, intergroup, and organizational) that exist at the human level. For example, we described the pervasive defensive strategy of faculty distancing themselves from issues that could upset people. But in order to begin to solve any of the issues just described, personal values and objectives will have to be explored. To illustrate: Some think the policy of admitting older students is supported by faculty who are not research-oriented, when actually the faculty supporting that policy are looking for academic and potential research performance regardless of age. Likewise, some professors maintain that their outside "moonlighting" work may be as valuable as being teaching assistants, while others claim with equal vehemence such work is not valuable because it calls for little reflection and analysis. But what makes these issues especially difficult to explore is that both sides know that the feelings are strong. To surface such feelings would violate Model I governing variables and such Model O-I defensive games as distancing and camouflage.

Another example of multilevel conflicts embedded in each other would be the tactics faculty use to obtain scarce financial resources. Some create and maintain close informal relationships with the Dean. Others who do not have such relationships may try to use influential alumni or student demand as possible levers. What makes it especially difficult to discuss these organizational strategies is that each side makes untested attributions about the motivations of the other. Those who are close to the Dean are seen as apple-polishers. Those who rely on student pressures are seen as using divisive political strategies. And neither of these perceptions would be explorable in a Model O-I learning system.

Finally, it would be desirable to inquire into the ways in which difficulties with structural organizational arrangements can be reinterpreted as "personality conflicts," thereby increasing the probability that they become undiscussable. For example, some of the so-called personality conflicts may be caused by each faculty member distorting the differences between programs, or negatively evaluating other programs, in order to set the stage to obtain scarce resources. When the others learn of this distortion, they reply in kind. Tensions mount but are suppressed. However, when such feelings erupt in the faculty meetings, even though momentarily, then given the Model I governing variables ("suppress feelings and be rational"), the behavior of those violating the variables is attributed to personality characteristics.

These examples illustrate the requirement that the senior faculty will have to explore thoroughly the degree of congruence between organizational espoused theories and organizational theory-in-use. But we would predict that the moment the faculty attempt to interact in order to problem-solve, they will find that features of the O-I learning system get in their way. For example, they will have to face the Model I tendency to smother possible conflict and emotionality by denying the relevance of important issues, or by polarizing opinion.

Recall that in the cases of Carlos and the others, there was a predisposition to withhold information that was important for understanding and resolving the problems. We have found that this tendency is especially strong with faculty when the information being withheld has a high probability of arousing strong feelings if it is communicated. For example, certain faculty members may have become obsolete; others may be very active but rarely spend adequate time with the students; still others may tend to favor their own graduates for jobs within the school, thereby creating a degree of sameness in intellectual perspective that could be dangerous to students who depend on receiving a broad education about the range of views in their discipline.

It is one thing to point out the areas of need for organizational inquiry (instrumental and interpersonal); it is quite another to implement these recommendations. If the faculty met to discuss these issues, their Model I theories-in-use, their competitive group and intergroup dynamics, and their organizational games would tend to operate to inhibit learning. Even if the faculty is motivated to double-loop learn, their individual theories-in-use and Model O-I learning system will make it highly unlikely that they would achieve their intentions. For example, the faculty would have to learn to surface their hidden assumptions and the problem areas that they consider taboo. They would have to learn to advocate their positions in ways that encourage confrontation of their views. This, in turn, would require that the faculty learn such skills as speaking in ways that make their views testable (e.g., by providing directly observable data to illustrate their concepts), make their inference processes publicly examinable, and minimize unilateral attributions and evaluations.

These are not, as we shall see, easy skills to develop. Moreover, most of the faculty not only do not have many of these skills, they tend to be unaware that they do not have them. Also, they tend to be unaware that they do not know how to go about learning them.

These and other requirements leading to an O-II learning system may seem formidable, and they are. They tend to produce feelings of frustration in adult participants who may be accustomed to learning new skills quickly. What these participants do not realize is that their major learning skills are for single-loop and not double-loop learning.

Although we have just begun to enumerate the challenges of moving toward an O-II learning system, the reader may justifiably wonder if it is realistic to believe that organizations can make such transformations. There are several reactions to this concern. First, we wonder if organizations have a serious choice of not facing up to double-loop learning, given the pressures on them to improve effectiveness and to confront debilitating conflicts of purpose. Second, we are also impressed with the help that can be given to clients, even though the field is primitive and the technology crude. Finally, as we shall show in the following chapter, we are heartened by the fact that the resistance and concerns individuals may have about transforming the organization's learning system are also sources for energy to learn and to change. The questioning of one's assumptions and the facing of one's resistances to this questioning, are not counterproductive; indeed, they can be the basis for double-loop learning and growth.

CHAPTER SEVEN

Introduction to intervention

To intervene is to enter into an ongoing set of relationships for the purpose of being of help. The kind of help on which we focus is to increase the capacity for good organizational dialectic—that is, the capacity for organizational inquiry which engages those mistakes, incongruities, and incompatibilities in organizational theory of action which necessarily emerge as the organization/environment system changes.

O-I learning systems make good dialectic impossible by preventing organizational double-loop learning and deutero-learning, which can remedy O-I systems.

Intervention appropriate to O-I systems must focus on deutero-learning in order to remove the O-I features which prevent good organizational dialectic, but such intervention itself requires an O-II learning system. Model O-II is necessary for the transformation of an O-I system, and this is the paradox of intervention to which our approach is addressed.

We must show how the intervenor can help an O-I organization to deutero-learn before it has the competence to do so. The approach we describe is one in which the intervenor seeks initially to map the O-I learning system, bypassing the features of the system which prevent it from mapping itself, interweaving work on the theories-in-use of individual members with the deutro-learning process.

Our focus is on double-loop learning. We are aware of the need for single-loop organizational learning, but choose not to focus upon it for two reasons. First, if an organization can double-loop learn, it can also single-loop learn. Capacity in the former assures capacity in the latter, but not vice versa.

Second, as we have suggested, the history of organizations shows that second- and third-order quality-control checks on first-order activities seem to be increasing in number, but not in effectiveness. Organizations seem to be increasing their control over first-order activities in order to assure a desired degree of effectiveness. However, the increase in control does not appear to bring proportional increase in effectiveness. Indeed, in many cases, it appears to reduce the present level of organizational effectiveness while adding activities that make the system more rigid. Our diagnosis suggests that the underlying problems are that changes of the single-loop variety have been used. It is time for organizations to reexamine their underlying values and norms of practice. We need radically different managerial concepts if we are to halt the stockpiling of increasingly ineffective unilateral controls.

The intervention perspective that we hold leads to theories-in-use that should be in essential ways the same for whoever uses them, be they insiders, outsiders, line, or staff. Moreover, the perspective should apply to large or small, temporary or permanent, and young or old systems. The criterion for applicability is whether or not the organization has an O-I learning system and whether it is willing to consider developing an O-II learning system.

It may be necessary that outsiders use somewhat different behavior than insiders, or they may use somewhat different timing; or both insiders and outsiders may design different interventions for young or old, large or small systems. However, we hope to show that the same theory of intervention ought to be used to design the different behaviors. Thus our position is not that intervention behavior may not vary; it is that the theory-in-use that informs the behavior will be the same.

MAPS, MAPPING, AND LEARNING

Learning (single- or double-loop) cannot proceed effectively without maps which can be used to relate errors to features within the organization. Maps, as we have pointed out, are organized pictures which show how the features of the system have been placed in some sort of pattern which illuminates the interdependence among the parts of the system. By interdependence, we mean the mechanisms by which the parts take from and give to each other the information needed to permit each part to accomplish its organic role and simultaneously help other parts to do the same, thereby creating and maintaining the system.

Maps not only locate the problem in an organizational problem-solving space, but having done so, they first provide insights into the system changes that may be necessary to solve the problems and then suggest how these changes might be achieved. The maps we will focus on must not only indicate the lay of the land with respect to the sources of organizational ineffectiveness, incongruity, and inconsistency; they must do so in ways that can help the system to move from where it is now to some new state.

A key resource in mapping is organizational memory. Organizational memory is a type of map, a map of the organization's past. Organizational memory, as we have seen, may be contained in individual heads, in files, in documents, or more recently, in computer memories. Organizational memory, therefore, may contain information that is scattered and inaccessible to the agents of organizational learning. One of the objectives of mapping is to bring this scattered information into a unified picture organized for the purpose of learning and for action.

There are three kinds of maps needed to help organizations to learn for action. The first is a map of where the organization is; the second is a map of where it wishes to go; the third is a map of how to get from here to there. Without the third map, knowing where you are may be interesting, but not helpful for change; knowing where you would like to go becomes an exercise in abstractions; and knowing only both can lead to frustration and a sense of helplessness.

If it is to inform action, the map of where the organization is should specify the mechanisms that create and maintain the ecological balance that is the system. The map should make explicit not only the role of each part, but also the interdependencies (the give-and-take relationships) that create the whole. The map should also suggest the mechanisms which create the ecological balance. A map for action should therefore tell us not only what the interdependencies are, but how they evolved. A map for action expresses the equilibrium conditions and the etiology of those conditions.

O-I LEARNING SYSTEMS AND MAPPING

Every organization will have several maps. Does that mean that nothing can be said about mapping that is generalizable to most organizations? We think not. Although the specific content of the individuals' theories-in-use varies widely, we have shown that it is possible to develop a model of the genotypic or underlying characteristics of most individuals' theories-in-use. We called that Model I.

Model O-I attempts to serve the same function for organizations. It purports to represent the ecological system and the etiology of the factors that inhibit and facilitate learning in most organizations. To what extent O-I model is representative of a particular organization is an empirical question best settled by research. For the purposes of the following argument, we are assuming that the O-I model holds for the systems in which we intend to intervene. On the basis of research such as that we reported in Parts II and IV, we believe that the O-I model holds for most mature organizations. If, as a result of future research, we find that Model O-I does not represent a wide range of cases, then we would doubt its value as the basis for intervention.

The thrust of Model O-I is that problem solving and decision making about double-loop issues at the levels of the individual and larger social units (groups, intergroups, and organizations) tend to be counterproductive, and that individual participants tend to be unaware of this phenomenon. Illustrations of this assertion at the group and individual levels are presented in the following section.

A BRIEF ILLUSTRATION OF MODELS I AND O-I

Let us return to the professional school described in Chapter 6. The school developed financial problems and action had to be taken. The President of the university encouraged the Dean and the faculty to consider all options, including enlarging the school. The President felt that new funds could be obtained, but only if the school generated a new and educationally exciting thrust. In our language, the President was connecting successful fund raising to double-loop changes in educational programs.

As was indicated above, given the O-I system, the faculty and the Dean were unable to arrive at any new statement of where the school might go. Indeed, the statements prepared by the Dean were utilized by professional fund raisers (who had an excellent track record in raising funds) with minimal success. The school was simply not producing a new and attractive map to the relevant public.

Finally, another attempt was made with a key group of faculty and administration to redesign the school. The results were again consistent with Model O-I. For example, the faculty members' theories-in-use led to competitive win/lose dynamics that rarely produced any progress during the meetings. At the end of each meeting, people left feeling that they knew more clearly how well they were divided or how sloppy other people thought about the issues.

The Dean struggled valiantly not to be overcontrolling. Given his Model I theory-in-use, this meant withdrawing and giving the group members the lead. However, as we have seen, Model II is not the opposite of Model I. The nonadditive problem solving continued until the frustration level was high enough that the Dean could warn the group, without appearing to be unilateral and punishing, that movement was necessary. Indeed, the punishing aspects were carried out by the faculty members toward each other. One senior professor condemned the group for talking abstractions and not saying anything specific. The same professor confided to the interventionist that he had a plan but was keeping it covered until he could flush out the plan that the Dean held. "When you are playing poker with a politician like the Dean, the best thing to do is to get him to lay his cards on the table."

The Dean eventually did lay out a plan that was exactly what was needed to unite the faculty—against it. However, consonant with Model I, the resistance was not angry or hostile. It was polite, focusing on the wording of the proposal, and insisting that all differences were minor, etc.

The alternatives discussed were related to such issues as size of budgets, number of students, and new extension-type programs to bring in more money. The issues that were almost never discussed included the barriers among departments (yet the faculty espoused interdisciplinary learning), the large number of overlapping courses (yet each faculty insisted that their course offerings were kept to a minimum), the declining academic standards (yet there were frequent pronouncements on the importance of academic excellence), and the resistance to reorganization of departments into more organic units on the basis of intellectual interests (yet the faculty espoused crossing administrative boundaries).

Other important issues not discussed included the allocation of scarce resources, how one gets and keeps power in the system, competitiveness in terms of numbers of students, the faculty's predisposition not to be available when the students requested assistance, and finally, how a system decides when an academic field is out of date and gone dry, or simply no longer necessary.

During one discussion, a senior faculty member suggested that the group consider designing some new courses that integrated the perspectives of different disciplines. The reaction may be illustrated by the remark of another senior colleague, who said, "That's a great idea, but does anyone know of any of these types of courses ever lasting longer than a few years? They never seem to take hold." The first faculty member agreed that the history of such courses was not too good. However, the probabilities for success might be enhanced if several senior faculty committed themselves and related their research interests to the thrust of the class. The second faculty member agreed and then added in disbelief, "But do you think that there is anybody here who would do that?" Instead of discussing the issue, he followed up his rhetorical question with, "Let's get back to reality; we have been meeting for too long and not gotten anywhere."

The committee eventually did develop a statement about the school that suggested single-loop changes. Most members felt that the exercise was a success because a package would be presented that the full faculty would not resist. As far as organizational double-loop learning was concerned, the system made no progress whatsoever. The existing primary and secondary loops were maintained; the organizational games were reinforced; the belief that the learning system cannot be altered was strengthened; the "natural" predisposition of systems to be ultrastable was confirmed; and the psychological withdrawal of the faculty regarding the effectiveness of the school as an organization was maintained.

Perhaps this is enough to illustrate the counterproductive problem-solving and decision-making dynamics that are likely when clients are programmed with Model I theories-in-use and embedded in O-I learning systems. The group did not tend to produce double-loop learning conditions, and hence was unable to detect and correct errors in a double-loop way. Instead, the group tended to create primary and secondary loops that encouraged the making of errors, that reinforced error, and that therefore led to increasing escalation of deception and camouflage, which, in turn led the members to doubt seriously the advisability and practicability of ever changing an O-I learning system; indeed, some came to see the task as inadvisable and dangerous to the functioning of the organization.

THE TENSION AMONG DIFFERENT VIEWS
OF THE OBJECTIVES OF INTERVENTION

We may now begin to see that clients and interventionists of our persuasion tend to hold rather different views of the purposes of the intervention. Some of these differences are presented here.

1. Clients usually identify problems in the instrumental domain.

1. Interventionists identify problems as existing in the instrumental and learning system.

2. Clients seek single-loop learning related to immediate problems.

2. Interventionists believe that the organization should learn to solve its immediate problem and learn how to solve more fundamental problems that require double-loop learning.

3. Clients believe that their knowledge and skills combined with those of the interventionists should be adequate to solve the problems identified.

3. Interventionists believe that clients are unaware that their organization needs double-loop learning processes, and that if they knew about double-loop learning, they still could not produce it.

4. Clients who become aware of the actual conditions and competences required for double-loop learning tend to evaluate them as difficult, if

4. Interventionists expect that if clients develop these views, the initial tendency will be to not express them openly lest they arouse negative feelings

not impossible, to produce in an O-I system.

on the part of the interventionists. If the latter persist in asserting their necessity, the clients will probably express their negative views in individual sessions with the interventionists.

5. Clients, because of the brittleness and hopelessness they ascribe to the existing O-I system, tend to feel that O-II is impractical.

5. Interventionists believe that each client is also personally and causally responsible for maintaining and reinforcing the ultrastability of O-I system.

6. Clients expect the interventionists to take the initiative and the major responsibility for diagnosing the instrumental problem and for making the concrete recommendations to solve it.

6. Interventionists expect to take the initiative and initial responsibility to help clients produce O-II learning systems which, once in operation, should lead the clients to set and solve their own problems.

7. Clients expect that the interventionists will not violate the rules, norms, and games of the O-I learning system, including the rule about not discussing publicly the dysfunctional aspects.

7. Interventionists tend to help the clients create conditions under which violating the rules, norms, and games of the O-I learning system is rewarded and encouraged.

8. Clients expect that if the interventionists ask or require risk taking, they will be responsible if anyone is hurt individually or organizationally.

8. Interventionists expect to recommend but not require risk taking, and to have it occur only when the clients can accept responsibility for designing procedures to make certain no one gets hurt individually or organizationally.

In our experience, attempts by the interventionist to down-play or deny the differences in order to be accepted by the client tend to lead to difficulties. Such actions ultimately backfire because either the interventionists are discovered covering up, or, at a later date, to have covered up differences (Argyris 1970). This leads the clients to conclude that when the interventionists are in difficulty, they too utilize Models I and O-I. If so, why should the clients consider learning Models II and O-II? After all, they want to learn new skills to deal with the difficult issues, not the old ones.

According to Model O-II, tensions and differences between the client and the interventionists should be neither hidden nor down-played. They exist and indeed may be a leverage for change. If the interventionists are able to model behavior that deals with the clients' doubts successfully, then the clients can begin to see evidence that Models II and O-II work.

Our intervention activity must therefore be concerned with three purposes. They are to (1) help the clients become aware of and un-freeze their existing Model I theories-in-use and O-I learning systems and (2) educate clients to use Model II and create O-II learning systems, in order (3) to use this new knowledge for the purposes of good organizational dialectic.

We call the intervention activity that includes all three purposes a comprehensive intervention. There may be occasions when constraints on time, resources, and client readiness make comprehensive intervention unfeasible. Limited interventions are those which help clients to achieve some of the elements of good dialectic, while bypassing the more fundamental transformations required by purposes (1) and (2) above. In a limited intervention, the primary and secondary inhibiting loops are, as we shall see, neutralized by the interventionist's activity. Interventionists may intervene to provide safeguards for people to become more open, while at the same time reducing some of the negative impacts of Model I theories-in-use in competitive group dynamics. Within such a temporary setting, the interventionist can help clients to carry out some of the organizational mapping and problem setting essential to good dialectic.

CHAPTER EIGHT

Comprehensive intervention

THE COMPONENTS OF A
COMPREHENSIVE INTERVENTION PROCESS

As we have seen, clients who hold Model I theories-in-use and who are embedded in an O-I organization's learning system tend not to know how to develop Model II theories-in-use and O-II learning systems and to be unaware of their inability to do so. The key activity in the comprehensive intervention process is to learn to double-loop learn. Instead of educating the clients to discover-invent-produce-generalize double-loop solutions directly, we first have to help them become aware that they are unable to do those things and that they have been unaware that they are unable to do so. Next, we must help them to learn how to discover double-loop problems which include (as we have seen in Chapter 6) learning how to: discover how to discover, invent ways to discover, produce the inventions that lead to discovery, and generalize the learning created as a result of going through these processes. Next, the client must go through the similar phases of invention, production, and generalization.

If the intervention process is to be comprehensive, then the clients must learn the above not only for changing their individual theories-in-use, but also for changing the O-I learning system to an O-II. In other words, double-loop learning that must go on at the individual level must also go on at the systemic level. The latter is carried out by individuals who are the agents of organizational learning. But these are the very same individuals who are attempting to learn to alter their Model I theories-in-use. As we shall see, learning oscillates continually between these two levels. The learning may be initiated at the individual level, but necessarily moves to the system level, then back to the individual, and so on.

In order for people to move away from Model I and O-I, they require a conception of what they are moving toward (a model of the end state) and a model of how to move toward it (the process of transformation). The second component of the intervention process, therefore, is surfacing the inconsistencies between I and II and O-I and O-II. The resulting conflict produces the energy and motivation for learning. The models may be used to inform the individuals how effectively they are moving in the direction of Models II and O-II, and of the extent to which they are using the appropriate processes.

First, in order to learn how to double-loop learn (at the individual or system level) the clients must become aware of what they (and the system they represent) are unable to do. This means that they must be helped to discover their present behavior and activities, and the reasons why they are unaware of their existing limitations. In order to do so, the organization members must be helped to discover their O-I learning system. To make this possible, they will have to become aware of their individual Model I theories-in-use, the primary and secondary inhibiting loops (at the group and intergroup levels), and the norms and games at the organizational level. Therefore, the first step in a comprehensive intervention process is a comprehensive diagnosis of the problems that will have to be overcome to create an O-II system. Again, if our diagnosis is correct, the probability is very high that the clients will not be able to conduct this diagnosis by themselves. The information that they need will tend to be scattered. It will probably exist in vague and unclear forms. There will be many inconsistencies and incongruities. It requires a great deal of skill to obtain valid information under these conditions.

But the situation is even more complicated. If our clients attempted to conduct a comprehensive diagnosis, they would do it armed with theories-in-use that, in interaction with data that are already vague, unclear, and inconsistent, may make the data even more vague, unclear, and inconsistent. Moreover, they would be greatly inhibited in their inquiry by the games of camouflage and deception that exist in their O-I system. For the clients to conduct the diagnosis would be tantamount to asking them to violate the games and norms of their learning system. If we combine the above with the clients' unawareness of their incompetence in diagnosing their theories-in-use or their learning system, as well as their inability to invent solutions to the problems they discover, or to produce solutions they have invented, we can predict that our intervention process will not be an easy one for the clients.

Second, the clients will then not know how to create a good dialectic. Since they are programmed with Model I and immersed in a Model O-I learning system, the probability is high that they will tend not to know how to invent a model whose basic assumptions and governing values question the existing organizational assumptions and governing values. If they knew how to do this, they would already have the skills for double-loop learning. Again, the clients will tend to find themselves in a situation that is difficult, frustrating, and tension producing.

It is therefore necessary to help the clients learn how to deal with feelings of surprise, inadequacy, incompetence, and embarrassment. These feelings will arise as the clients realize how dysfunctional are their theories-in-use and the learning system that they created and continue to maintain. Also, they will need help to learn to cope with the feelings of helplessness and frustration that will result from the fact that during the early stages of the intervention process, almost every action they take to change their Model I theories-in-use or their O-I learning system will tend to be counter-productive. Because of their unawareness, they will tend not to realize that this is so until it happens.

But as the clients progress, they will encounter new dilemmas. Every new discovery will seem to unearth the kinds of problems for which they have not been educated, or which they maintained did not exist in their organization, or which (if they did exist) appeared intractable. These discoveries trigger additional feelings of frustration and failure. Since the clients know neither how to solve the substantive problem (i.e., create an O-II system) nor how to deal with feelings of failure and frustration effectively, there is a high probability that the discoveries could create a process that culminates in failure and/or denial that the problems discovered are the ones that the organization should work on. Thus, the intervention process seems to assert that the clients must be exposed to threatening experiences in order to learn. Another requirement, therefore, is for the clients to learn to see threat as an opportunity for growth, and some degree of fear as a necessary component of double-loop learning. In other words, the feelings that they have probably learned over the years to consider as bad and dysfunctional are the ones that they must now learn to use as a springboard for learning and change. This means that the clients will be faced continually with dilemmas and that they will need to learn to use those dilemmas as the basis for learning.

As these requirements are met, the next step in the intervention process is to help the agents select a few instrumental problems for which they can invent solutions. The success experiences obtained from these inventions can begin to increase the clients' sense of confidence and decrease their feelings that the problems are insurmountable. This, in turn, can lead the clients to develop a more realistic time perspective and level of aspiration about how long it will take the organization to learn. Next, the clients are helped to produce these inventions in their organizations and to monitor their implementation in ways that they can correct for errors, as well as generalize about future actions.

As the clients begin to experience an initial success in the requirements embedded in learning to discover, the next phase may be initiated, namely, to invent solutions to the problems discovered. To invent effectively, the clients will have to learn how to discover how to invent, how to invent solutions, how to produce these inventions, and so on. This means, in turn, that the clients will now tend to experience the same tensions and frustrations that they experienced when learning to discover. If they have had even a little success in learning to discover, then their newly earned confidence will help them to tackle the problems of invention more effectively. Moreover, the very success experienced in the previous stage will tend to reduce their sense of helplessness and hopelessness, because they now have evidence that they can overcome and learn from these difficulties.

As the clients begin to gain some small degree of confidence in their ability to discover and invent, they will seek to learn to produce their inventions. Again, there will be the difficulties and tensions described above. But because of their previous success, they will probably feel less threatened by the difficulties and tensions—and this increases the probability that they will succeed.

INTERVENTION: THE INITIAL PHASE

Objectives of the initial meetings

The first step in any intervention is for the clients and the interventionists to become acquainted. The initial sessions cannot tell each party all they need to know—that will become an ongoing process—but they will have to be used by both parties to decide whether they will work together. The decision will no doubt be made on incomplete data, therefore it is incumbent upon the interventionists to help create a milieu where as much information as possible can be generated about both parties.

One way for the dialogue to begin is for the interventionists to ask how the clients would like to begin. If the clients indicate that they would prefer it, the interventionists can begin by advocating their views, and do so in such a way as to invite confrontation and inquiry from the clients.

The first order of business is for the interventionists to provide some information about what they do and how they go about doing it. The interventionists may say, for example, that they know how to help organizations learn how to double-loop learn, how to overcome the factors that inhibit learning at all levels, how to help clients develop competences to enhance learning, and how this knowledge serves, in turn, to solve important instrumental problems. Examples could be introduced, at this point, from several different previous client relationships, but care should be taken not to reveal the names of clients or information about systems.

The second objective is for the interventionists to focus on issues related to the design and control of the working relationships required for effective comprehensive intervention. For example, the interventionist will need a scope of free movement, and the position of any individual who participates in good faith in the program should be protected. These are critical points and should be made explicit. If Model O-I is applicable, then the subordinates would be jeopardizing themselves with their superiors, their peers, and (in some cases) their subordinates if they became candid about hitherto undiscussable issues. Consequently, part of the agreement will be the development of a set of policies and procedures to protect individual clients.

The interventionists can take the lead in beginning to equalize power around the intervention activity by stipulating that they do not wish to report to one individual (e.g., the president). Nor will they provide separate reports to the top. Nor will they provide feedback first to the top and then to the immediate subordinates. The purpose of these rules is to increase the power of the subordinates to control the fate of the interventionists and decrease the probability that the interventionists can be controlled by a few power people.

The interventionists should also make it explicit that all individuals, including the interventionists, will be free to behave according to their values—but that their behavior and values will be discussable. The interventionists seek the freedom to ask for directly observable data, to define issues in ways that are disconfirmable, to test issues publicly, and to confront self-sealing processes constructively.

Failure and success of any aspects of the intervention activities may be examined in order to understand their causes. In this connection, it is important for the behavior of both the interventionists and the clients to be examined continuously. Indeed, if the program becomes a long and extensive one, the clients may wish to obtain periodic outside evaluation of the interventionists' activities.

The third objective of the initial sessions is for the interventionists to assess the degree of understanding and awareness that the clients have about their problems. For example:

1. The clients may have identified the correct problem and its causes, but do not know how to solve it.

2. The clients may have identified the problem and know how to solve it, but cannot do so because they may lack the ability or willingness to implement the solution.

3. Some participants may feel helpless to change others and seek the interventionist as a person to create the changes.

4. The clients may not understand their problem, nor, therefore, have a solution. They seek an interventionist to help them define their problem and develop their own solution.

It is important to surface these beliefs because they imply a different psychological set of the clients and, in turn, a different starting point. For example, a client system that has identified its problems correctly tends to have significantly greater problem-solving capacity than one which has not been able to do so. A client system that feels helpless and is able to admit it is at a different stage of readiness than one that feels helpless but cannot admit it.

This leads to the fourth objective of the initial contacts: an assessment by the interventionists of the readiness and capacity of the system to learn and change. Again, such assessments will be made on incomplete data and will probably require revision. However, it is important that they be made and be tested publicly, so that the interventionists can estimate for themselves and the clients the probability that they can help.

The interventionists can obtain much information that will help them assess and test the readiness of the system if they observe: the way the clients formulate questions, the quality of the interaction, the depth of the confrontation, the degree of the clients' embarrassment about requiring outside help, the clients' fears of losing control, their view of the brittleness of the system, the degree to which they confront the interventionists about their values and perspectives, the way they react to the interventionists' contractual conditions (e.g., being hired by and reporting to a group), and the way they design the process to decide if they wish to go ahead.

Client reaction to the interventionist's initial actions

The first meeting is not simply for rational planning and contract-defining. It includes a whole host of issues and feelings that are probably suppressed. The clients act as people who wish help; they simply hide (even to themselves and to each other) the boundaries beyond which receiving help is painful.

One way for the clients to minimize the dilemmas and binds that they may be experiencing is to strive to make the intervention activities as much as possible the responsibility of the interventionists. If the outsiders can become responsible for what the insiders are required to say and do, then the insiders can play their own defensive games, and/or if these games are surfaced, they can place the blame on the interventionists.

But this stance is contrary to the stance of the interventionist interested in helping clients to develop an O-II learning system. The underlying intent of the interventionist is to surface and maximize, as quickly as possible, the personal responsibility of the clients for the causes and solutions of the problems. As this is done, then the clients will develop a genuinely autonomous self-manageable system.

The first meeting is full of opportunities for misunderstanding, miscommunication, camouflage, and eventual rejection. Some interventionists strive to design the meeting in ways that do not knowingly surface any of these problems. The logic is to get the assignment and later to confront the issues. As we stated, earlier, this strategy is doomed to failure. If the clients succeed in making the interventionists stay away from threatening issues, then their use of these defensive activities will be reinforced and their expectation that Pandora's Box will not be opened will be increased. As these two factors increase, the pressures to stay away from the taboo areas become even stronger. The result is that the interventionists may find themselves in a double bind. If they choose to go along with the clients' defensive activities, they will have embedded themselves in the learning system and therefore make it unlikely that they will help the clients alter it. If they choose to be candid about their early behavior, they will have provided a role model that Model II theories-in-use are not credible under moderate stress. Why should clients go through all the trials and tribulations to develop theories-in-use that are not viable for the very conditions that plague them in the first place?

A second way for clients to react is for their top people to pressure the interventionists to relax their minimum conditions. Standing up to such client pressure early in the relationship tends to have several positive effects. The subordinates can see, in action, that their superiors cannot cause the interventionists to violate their professional standards. Also, the clients obtain a living sample of the interventionists' behavior under stress. This is a crucial sample because many subordinates in a client system may have fears concerning the interventionists' behavior under stress. If they pass the test, they are admired, since the test of operating under pressure is the one most respected. If they take the stress in stride, they may be the people to whom the clients can trust their organization.

It is important to know that if the diagnosis uncovers deep problems, the organization is in the hands of competent professionals. This need for dependence is similar to the dependence people usually have on their surgeon. They want to see him as internally secure and open about the chances for success. Unlike the surgeon, however, the interventionists will use the dependent relationship differently. They will strive to use dependency in the service of growth, so that the clients can begin to stand on their own two feet at the earliest possible moment. If the interventionists are willing to drop an opportunity rather than violate their professional standards, the clients are assured that the interventionists will not attempt to prolong the relationship or push the clients into activities that have not been well thought out.

A third mode that the clients may use to adapt is to hesitate, ignore, and/or resist defining the problems as they see them. If they do not do so, the interventionists may ask them to describe their problem as they see it without trying to present a coherent picture to which they all agree. If there is a divergence of views, they would prefer to learn the variance. If the clients feel the diagnosis is not complete, the interventionists want to know the reasons.

It is during this discussion that the interventionists may pick up important cues regarding the relationships among the clients. How openly do they disagree? How comfortable are they about thinking out loud? How much pressure do they feel to insist their diagnoses are accurate?

If the interventionists sense that the clients are not confronting each other or that they are not listening to each other, they may use the data as good examples of some of the phenomena on which they will focus. However, a prolonged discussion of these issues is not recommended for the first meeting. The objective of this meeting is to help the clients learn what the consultants may do if they are invited to work with them.

Minimum structural requirements

At this session the interventionists should also make explicit the minimum structural requirements for the conduct of the diagnostic phase. For example, it should be emphasized that they are asking the clients to consider a binding agreement only on the first phase. After the diagnosis and feedback, the clients will decide whether or not they want to proceed. The interventionists will also determine their ability to be of further help.

It may be helpful for both the client and the interventionists to have the freedom to terminate the relationship on 60-seconds notice. However, once the notice is given, it is not necessarily binding on either one unless there is a meeting in which the issues for termination are described by the aggrieved party.

The following structural arrangements have been found to be helpful.

1. If the top administrators agree to the proposal, a top-level steering committee should be appointed. This committee would act as the host subsystem by which the diagnosticians could enter the various parts of the organization. The committee should be able to provide all the organizational conditions necessary for the research.

It is advisable that representatives of all the levels being studied be included as members. They can ease the way for the research team as it comes down the hierarchy.

In addition to a steering committee, a liaison individual should be appointed to handle day-to-day matters. He or she usually generates the interview schedules, makes appointments for observations, calls meetings to discuss questionnaire data, etc. Preferably this liaison individual would be from the highest possible level.

The steering committee and liaison person should act as central points to which client interests can be brought and woven into the research design.

2. Selection of subjects, the length of interviews, the taping and transcribing of interviews and observations, and the analysis of data should all be the primary responsibility of the interventionists, although as indicated earlier, the group will be invited to share the responsibility with appropriate representatives. No typed material should be kept in the organization even if the security is good.

3. Selection of the time and location for interviews, or for the completion of questionnaires, should be under partial control of the interventionists. The time issue is usually a small problem because research activities are scheduled to fit within the stream of the ongoing activities. The researcher should make certain that the research activities are not scheduled at times that are inconvenient for data collection (for example, just before lunch or at the end of the day). Any employee who loses free time as a result of research activities, especially at the lower levels, should be fully compensated.

4. The amount of time necessary for the diagnostic phase should be realistically assessed at the outset. It is not difficult to predict the time necessary to fill out questionnaires and conduct interviews. Observations are more difficult to preschedule, but they seldom interfere with the ongoing organizational activities.

Feedback activity is the most difficult to preschedule. Often the administrators and, in many cases, the interventionists grossly underestimate the time necessary to analyze and organize the results.

The time period between the end of data collection and the feedback of results is a crucial one in the relationship between researcher and client. Administrators tend to use this period as a real test of the diagnostician's concern for the organization; as a consequence, they would like the results back as soon as possible. The interventionists should also be concerned, especially if they hope to participate in further studies of change. The longer they remain away from the organization, the colder their relationships become, and the more numerous the difficulties to be encountered in future research. However, these pressures should not cause the interventionists to develop inadequate analysis.

5. Interventionists should publish results and thereby add to the stream of basic knowledge. This responsibility should be taken seriously. If added knowledge from a research project is not published, the result is an erosion of the public viewpoint that the researcher has a commitment to inquiry and addition to knowledge. Publication is also one of the best quality controls that clients have over interventionists. Having one's work reviewed by one's professional peers produces considerable anxiety. The alert clients will use this reaction to their benefit.

It may be necessary to give the clients censorship power over information that they feel will harm the system. However, the organization does not have veto power over publication. The final disposition of a manuscript is the joint responsibility of both clients and interventionists.

Discovery or diagnostic mapping

The beginning point for intervention is a map that describes the learning system of the organization. The map will not only describe the capacity of the organization to single- and double-loop learn, but it will also describe how the organization developed to its present state. This map represents one anchor of the dialectic of intervention; the other anchor is the map of an O-II system.

The methodology used should permit the development of any map that fits reality, be it O-I, O-II, or some other category. Although it is our hypothesis that most organizations have learning systems, the hypothesis must be subject to disconfirmation.

The requirement that all the methods used to collect data should provide for the development of other than O-I or O-II learning systems is not simply based on research needs. A map that incorrectly confirms the biases of the interventionists and incorrectly describes reality is not only empirically misleading but also useless to the clients—and indeed, may be dangerous if they base their strategy for change on it.

The underlying purpose of the map is to inform the clients of the degree to which their organization is capable of discovering and correcting error (related to single- or double-loop problems), and the degree to which it is aware of its abilities to detect and correct error about any kind of problem, as well as the probable capacity to learn how to learn.

Census of problems

The first step is to develop a description of the immediate problem troubling the clients. The description should include: the range of views about the problem, the clarity of those views, the accessibility and availability of the information needed to understand it more fully, and why the clients regard the problem as unsolvable.

Typically, as one problem is described in detail, other problems surface. The same information should be obtained about those problems. This should lead to a mapping of the problems into a cluster or pattern, including the degree of accessibility, clarity, etc. of the information relative to the pattern of problems.

As the clients unfreeze even further to discuss their problems, it would be useful to develop a list of problems that the clients consider important but unsolvable. Such a list could represent one criterion of the effectiveness of the intervention. The effectiveness would be assessed in terms of the number of unsolvable problems that became solvable and were indeed solved. For example, in the study of a newspaper, clients agreed that getting the managing editor and the editor of the editorial page to discuss certain issues was necessary and yet highly improbable. The intervention resulted in the meetings being held and some of the issues being resolved.

Individual theories-in-use

The theories-in-use of individual clients may be collected in several ways, none of which is time consuming or interferes with the clients' work schedules. First, the clients could be asked to complete a case of an intervention that they made (or are likely to make), using the outline described in the cases of Carlos or the school principal (Chapter 3). A shorter version can be used, if necessary, as was illustrated in the case of the financial and line executives (Chapter 3). Finally, theories-in-use can be inferred from tape recordings of people in actual problem-solving meetings. For example, six presidents, with the agreement of their vice-presidents, recorded several sessions of their executive committee meetings. These were then transcribed. Initially, the interventionists analyzed them in terms of Model I and II. As the presidents became competent in analyzing their own tapes, they did so.

The first method usually consumes about an hour of the clients' time; the second, about half an hour; and the third method consumes none of the clients' time as long as they are not analyzing the tapes. The advantages of the case method are that they make explicit the taboo areas and require that the individuals reflect on and make explicit their intervention strategies and theories-in-use, which in turn may lead to a heightened awareness of the individual's personal causality. The advantage of the tape recordings is that the clients are not required to interrupt their busy schedule nor to reflect. This may be an easier strategy for the clients who have yet to commit themselves internally to reflecting on their theories-in-use. Once they have gotten their feet wet in reflection and inquiry, they may then turn to developing the cases.

Tape recording may present a problem for the client. In our experience, the problems should be discussed. Possible ways of confronting and resolving the issues will be presented below. The reader may wonder about the probability that cases may be written in ways that distort individuals' theories-in-use. To date, our experience suggests that conscious distortion is highly improbable. The first reason is that the respondents do not describe their theories-in-use in the cases. They describe their behavioral strategies. They may try to shape these strategies in ways that approximate Model II. But, as we have indicated, their only available alternative is to describe behavioral strategies that are opposite to Model I or are oscillating Model I. The second reason is that their description of what they thought and felt but did not say provides important clues to the taboo areas. But if neither reason applied (because they were able to distort the case successfully), the individuals' true theories-in-use will surface when they discuss their case and/or when they attempt to help others.

To date, we have experienced little resistance to any of these methods. The lack of resistance, we believe, has been due less to the simplicity of collecting information than to the fact that the cases and the transcriptions were eventually used as bases for designing learning environments to reeducate the clients. This, by the way, is a characteristic of all our data-gathering methods. They are all designed to provide the basis for learning experiences. Hence, the clients are not completing instruments simply to satisfy research or diagnostic requirements. One very important limitation that this requirement places on our diagnostic instruments is that they produce directly observable data, be they taped or recollected. Indirectly observable categories, such as data from questionnaires, are not helpful in changing theories-in-use because questionnaire data tap the espoused theories-in-use.

Primary and secondary inhibiting loops

A map of a learning system should identify the primary and secondary loops that inhibit (or facilitate) single- and double-loop learning about organizational problems. The primary loops would indicate how individual theories-in-use, interacting with features of the behavioral environment, make error detection and correction unlikely.

For example, the line and financial officers discussed earlier held Model I theories-in-use. When the issue of who ran the company (the line or the staff) began to surface, it became undiscussable. As a result, whenever line and financial executives interacted about the problem, instead of discussing the relevant issues they focused on the more trivial and discussable issues, such as the amount of paper work and the requirements of the banks for information. The faculty of the professional schools avoided discussing double-loop educational reform by maintaining distance from each other, from the administration, and from the students. To violate "distancing" would mean to become a deviant and risk being rejected or rejecting others. Both conditions would in turn violate their Model I theories-in-use.

In the study of the newspaper, the win/lose group dynamics plus the competitiveness of the members were shown to lead people to attempt to control each other rather than to generate additive problem solving or to take risks. These conditions led people to consider meetings and groups a waste of time. These beliefs, in turn, increased the probability that future meetings would be less effective. As a result, interpersonal and group conflict were avoided, information that might have been threatening was suppressed, and, consequently, group problem solving was less than effective.

The result was for top management to control tightly the problem-solving and decision-making processes and to keep secret negative management decisions in order not to upset people—who, of course, learned the secrets. Indeed, making secrets open but keeping the openness secret was one of the most powerful games played by the newspaper people.

The map could show how each of these consequences contributed to the others and how they fed back to reinforce the primary inhibiting loops.

An illustration of the intergroup dynamics that may be included in a map of an O-I learning system comes from some research in the State Department (Argyris 1967). A group of senior foreign-service officers was subdivided into two groups. Group A was composed primarily of top-level substantive officers. Group B was composed primarily of top-level administrative officers. Each group was asked to discuss three questions and to develop a list of words or phrases that would summarize their answers. Each group's list was then to be shared with the other group. The three questions were:

1. What qualities best describe our group?
2. What qualities best describe the other group?
3. What qualities do we predict the other group would assign to us?

The results were as follows:
The substantive officers saw themselves as reflective, qualitative, humanistic-subjective, generalizers, detached from personal conflicts, with broad cultural interests and intercultural sensitivity. They saw the administrative officers as doers and implementers, quantitative, decisive and forceful, noncultural, with limited goals, jealous of the substantive officers, interested more in form than in substance, wave-of-the-future! (exclamation point theirs), and drones but necessary evils. The substantive officers predicted that the administrative officers would see them as arrogant, snobs, intellectuals, cliquish, resistant to change, inefficient, dysfunctional, vacillating, compromising, and effete.

The administrative officers saw themselves as decisive, gutsy, resourceful, adaptive, pragmatic, service-oriented, able to get along, receptive to change, dedicated to job, misunderstood, useful, and modest. They saw the substantive officers as masked, isolated, resourceful, serious, respected, inclined to stability, dedicated to job, necessary, externally oriented, cautious, rational, surrounded by mystique, manipulative, and defensive. The administrative officers predicted that the substantive officers would see them as necessary evil, defensive, inflexible, preoccupied with minutiae, negative and bureaucratic, with limited perspective, less cultural (educated clerks), misunderstood, practical, protected, and resourceful.

These data could be used to illustrate the intergroup win/lose dynamics that caused each group to mistrust the other and hold certain biases or expectations about what the other group said and meant. They also illustrate how these biases acted not only to filter what was heard, but also to influence what was in turn communicated. Again, the feedback processes reinforcing the previous primary and secondary loops would be made explicit.

ORGANIZATIONAL GAMES

As we suggested in Model O-I, the tendency of people will be to strive to maximize their survival. Monsen and Downes (1968) have stated that the two central hypotheses of their theory of large organizations are that managerial participants will act to maximize their own lifetime incomes (p. 41) and minimize the probability of error because the punishment for grievous error is greater than the reward for outstanding success (p. 42). The result, as we have seen in system O-I, is that managers at all levels will tend to screen information in their possession so that only data favorable to them are made public.

The result is that games arise to achieve these objectives. Games may be defined as schemes and procedures designed to achieve the purpose of maximizing lifetime income and minimizing the probability of being held responsible for major errors. The result of these games is that the top levels fail to learn important information and the lower levels systematically alter the orders given to them, and both create camouflages; the subordinates hide the fact that they may be carrying out only part of the orders given to them and the top hides the fact that they sense the "disloyal" behavior.

There does not yet exist a systematic microtheory of organizational games that may be utilized by the interventionists to develop their diagnostic categories.

Examples of games and their consequences are:

1. Before you give any bad news, give good news. Especially emphasize the capacity of the department to work hard and to rebound from a failure.

2. Play down the impact of a failure by emphasizing how close you came to achieving the target or how soon the target can be reached. If neither seems reasonable, emphasize how difficult it is to define such targets, and point out that because the state of the art is so primitive, the original commitment was not a wise one.

3. In meeting with the president it is unfair to take advantage of another department that is in trouble, even if it is a natural enemy. The sporting thing to do is to say something nice about the other department and offer to help it in any way possible. (The offer is usually not made in concrete form, nor does the department in difficulty respond with the famous phrase, "What did you have in mind?")

4. If one department is competing with other departments for scarce resources and is losing, it should polarize the issues and insist that a meeting be held with the president. If the representatives from the department lose at that meeting, they can return to their group, place the responsibility for the loss on the president, and thereby reduce the probability of being viewed as losers or, worse yet, as traitors.

These games do not go completely undetected by those on the receiving end. Although they are rarely dealt with openly (because that would violate the values of the system), the top executives tend to develop their own games. Several examples frequently found are: (a) the constant alteration of organizational positions and charts, and keeping the most up-to-date versions semiconfidential; (b) shifting top executives without adequate discussion with all executives involved and without clearly communicating the real reasons for the move; and (c) developing new departments with production goals that overlap and compete with the goals of already existing departments.

There are several rationales usually given for these practices: "If you tell them everything, all they do is worry, and we get a flood of rumors." "The changes do not really affect them." "It will only cut in on their schedule and interrupt their productivity." The subordinates respond, in turn, by creating their own explanations: "They must be changing things because they are not happy with the way things are going; the unhappiness is so strong they do not tell us."

These examples suggest that some meaningful questions about games would include:

1. How are bad news and good news handled (especially when the former may be threatening)?

2. How do rival factions cope with their differences and strive to win, yet act in ways to show the top that they are loyal and cooperative subordinates?

3. How do superiors try to uncover hidden errors and camouflage, especially when they maintain publicly that most of their subordinates are loyal and honest?

4. What rationalizations do the people at all levels develop to make acceptable the necessity both to deceive and to deny the deception?

5. How do many superiors try to make their control systems transfer-proof, and how do subordinates overcome these qualities yet act as if they do not strive to do so?

6. How do the games at different levels interact to create a cumulative equilibrium of increasing dysfunctionality?

Learning-systems maps as the foundations for inventions

Experience has shown several other uses for maps of learning systems besides the obvious one of diagnosis. One specific and important use is as the basis for effective predictions about certain long-range consequences. For example, in the case of a particular newspaper, predictions were made that: (1) the system would be unable to surface threatening issues and would become a compulsive, uncorrectable organization; (2) professional employees would see innovation and individual development as decreasingly associated with internal organizational factors; and (3) the organization would magnify conflict and fear, and employees would demand increased benefits and wages as compensation for the tension that results from that magnification. These predictions were supported by the data collected (Argyris 1974).

It was also possible to use the map of the newspapers learning system to predict the nature of clients' resistance to pressures for cost cutting, to increase interdependence between news and administration, and to predict resistance toward increased understanding between news and editorial.

The identification of dysfunctional consequences and the long-range predictions caught the attention of the executives because these were the problems that plagued them. They were experiencing the ineffective meetings, the destructive intergroup relationships, the decreasing commitment to the organization, and the increasing costs increasingly disconnected from performance. The map became an important tool for the executives to think about invention because it brought together apparently disconnected and scattered information, and it organized that information into a pattern of relationships from which it was possible to make predictions about short- and long-term consequences.

The diagnostic map may also be used as a basis for understanding the ecological steady state of the system and making *a priori* predictions concerning the impact of changes being considered. An example of the former was when the interventionists made predictions that the learning system of the newspaper would not be altered as long as the individuals' Model I theories-in-use were not altered. This prediction, in turn, had important practical consequences. It stated that a whole host of educational programs which top management was considering to increase leadership effectiveness would not achieve their objectives because they did not focus on the theories-in-use of the individuals taking them.

As an example of the latter, the interventionist predicted that the finanical-information systems and the long-range planning would assist the organization in its first-order work activities. However, he was able to predict that the new systems would eventually take on all the characteristics of the learning system, and thereby simultaneously reduce both their effectiveness and the probability of correcting them. This, in turn, would increase the sense of brittleness and hopelessness the executives felt about the probabilities of changing their organization. These predictions were supported by the follow-up diagnosis and confirmed by all the executives, especially the two who disbelieved them when they were first made.

Assessing the validity of the learning-system map

The most powerful way to test the map is to generate predictions from it and see whether they are confirmed or disconfirmed. For example, the predictions made above about the probable lack of effectiveness of the proposed leadership program and the new financial system could be checked. If the executives took the courses, before-and-after studies could be made of their effectiveness. Also, an experiment might be designed where some executives took a course in which there was no focus on theory-in-use while others took courses where the theories-in-use were central.

The prediction about the financial system was that it would show initial success and then the games of deception and camouflage would penetrate it. The result would be to reduce the probability of correcting important errors in the system and simultaneously make the system more difficult to correct. These predictions could be tested by interviewing the line and financial people as well as by observing financial meetings.

Another possible test would be to specify ahead of time the probable kinds of resistance the clients would manifest to unfreezing Models I and O-I and to learning Models II and O-II. These predictions could then be used to generate a learning environment designed to surface the resistances and overcome them. Consequently, the entire educational program could provide many opportunities to test the validity of the model. The research conducted for such a test would, at the same time, be useful in evaluating the effectiveness of the learning environment.

A third possible test is related to the changes that may or may not occur in the organization. For example, in the newspaper study, one of the consequences of the learning environment was to make it impossible for the editorial and news people to collaborate. The map specified how the primary loops involving the two respective editors played a key role in creating the problems. When the interventions were designed to overcome the problems, the primary actors first had to confirm those aspects of the map. If they did not, then the map would be placed in question. As was the case, not only did the protagonists agree, they presented directly observable evidence of the primary loops as each discussed the problem. Subsequently, three sessions were held with the protagonists to resolve the problem. These sessions provided further evidence of the problem's existence. However, as the problem began to be resolved, we observed that the secondary loops began to be altered. Interviews with people who were not present during the sessions (but were involved in the loops) confirmed the changes. The tapes from the meetings and the interviews also generated data about what aspects were not changing and the probable reasons for this resistance to change. Again, these data should not operate to disconfirm the original map by, for example, surfacing new components of the learning system that were counter to those developed.

Every intervention session designed and executed to generate learning and overcome problems becomes a demonstration-experiment where aspects of the map are confronted. Consequently, a set of tests of the map be generated through predictions of what will and will not happen in the organization given the learning system. For example, in the newspaper, an episode called "the great fiasco" occurred which involved resignations of several key people. The interventionist was able to predict that should a similar problem occur, the fiasco would reoccur even though the (remaining) participants vowed that it would not. By a strange set of events, the condition did reoccur, and so did the fiasco.

Finally, the validity of the map may be tested by asking the clients to confirm or disconfirm it. This opportunity usually comes before the others, during the feedback sessions of the initial diagnosis.

Feedback and testing the diagnosis

There are four purposes to the feedback session. The first is to present to the clients the map of the learning system developed by the interventionists. The second is to utilize the clients' discussion of the map as further confirmation or disconfirmation of the map. The clients may or may not agree with the factors identified by the interventionists as composing the learning system. Or they may agree that they utilize Model I theories-in-use and are embedded in an O-I learning system. If the latter, they should produce examples of primary and secondary inhibiting loops as they discuss the map.

The third purpose is to use the presentation as the first step by which the clients can internalize those aspects of the map that make sense to them and develop new aspects of the map. The fourth purpose is to utilize the map and the learning generated by reflecting on the discussion in order to invent next steps in the intervention process.

Experience to date suggests that the clients' reactions toward a relatively comprehensive map of their learning system produces questions that are understandable in terms of an O-I system. The first reaction is one of dismay and disheartenment. It is not easy for a group of top administrators to accept the possibility that they are embedded in a system of interconnected factors that inhibit learning. Moreover, to accept the possibility is to also accept that they have not been managing their organization effectively and/or that they have not been aware of the complexities of the organization.

Questions are therefore raised as to how likely it is that organizations with other than O-I learning systems may be created. If the answer is that it is highly unlikely (and most clients know that by simply observing their own and others' organizations), then they may feel less of a sense of shame or responsibility for managing, in other eyes, irresponsibly.

The second set of questions is also related to reducing the dissonance that the clients may be feeling once they realize the discrepancy between what they espouse as good organization, and the organization as mapped by the interventionists. Two of the most frequent questions are: "How do the findings compare with those generated in other studies?" and "Is our organization better, worse, or about the same as other systems studied?" Again, if the interventionists reply that most organizations have O-I learning systems, and this one is about as complex as the others (two responses that almost certainly would be made), then the clients may reduce their anxiety and prepare themselves for learning.

The reduction of this type of anxiety could facilitate the clients' turning to the invention of solutions to the problems. However, this rarely happens during the early phases of feedback. Rather, the clients may attempt to find gaps and errors in the research. Requests are made for clarification about statistical analyses, definitions of categories, samples used, and so on.

Another set of questions is related to probing the substantive findings. For example, the clients may ask, with a sense of disbelief,

"Are you really suggesting that you rarely observed trust or openness of feelings in our meetings?" Straightforward and direct answers are usually most effective. If our response is affirmative, we add, "We have brought with us the tape recordings of the meetings and would be glad to play any one where you believe there are instances of trust and openness." Thus the interventionists make themselves open for confrontation and public testing of their findings.

Generating new data and increasing
internal commitment to the diagnosis

To date, the focus of the learning has been on confirming or disconfirming the maps and striving to reduce feelings of discomfort due to the gap between what the clients may have expected and the results that they actually received. There is another quite different level of learning that goes on during the feedback sessions. In this phase, there is new learning that goes beyond the map; it is a more clear connection between the map and the behavior of the top and the experience of seeing Model II in action as performed by the interventionists.

For example, one of the newspaper executives reacted angrily that his subordinates misunderstood his motivations in holding certain meetings. Note, in the following dialogue, that the interventionist did not become seduced by the executive's anger, nor did he attempt to tell the executive (identified as C) to suppress his feelings. The interventionist (Int) tried to make clear his position, yet he also invited confrontation of his views even though some of the clients insisted that they did not mean to fight him. The interventionist also attempted to encourage the expressions of frustration and anger by noting that he too had experienced similar feelings when he received feedback similar to some the clients had received:

C: (Angrily) Hell, people below may think that, but that is not our intention.

Int: I'm not trying to attribute a particular motivation to you. I'm suggesting that there may be a gap between how you see the situation and how your subordinates experience it.

C: (Still angry) I'm just setting the record straight.

A: Why don't we go on? We don't mean to fight you, you know.

Int: There will be times when people will mean to fight me. I welcome it. It's important to express all our views. I'll express mine!

D: These are all new ideas and sometimes they're not easy to accept.

Int: I understand how you feel. I have similar feelings when I get the same type of feedback about my own behavior or about the organization I work in.

In another example, the interventionist did not permit others to attribute that he was blaming the clients. Instead, he was able to help the clients express their astonishment and then reflect on the fact that they were astonished. What does it say about their perceptions of reality and their relationship with the subordinates if the findings astonished them? Such questions begin to give the clients preliminary experience in using research findings to explore the learning system of their organization.

A: I thought those meetings were one of the most valuable innovations we had.

Int: Some people would agree with you.

A: I thought they were well conducted and very productive. Are you saying I'm wrong about all that?

Int: I'm not saying that you're wrong. I'm saying that almost none of the people I interviewed would agree with you.

A: (Laughing) That's a perfectly valid answer.

B: What's happened to that idea? What is causing that meeting to lose its effectiveness?

Int: One reason that was reported was related to the way the meetings were led.

B: That astonished me.

Int: That raises an interesting question. (Looking at several people) Why weren't any of you aware of this information? What does it mean about your relationship with these people?

B: Yes, I see your point.

During another interchange, the interventionist responded to a question about sample size and then asked the clients if they were not also having doubts about the results. For example, in one organization, the executive wondered if the interventionist had not attended "too few meetings." The interventionist responded by describing the number of meetings attended, the sampling theory behind the selection, and his experiences in other organizations. Then he went on:

Int: Sometimes when people question my sample, they mean to question the results. Would you be willing to tell me if there are any results that you find hard to believe, that do not square with your experience?

A: I can't believe there isn't any risk-taking in our meetings.

Int: May I suggest several ways of tackling this issue? One is for us to go on to the data on the meetings in which you were involved. Perhaps you can give examples of risk taking. Another is to ask others to give us their views. A third is to listen to parts of the tape recordings I have brought with me.

Whenever the executives recalled a particular meeting, they had difficulty recalling what they and others had said. If they could recall, they could seldom agree on one description of a particular behavior—whether for example, one man's statement was an example of risk taking. (Whenever possible, the interventionist may urge listening to the tape recording. But to date, even the most vociferous doubters have not agreed to playing back portions of the tape. They should not be pressed to do so.)

As the interventionist was able to answer questions to the clients' satisfaction, the latter begin to realize that they were embedded in an organization with important learning difficulties. At the outset, it was not surprising, therefore, that the clients dealt with the findings by describing their disappointment in the results, in general, and in their subordinates, in particular.

These discussions can be used by the interventionist to reinforce the findings, yet in a way that will help the clients to get on with the task of inventing solutions to the problems. For example:

A: Everything you say is true. Do they realize the pressure that we're under?

C: That's true—all of us are under pressure. Sometimes we get so preoccupied with a deadline that we don't look at the human problems.

In the discussion that follows, the interventionist first encouraged the clients to speak about their feelings of pressure, then prevented A from sidetracking such expression of feelings, and became a representative of the subordinate's views to the top officials. Later, he was careful not to be seduced into polarizing the diagnosis, yet did not hesitate to state unequivocally to C just what he believed the subordinates felt and thought. When C stated that the subordinates were wrong, the interventionist used the opportunity to test the findings with others. This led others to provide even further illustrations of the problems that confirmed the original diagnosis.

A: Are we sidetracking your presentation?

Int: I think we should discuss these feelings as they come up. We've scheduled plenty of time so that issues like these can be fully explored.

A: Well, do they want to ask us if the elevators should be painted blue, or do they want us to tell them to do it?

Int: As I understand their views, they are as follows: On unimportant issues, like the color of the elevators, tell them. On important, long-range policy issues, many want to be more involved. Also, if you want to be directive and not involve them, they will go along with this policy, but they question the validity of all the talk about increasing their participation in decision making. Finally, I'd like to emphasize that they are aware that all of you are under pressures. They sympathize with you, and this is one reason that they rarely discuss these issues with you.

Later on in the meeting:

A: I suspect that (in discussions) he cuts off the dumb ones and encourages the bright ones. It seems to me that you're suggesting that everyone, dumb or bright, should be encouraged.

Int: I'm asking, how do you know they are dumb? Could this be a self-fulfilling prophecy? Also, why do you invite the dumb ones to the meetings?

A: You can't afford to exclude them.

Int: That's not their view. If they are going to be treated as machines, many prefer to be excluded. Maybe it's time that they were helped to see exactly how their superiors evaluate them.

C: He's right. We rarely tell people about these evaluations.

Still later:

Int: What would you predict as their view of that news meeting?

C: I think they think it is practically useless.

D: Well, it's a kind of nostalgia.

Int: That's their feeling about it—that they're being used to serve nostalgia.

C: Not my nostalgia.

Int: That's their view.

C: I must say that they're wrong.

Int: Let's check it out with others around the table.

D: (He the interventionist) is correct. These have been your meetings for years.

C: Well, hell, let's drop them!

And finally:

Int: I gave an example where, in order to save face, management created two bosses for a particular group.

P: Yes, we did that and it was wrong.

Int: But as far as I can see, you're still doing it.

P: Yes, you're right. It won't be easy to change.

E: But why is this wrong? Doesn't it show that our organization has a heart?

F: Well, I can give you several examples of how this has harmed us, especially with our better younger people. They believe we prefer to reward dead wood.

D: Frankly, I feel we also destroy the people we think we're helping. They know that their jobs are meaningless.

E: I think a certain amount of subterfuge works because people like it.

Int: If it does, I would say that could be a sign of sickness in the system.

Is this trip necessary: the tacit agenda

Some reasons for the clients raising the questions described above include: (1) to explore the validity of the findings; (2) to learn the degree to which the findings are common to other organizations; and (3) to assess the degree to which it is possible to manage organizations with other learning systems.

Another reason, equally important and usually held more tacitly than explicitly, is that the clients wonder if it is really necessary to focus on the theories-in-use, the primary and secondary inhibiting loops, and the organizational games in order to create genuine solutions. Is such a learning trip necessary?

The interventionists' stance to the latter question is to assert that the trip is necessary but the commitment to it must be internal; otherwise it will be ineffective. The interventionists advocate the position candidly and simultaneously encourage confrontation of it. The clients may then raise questions and invent other possible strategies. The interventionists attempt to explain why and how the bypass strategies would leave the theories-in-use and the inhibiting loops as they are, ready to operate on the next set of problems. Moreover, the common client reaction is similar to that in the example above. In that case, the reaction of the clients to the feedback indicated that they were surprised by some of the findings, and they felt misunderstood. The surprise was evidence that the clients were unaware, which in turn was evidence that inhibiting loops are working to keep them ignorant. Their reactions of feeling misunderstood and therefore annoyed were evidence that they were placing the blame on the subordinates. They did not consider that the subordinates could have withheld the information because the system dictated such action; that the system dictated such action in order to protect the superiors and the subordinates; and that therefore they were not seeking to explore their personal responsibility for the very problem they were lamenting.

The degree of client defensiveness over taking the trip suggested by the interventionists varies widely depending on several different conditions. Client defensiveness is related to the degree of openness to learning that exists in the client system, the degree of openness of the key power members (especially the leader), the members' conception of what the trip will be like, and the degree to which they believe that the required skills are dangerous.

For example, in one case on record, the group began by talking about their discomfort in dealing with primary and secondary inhibiting loops. This soon led them to explore their discomfort. Several mentioned the fear that to be open is "to clobber" people. Others mentioned that their dilemma was that the organization was managed by fear. The president interrupted and said:

P: I don't think that we run this company by fear and I don't think that you should have said that.

There was an excruciatingly lengthy silence of five seconds, and the vice president replied:

VP: I still believe that we manage this company by fear and I agree with you that I should not have said it!

Before the interventionist could try to help, the president said:

P: Before you (the interventionist) jump in, let me say that I see what I just did. I have been asking for openness and risk-taking, and I clobber the first peron that takes a risk. I'm sorry; it's not easy to hear such things.

VP: I too am sorry, but it is not easy to say them.

The level of candor was achieved in several hours of discussion which in turn made it possible for the group to explore their learning system in great detail and with minimal resistance (Argyris 1962).

The other end of the continuum may be illustrated by another example from the newspaper case. The managing editor of the news department wanted to try to build more of a double-loop inquiring system than existed at the time. He was aware that this meant that he and others would have to explore the primary and secondary loops and was prepared to do so. Several sessions were held with subordinates to explore the issue. Relatively quickly, they validated the diagnoses made by the interventionist and almost as quickly stated that they had doubts about the advisability of exploring their learning system. They gave two reasons for their doubts, saying that (1) they already had an open relationship among each other, and (2) they did not need an open relationship because they performed their duties with little interdependence among them.

Leaving aside for the moment the partial contradiction implied in the assertions that they were open and that they did not need openness, there is the question of validity of the latter. If it is structurally true that they did not have many interdependent relationships, then why focus on interdependence?

The managing editor had several views on this question. First, he agreed that historically the assistant editors rarely had to talk to each other. But with the new financial pressures, it was no longer possible to give any one of them all the financial resources he or she asked for without taking money away from the others. He believed that giving the assistant editors more influence in how the pie was cut would give them greater control and encourage them to put less padding in their requests. Moreover, journalism was becoming more interdependent by the introduction of news analysis as distinct from hard news reporting. The younger reporters wanted to do more of the former and were increasingly doing "subjective" reporting. The criteria for objective and subjective reporting were very difficult to develop. The managing editor believed that this kind of issue required discussion among all the editors. Finally, as the amount of reportable news increased, and as the size of the news-hole decreased, there were difficult decisions to be made about what to exclude and include. Again, the managing editor believed that this required greater interdependence.

The managing editor also believed that he could not state any of these reasons and give the concrete examples that would be necessary without plunging headlong into many of the win/lose dynamics, intergroup rivalries, and games that news people played. He also believed that he could not state these things because in the past, when he had made some carefully designed attempts to do so, subordinates had insisted that he go right ahead because they trusted each other—and this "trust" had resulted in some highly defensive discussions.

A six-hour session was held to discuss the possibility of exploring the learning system. A reading of the transcripts indicates that it was one of the most defensive meetings reported in the literature (Argyris 1974, pp. 182–217), where the clients were highly inconsistent and apparently unaware of their inconsistencies.

For example, listed below are the positions maintained by the subordinates (left hand column) and what the same people said to the interventionist during subsequent individual interviews:

What subordinates said to superiors	What they said to the interventionists
We are a group that understands each other. We understand each other even without talking. We know each other well.	We don't want to say things that might hurt our relationships with others. We behave in ways that range from fear of punishment to diplomacy. I'm not really sure how the others would have responded.
We trust each other.	People do things secretly around here. There is a lot that we don't tell each other. I think we may be afraid of what we can do to each other if we really leveled.
Things are much better in our department. Morale is much higher.	Yes, there is a decrease in tension but there is an increase in mistrust. I predict a blowup in two years.
We face issues squarely.	There are some big professional egos in our group. We're always externalizing causes; the problems are always out there.
People are our most important resources.	The truth is that most of us cannot put this learning project on a high priority.
We prefer to make our own decisions.	(The subordinates, when asked how they preferred to vote for the program, asked that the superior make the decision. Also, those who came to the meeting feeling receptive to the idea of attending an off-site learning experience expected that the interventionist or the superior would say something that was convincing and compelling.)

These inconsistent positions and the subordinates' unawareness of their inconsistencies are not surprising. We would expect such results in an O-I system. The subordinates focused so intensely on defending against the exploration of their learning system that they had little energy to reflect on what they were saying. Their purpose was not to advocate and inquire but to win and not lose, where winning meant not to enter a learning environment in which they would discuss these difficult issues.

After the session, the subordinates maintained that they were against such an exercise because the managing editor did not really want it; he was pressured by the publisher to hold it. When asked what prevented them from raising that issue, they all said it would have been too risky (yet they maintained that the group was open and trusting). And finally, the members felt that the proposed exercise could do psychological harm to member F. They presented cases in which they felt F showed a high degree of sensitivity. The interventionist recognized these cases because F had discussed them with him. Member F was aware that he acted defensively during these sessions, but part of the cause was, in his view, the sense that his colleagues were holding back information from him!

In this case, the subordinates voted unanimously not to participate (the managing editor voted to participate). The managing editor's immediate response was to wonder out loud if he should not order them to go to a session. They responded that if he ordered them to go, they would do so. The interventionist intervened to support and reinforce the subordinates' prerogative to vote as they did. The managing editor quickly accepted the vote and said that it would not make sense to coerce people. He told the interventionist privately that the decision also hurt, because it indicated the lack of trust the subordinates had in him and in each other.

The causes for the resistance are understandable in terms of Models I and O-I. People programmed with Model I theories-in-use tend to resist exploring issues that might surface threatening information and arouse feelings. Their major skill for dealing with these issues is to hide them. The result is if the issues are ever dealt with openly, it is usually done in a crisis atmosphere, and when it occurs, a lot of pent-up information and feelings gush out. This in turn tends to overwhelm both parties because they usually do not have the experience or skills to deal with threatening information and pent-up feelings. The feelings of being overwhelmed are rarely described in these terms. In accordance with Model I theories-in-use, most recipients explain their defensiveness by attributing the cause to the other. Hence, the feelings of being overwhelmed are usually translated into, "The other person clobbered me."

Most people embedded in an O-I learning environment do not have the Model II skills to deal with these issues effectively, and, as we have illustrated at several points, they tend to be unaware that they do not. Once they become aware of the skills, they tend to see them as impractical and unrealistic. This is a valid perception if the world remains O-I.

Inventing, producing, and generalizing

As the clients listen to their discussions of the data and satisfy themselves that the diagnosis is valid, they begin to accept the fact that the trip is necessary and that it is time to think about taking action. In terms of our model, the clients now plunge into the phases of inventing, producing, and generalizing.

Inventing, producing, and generalizing occur at the individual, group, and organizational levels for theory-of-action problems, as well as for instrumental ones. Perhaps because of the way we design the intervention process, people focus on inventing and producing a new theory-in-use before they attempt to invent and produce solutions to secondary loops, organizational games, and instrumental problems that involve double-loop issues. They learn to use progress in moving from Model I to Model II as evidence that they really mean to change. Only after they show such commitment to changing their theories-in-use does progress spread to other levels.

For example, a president and the nine vice-presidents became involved in an intervention program. The first stage was to help each other move from Model I toward Model II. During the early phases, this was very difficult, because in trying to help each other they generated behavior that was counter-productive for problem solving. Thus, they counseled each other by making unsubstantiated evaluations, unilateral attributions, and untestable assertions. It was not long before the members realized that they would never help each other by such behavior.

They decided to attempt to invent statements that approximated Model II. As would be predictable from our view, they remained within Model I, the opposite to Model I, or the oscillating Model I relationships. In desperation, they asked the interventionists to demonstrate Model II responses. The interventionists were able to help the members design Model II statements, but when these statements were written on the chalkboard, most of the members threw up their arms. They would never say anything like that. Indeed, they would never *think* anything like it. It would be foolish to say it in such a way in the group.

For example, the group spent several hours trying to invent a new approach to a subordinate who was not present. They wanted to keep him but he was performing poorly. The interventionist asked, "How do you feel about the problems?" A composite answer was: "We are in a dilemma. On the one hand we do not want to lose him and on the other hand we cannot continue to have him on the payroll with such poor performance. But we do not know what to do because everything we have tried seem ineffective. He appears to us to be impossible to influence."

The interventionist then suggested that that very statement would make a good beginning. The executives were surprised; in spite of the fact that they had said they would never do so, they had no trouble in *thinking* those thoughts. However, they would be very uncomfortable in *saying* what they thought. So we have executives who can invent solutions but would neither see them as appropriate nor think of producing them.

"What prevents you from using these solutions in the room, right here where we are practicing?" asked the interventionist. The resulting intense discussion developed several answers. First, the reply above appeared to them to be "mushy"; it suggested that the leader was unsure and ambivalent. Leaders should not communicate such feelings because they would lose their effectiveness. Second, making such a reply would increase the probability that the subordinate may respond in such a way that the leader would lose. As one man said, "I would feel naked making a statement like that."

The executives realized that they were saying that they would not make such statements because they would violate their existing Model I theories-in-use. But if they did not try out their statements to see how well they worked, they would never move toward Model II and entertain a new set of values.

What is it about a group in the learning environment that makes it difficult to experiment with inventions? The executives concluded that they did not wish to fail and look foolish in front of the group. If and when they were to make a Model II intervention, they wanted it to be "a gem," or "a thing of beauty." But who expects these interventions to be perfect on the first try? The answer was that the executives themselves did. Thus the competitiveness among the members in the learning seminar precluded their experimenting, which practically guaranteed they would not learn.

The executives saw their bind. If they continued this way, there was little hope of learning. One man said, "If we could only reduce the competitiveness!" Another asked, "What is there to stop us? If we want to try to become less competitive, we can do it." So the group invented some of the first norms to guide their behavior. Having done so, they learned that these norms did not guarantee Model II behavior. Indeed, behavior continued to be competitive. However, the actors were more deliberate in trying to design new behavior and therefore more open to experimenting. Also, whenever competitiveness arose that inhibited learning, it was identified by the members. Over time and many experiments, the members began to reduce the level of competitiveness.

The interventionist noted that although competitiveness had generally been reduced, there still seemed to be competitive feelings toward A (a financial vice-president). Was this inference valid? There was a period of silence. One executive asked for some directly observable data to illustrate the inference. Before the interventionist could reply, A said that he felt it too, and proceeded to give two examples. Both examples were related to jokes about the "misers" in the finance department who think the company would go broke without them.

This opened up a new set of issues. Many of the line vice-presidents admitted that they felt that A did not trust them. Indeed, they were tired of the innuendos, emanating from his offices, that the finance people were the eyes and ears of the company. Moreover, they did not like the innuendos made during the meetings at which their financial performance was being examined.

The discussion continued, with A asserting that he did not wish to mistrust them, but that he had learned to do so. He found evidence, for example, that budgets were being padded. Several line executives admitted that they padded their budgets to protect themselves from unpredictable errors or disasters. They simply did not feel the financial vice-president would recommend that their budget be increased if some unforeseen problem arose.

The discussion continued with everybody surfacing the mistrust they felt toward one another concerning the allocation of scarce financial resources. Each statement was documented with several business examples.

After several hours, the president asked if there was not a way that the group could design a process to define financial goals, allocate resources, and monitor the use of those resources. Could not the group invent a procedure for control such that no one individual, including himself, would have undue influence? This question opened up even further issues of administrative warfare, because as one man said to the president, "If we really mean this, then we ought to include some other games that we play around here that cost money and are divisive."

Several meetings were allocated to this issue. The result was that a new process for financial allocation was designed to be used as an experiment. If any member (including the president or vice-president of finance) felt that the new system was jeopardizing the organization, they could call a meeting to recommend the discontinuance of the idea.

Not only was the idea not discontinued, it led to a drastic reduction in: (1) padded budget requests (thereby saving several million dollars a year), (2) clique meetings to find out who was getting how much money and why, (3) "JIC" files ("Just In Case the boss asks" files), and (4) the amount of deception and camouflage around financial issues.

Note what happened. The group began with a task of moving from Model I to Model II theories-in-use. This led them to explore primary and secondary inhibiting loops within their learning group. One incident led to the identification of the line-finance issue, the intergroup rivalries, and the games of deception and mistrust. Once these became discussable, it became clear to all that they were alterable.

This led to the invention of new solutions and experimentation with these new solutions in the back-home situation.

The experiments did not work perfectly at first. There were many errors. But everyone was on the lookout for errors, and since the errors were discussable, they became correctable. Thus, after six months, the organization had a new budgetary process that was being continually monitored and which was saving the organization considerable sums of money.

In other words, a process whereby people begin to behave according to Model II theories-in-use leads them to explore primary and secondary inhibiting loops and organizational games. Once people begin to hold the values of valid information, free choice, and internal commitment; once they begin to combine advocacy with inquiry; once they seek to eliminate self-sealing processes and experience public testing and experimentation, then the entire O-I learning system is confronted. Model II theories-in-use make it possible for people to generate double-loop learning and pursue good dialectic. With these theories-in-use, members are able to identify and discuss many group, intergroup, and organizational norms and games that inhibit learning. They can, in many cases, eliminate the inhibiting loops. It is more difficult to invent and produce new solutions, but: (1) the members know it is more difficult; (2) they have a realistic level of aspiration; (3) they know how to decompose the problem; (4) they are able to experiment with new solutions without hindering the organization's cost-benefit ratios or outputs; (5) they know how to monitor, how to learn iteratively, and how to evaluate their learning in order to (6) discover new problems and then repeat the cycles.

The case of F also relates changes in theories-in-use to changes in the learning system and to the solution of important instrumental problems. The case of F is presented because in addition to the above, it also illustrates how focusing on changing one's theory-in-use can lead to the discovery that phenomena evaluated as strengths of individuals and organizations may actually be weaknesses, and vice versa.

The owner of a successful firm, F was a participant, along with five other presidents, in a series of seminars to move from Model I toward Model II (Argyris 1976a). During the early seminars, F had difficulty in relating effectively with the other presidents. He would remark how helpful Model II was, and that he and the new president he had selected for his firm had a Model II relationship. The assertions

irked the others, partly because F did not appear to behave according
to Model II in the seminar and partly because they attributed to F a
motivation to put them down and to continuously look good. The
others spoke about F with anger when he was not present. When the
interventionists were asked to present their views, they kept suggesting that the problem be discussed with F.

The other presidents hesitated to do this because they feared it
would upset F to realize that he was not behaving according to Model
II. The first reason for the inference was the (to them) obvious blindness of F to the fact that the examples he used to illustrate a Model II
relationship were Model I. The second reason was the discrepancy between how F described himself and how the others experienced him.
For example, F described himself as emotional, intuitive, and nonra-
tional. They saw him as intellectual (denying and suppressing his feelings), compulsively planning, and highly rational.

One day, when F was remarking about how great it was to use
Model II (in a Model I manner), the confrontation occurred. It was
carefully expressed, openly discussed and competently carried out by
others in the seminar. As a result of several long discussions, F began
to see that he was suppressing his feelings, and that he was highly
competitive and prone to intellectualization. He also realized that he
had been blind, and explored how he and others designed the world to
keep him blind.

He realized that many of his questions and assertions were made
in ways that encouraged self-sealing responses from others, and the
other presidents were able to describe how they had adapted to him by
withholding information and deceiving him.

The new awareness led F to a heightened capacity to see others
more accurately. He began to see that his president (X) was indeed
highly rational and that he suppressed his feelings. Seeing the world
differently led F to begin to inquire differently. The vice-presidents
sensed the difference and they began to be more candid about their
frustrations. In turn, F attempted to validate the assertions made by
the subordinates about X, only to find out that X did not want to discuss such issues. While X was prepared to discuss business or instrumental issues, he was not prepared to discuss his theory-in-use.

Although X communicated that view to the vice-presidents, F
learned, they did not communicate important business or instrumental issues to X because they felt it would upset him. For example, they

questioned whether a particular plant would be able to produce the goals for the year, but hesitated to say anything because X sounded certain that it would. Others had serious doubts about the marketability of a new product, but hesitated to say so because X appeared enthusiastic about it.

Again F tried to discuss these issues with X and had the same difficulties the vice-presidents had experienced with him. But F understood these difficulties differently because he knew that he had created similar communication blockages with the other presidents in the learning seminars.

Although he tried several times to do so, F found it difficult to communicate with X. Soon the predictions made by the subordinates began to be confirmed, and the firm was developing serious cash-flow problems. When F and X went to the banks to borrow money, F saw even more clearly how inept X was. Apparently so did the bankers, who said that they would loan the money only if F returned to more active leadership in the firm.

Reluctantly, F agreed though he would have preferred to leave X alone (note the strategy of going from Model I to the opposite of Model I). Now F was in a position to see more clearly the frustrations of the vice-presidents and the impact the poor relationship had on developing valid manufacturing, marketing, and financial plans. During a particularly stormy session between X and the vice-presidents, the former told the latter that they were not paid to disagree with him but to follow his orders and to say that they would do so willingly!

Knowing that X was under great pressure, F talked with him at length about the short- and long-range dangers of his approach. The only response X gave was to remind F that he had promised to let X manage the firm.

The situation became worse, and one day F decided that X should be relieved of the presidency. His new design was to discuss this openly with X and later with X and the vice-presidents. Several members of his board warned him against such openness. They recommended a sudden firing of X in order to "cut clean".

Deciding not to follow their advice, F first talked with X, to see if there was a way that he and X could team up to work together. But X was adamant, so F then said that he wanted to discuss with the vice-presidents the possibility of relieving X of the presidency. The latter responded that F could do what he wished.

Having tried to straighten things out with X, F did discuss the problem with the vice-presidents, who felt greatly relieved that the action was being taken. They united with F to build a team approach to undoing the damage that had been created by X's style of leadership. As a result, they were able to solve the plant-production and marketing problems. They not only reversed a dangerous trend, but they also brought the company back into a sound financial position.

The new team not only gained increasing confidence with each success, but they spent much time reexamining their learning system in order to reduce the probability that the organization would get into a similar position. They identified as many games, acts of deception, and camouflage as possible. Then they found ways to reduce those counterproductive activities and to create, wherever helpful, policies to help ensure that they would not be reintroduced.

CHAPTER NINE

Limited intervention

Let us suppose that clients have defined an instrumental problem, but have made it very clear that they want to meet to discuss this problem and not others—that, in particular, they are not prepared to address the limitations of their own learning system. Then it is still possible to intervene so as to help the client organization restructure its instrumental problem—and to do so, moreover, in ways that help members of the organization to learn about organizational problem setting and solving.

In this sort of case, the interventionists can help the clients to engage fundamental conditions for error such as organizational scatter and incongruity of espoused theory with theory-in-use. They can guide the process of organizational inquiry both by modeling an approach to that inquiry and by acting to suspend some of the dysfunctional consequences of an O-I learning system.

In this approach, the interventionists' responsibility is to generate as much valid information as possible from the clients by: (1) intervening when necessary to bypass the clients' primary and secondary inhibiting loops; (2) confronting any instances of organizational defensive games, such as deception and camouflage, whenever necessary; and (3) healing any damage done by clients to each other and to the problem-solving process as they behave congruently with Model I theories-in-use and in keeping with the constraints of an O-I learning system.

Moreover, the interventionists can help the clients to elicit organizational knowledge which is buried and scattered, and inaccessible to organizational inquiry. They can encourage the clients to look at the problem in different ways, of leading to a fuller and more complex representation of it than is likely in the normal contexts of organizational inquiry. And they can support the clients when the clients surface and inquire into conflicts which would normally be suppressed or resolved without inquiry.

But in this limited mode, interventionists cannot help their clients to implement the solutions resulting from inquiry, if effective implementation depends on Model II behavior. And they cannot help them to modify their living system as to make such problems more amenable to good inquiry in the future.

It is difficult to state ahead of time exactly how the responsibilities of limited intervention are to be fulfilled in any given situation. We can, however, describe what we have found to be some of the key phases, and how the interventionists may behave in order to carry them out.

MORE OF THE MERCURY STORY

We will take as an example the Mercury Corporation, which was discussed in Chapter 2. You will recall that although the corporation has based its growth on new technology, building a new business area on a new family of technologies every ten years or so, the development of new products and processes had always been seen as problematic. In the 1950s, the problem of corporate development was understood primarily in terms of research competence. By the 1960s, managers had evolved a new diagnosis. They recognized an "entrepreneurial gap," the need for a new business structure which could explore markets for research results and incubate new businesses until they were ready to be turned over to existing divisions. The problem, as the managers saw it, was that the heads of existing businesses tended to resist new products and processes until they had proven their worth.

Accordingly, in the middle 1960s, Mercury created a New Business Division (NBD). Over a decade, they invested a significant percentage of their R&D dollars in NBD. But they found the results ambiguous and troublesome, which led finally to their bringing in a consultant. The NBS manager proposed to discuss ". . . new venture management in a mature organization in view of the dramatic social, political, and especially economic changes that are taking place in the world today. Is the pursuit of new ventures still a viable alternative to growth for a mature corporation in these changing times?"

The consultant's first step was to develop a map of the problem. But, characteristically, there is more than one such map. Members of the organization hold different views of the problem, views which they have often withheld or expressed incompletely to one another. During the early stages, it is important that interventionists help their clients to surface these views, avoiding a focus on inconsistencies or negative consequences of the first views given (since this might trigger competition and the inappropriate punishment of those who were willing to start the discussion) in order to increase the probability that people will communicate with each other about the problem more fully than before.

Given what we know about O-I learning systems, there is a high probability that people have not fully communicated to each other all they know about the problem. The challenge to the interventionists is to surface the different views as completely and clearly as possible. In doing so, they tend to make the familiar foreign ("We thought we understood the problem, but now we realize that we do not") and the simple, rich and complex ("The problem is more complicated than we realized.").

In the early discussions of corporate development at Mercury, the clients expressed different views of the problem:

> We're not organized to do the job, not only in development but in the whole technological area . . . costs of technological development are going up . . . 50 percent of our profits come from 30 percent of the products, the proprietary ones. . . . We know how to manage capital much better than we do technology.

> NBD is constrained by its charter.

> NBD tends to take the path of least resistance, placing new technology within existing divisional boundaries.

> We have been going for 10 years and not produced anything of real consequence. Projects that have made it are not NBD projects. We have entertained lots of projects rather than pick an area and try to figure out how to get there.

You need lots of balls in the air, because the odds on any one are so low. You must look at lots of possibilities. Over 10 years, we've looked at more than 200 business opportunities.

The consultant proposed to get underneath these different views by asking the clients to reconstruct case histories of corporate development over the previous decade. He suggested that they address the following questions:

1. How have we actually gone about the process of development, particularly in the successful cases?

2. What can we learn from a consideration of these histories? In particular, how do these experiences illuminate (in what ways do they confirm or disconfirm) the pieces of theories about effective technological development now held in various quarters in Mercury?

3. What inferences can we draw about the design of organizational structures and practices for technological development?

This exercise in story-telling was not intended to discover recipes for effective development based on invariant features of "successful" developments which distinguished these from "unsuccessful" ones. It was intended, however, to elicit themes of development and patterns of informal and often tacit practice which were likely to be more subtle and complex than the theories advanced to account for those processes.

The effort at recreating history was based on the assumption that the organization is often able to do more than it can say. With a better picture of actual practice, members of the organization would be able to test and improve their own theories of effective performance and to criticize proposed designs for corporate development which were based on inadequate theories of organizational practice.

Further, as participants reviewed the stories of development, they would be likely to give different views of them. The attempt to explain differences could lead to insights into the learning system, and the way in which members reacted to the differences of views could provide another kind of evidence about the prevailing processes for setting and solving organizational problems.

These, in summary form, are some of the stories that were told:

Product X

In the early 1960s, we bought a fabricating company, based on the raw material, R. We built a division around it. At this time, we had no materials developed especially for this kind of fabrication. We depended on other kinds of materials which were adapted for this purpose.

But within one of our materials divisions, we had a process for producing materials which looked as though they might offer special advantages for the new fabricating process.

The new division had a good share of market but was up against strong competition. We were aware of needing new market applications, something bigger than our existing market. We set up a task force under a chairman who had both technical savvy and commercial knowledge, and they came back with a range of possible applications, recommending X in particular.

A two-year feasibility study then began. It required collaboration between the fabrication and materials divisions, and their relations were not of the best.

It was not at first evident to the materials division that, in this product, they could actually lose market for materials sold to customers with whom the new fabrication division would compete, though in the long run they would have materials to sell.

It was decided that not central research, but the divisions, through the pooling of people, should manage the development. The corporation funded this effort. There was a great cooperative atmosphere, but there were also misgivings.

This development represented more than $1,000,000, and existing businesses felt they could have used it better. Such a new business tends to look like a business that's failing. The project nearly died twice.

Nevertheless, it survived. In part, this was due to corporate funding. No division's P&L was at stake. And what was more, a big potential customer became interested within a year of the start of the feasibility study and said, in effect, "If you can make them, I'll buy them."

The managements of the two divisions gave the project their best people and were hurt by the drain on resources.

The product is now in test market. It has been an eight-year process, the largest and most expensive we've every undertaken. Its volume promises to swamp the previous scope of the fabricating division.

The New-Business Division did not have this product, though they thought they should have. In the late 1960s, the section had just been formed and its relations with the operating divisions were worse than now, but the Chairman of the Board was a staunch and dependable advocate of the project.

To the extent that the model of the O-I learning system is valid and applicable to client organizations, there is a high probability that some actions will be described that are consistent with the requirements of the system and counterproductive to effective problem solving. For example, when A told the consultant that they had not told the head of the materials division that he might actually lose market through the new development, the consultant asked why, and the following dialogue took place:

A: If we had told him, given our management policies, he would have been a fool to go along.

C: Did you test this assumption about his reaction?

A: Of course not. How can you test something like that?

C: What happened when he found out that the information had been withheld?

A: He blew his top, but he calmed down.

B: And some of us there wondered when someone was going to play that game on us.

C: Did this make you wary and mistrustful?

A: You're right. You have to be that way if you're going to survive.

Information such as this, made public, not only provides insight into the learning system, but also becomes part of the group's map of the problem which can then be retrieved for later analysis.

On the other hand, in an O-I learning system such discussions are apt to make participants uncomfortable. Hence, the consultant is faced with an additional challenge, namely, to forestall too-early surfacing of different points of view. The clients, being accustomed to O-I problem solving, may feel increasingly uneasy with the complexity and foreignness of the problem, and with the discussion of things previously considered undiscussable. They may call for closure, rarely in the name of being anxious but rather in the name of getting on with the task.

The consultant can accept the clients' reactions, but he is also responsible for alerting the clients to the consequences of stopping. If he experiences a great deal of resistance, he can at least test the clients' perceptions as to why discussions should stop (for example, "What is it that leads you to conclude that we have enough data?").

Product Y

We made a chart to show a spectrum of materials properties along a certain dimension, and we asked, "Could you tailor a material to fill the middle region of the chart?"

We had never been in that business, but we knew that several of our existing businesses would be relevant to it. We had here a material with many possible markets rather than one market looking for a special material.

The head of central research, presiding over the task force, asked, "Let's see if there's anything worth fighting over." The task force was temporary and part-time. There was significantly less commitment than in the case of Product X. Nobody's job depended on making it go.

The business went to one of the existing divisions.

Had we been going to go big, we would have gone after the Z business. Instead, the decision was made to go over a smaller specialty market.

The Z charter belonged to another division. NBS couldn't go forward unless we looked at it as a fabricated part. And the division thought in terms of intermediate materials. They said, "It's not that different. And the cost of maintaining a separate technology would be high." Meanwhile, they had a plan for the specialty market.

We gave it to them.

Product X

One of our old-time investigators had been told that if he took on a disagreeable task, he could devote the rest of his time to anything he chose. He came back with a proposal for Z. This was a technology intriguing to him, a phenomenon he had helped to develop.

He asked, "What have we got?" and "What technology do we bring?"

He thought in terms of the phenomenon, Z, and a business theme ("adhesion") shared by many of Mercury's operations. Here we have a tailored material for adhesion, at lower cost than our current materials.

So we looked across the corporation for those instances of adhesion that cost more than a certain amount. We picked internal applications where it would be easier to prove out the applications.

In their reactions to these stories, the participants made a number of observations.

Effective developments often seemed to involve three directional processes. The first had to do with phenomenology, with exploration of the potentials inherent in certain technological phenomena; the second, with the identification and description of the problems in existing businesses; and the third, with external problem-scanning, a kind of intelligence function through which problems identified in Mercury's environment could be related to Mercury's capabilities.

Development possibilities arose out of the matching of the problems and capabilities discerned through these three processes. For example, a technological phenomenon might be matched with an internal business problem or with a problem detected in the external environment. Often these matches seemed to occur through happy accident.

All of these processes required a very highly developed self-knowledge. Useful descriptions of capabilities were those that were readily connectable with descriptions of business themes and needs. The participants felt they were able to recognize "a Mercury problem" ("our kind of problem"), and that recognition seemed to grow out of their ability to keep in mind, at least tacitly, descriptions of internal capabilities and business themes, and to match them on occasion with descriptions of troubles experienced in the outside world. The participants were not able, however, to make explicit the features that enabled them to identify "our kind of problem."

The consultant attempted to be attentive to the clients' language for describing phenomena and processes familiar to them. He did not try to convert that language into more apparently rigorous formulations. Thus, "a Mercury problem" became a take-off point for exploring their sense of their own special business, a sense they felt and strongly shared but were not able to formulate as part of a theory of corporate development.

Slogans emerged that resonated with people's sense of capabilities and market potentials. The ability to describe targets and results in this way seemed to be an important part of the process for mobilizing energy and management commitment for development.

It was as though development depended on certain related languages, present in the minds of very useful old-timers. These languages, and the images related to them (such as "crying baby" for a project whose visibility results from internal trouble rather than inherent potential), were part of the tacit theory of development present in the organization, which the mapping process was designed to surface.

As the story-telling proceeded, it became apparent that there were only a few major stories. The many small ones fell into a pattern. They tended either to be "crying babies" or to be "fliers" into unknown territory, fliers that were generally cut off in mid-flight when the risks of the unfamiliar became fully apparent.

When the stories began to display a high degree of redundancy, the consultant worked with the participants to generate a model which revealed underlying themes. The attempt now was to diagnose the complex problem of development and to break it into subparts.

As the model was developed in group discussion, it was tested in several ways. How well did it explain and integrate the many different perspectives into one whole that was acceptable to the clients as an accurate description of reality? Could one predict from the model the events that should not occur? Or could one predict under what conditions events opposite to those explained in the model would occur? For example, if the model attempted to explain the conditions for success of certain organizational endeavors, one should not find any failures of similar endeavors under these conditions. The group therefore strove to recall examples that confirmed or disconfirmed the predictions.

The Mercury discussions led to the formulation of several themes of effective corporate developments in Mercury.

The development problem, first of all, appeared to be to mobilize corporate-wide capabilities which were apt to be found in any central or operating unit of the corporation, and to vary from project to proj-

ect. Moreover, certain capabilities ("a savvy, commercially experienced man," "someone who knows the Z business") were likely to be
necessary at particular stages of the process and to drop out later on.

The development task force had been an essential part of
Mercury's ability in the past to achieve these temporary fusions of
widespread corporate capabilities. Indeed, something like a "task-
force technology" appeared to have developed as an art form.

But the task-force approach could not be a solution to the problem of getting embryonic developments to the point where the need
to establish a task force could be perceived.

There was a need in each development venture to harness resources—to liberate energy in the system for the purposes of development—often from those parts of the system least willing to give them
up. This generated a dilemma. For the most effective developments
(for example, product X) were those in which Mercury combined and
transformed pieces of the existing business. From this point of view,
development was a kind of puzzle solving in which existing pieces
came to be seen in new ways, and were combined, transformed, and
infused with resources which allowed them to be made into new businesses.

This dependence on existing "pieces" is understandable as a way
of building on strength. But it is also understandable as a way of generating commitment, because managers are most likely to grasp and become committed to ventures which contain an element of the familiar.

On the other hand, what is from development's point of view a
"piece of the puzzle" is, from the point of view of corporate control, a
territory with its own charter and mandate for growth. Managers of
territories experience conflicting requirements. They are responsible
for maintaining and enhancing the integrity of their territory, but they
are also asked from time to time to regard themselves as pieces of a
larger or different puzzle. In that capacity they must give up a part of
themselves that is then to be combined with something else and transformed.

Hence, the combinations and transformations inherent in the
stories of successful development can also be seen as examples of
"tromping across existing charters." One participant described the
process as one in which "The best marriages are those in which there is
at least one unwilling partner." This is particularly true where the territory in question is profitable and full of potential for more profit. If
such divisions are the most likely to contain pieces whose combination

with others will tend to yield the most promising developments, then the most promising developments are precisely the ones most likely to be resisted by existing divisions.

In the field of force created by this dilemma, it would not be surprising to find development energy side-tracked to rescue operations on "crying babies" or to "fliers" which lie outside existing charters. It also would not be surprising to find development undertaken under the auspices of a single existing division, even when this may not be the most promising option. And it would not be surprising to find that people tend to suppress or disguise, in the early stages, the price an existing division must pay for development.

In its response to the problems of managing a corporation of enormous scale, Mercury managers had created semiautonomous territories whose barons were held accountable for short-term profits and were invited to compete for resources. The corporation had become a kind of oligarchy. But the development process required these barons to function as pieces of a larger puzzle, counter to existing sanctions and incentives.

Hence, it was not surprising that the successful developments were those that captured the attention of top management, who alone could compel divisional barons to give up resources.

The creation of the NBD as a development arm apart from existing divisions was based on a theory of development which ignored both the central dilemma of development and the processes by which the corporation had actually, on rare occasions, resolved it. Given the dilemma of development, and the disposition in an O-I learning system neither to discuss nor confront it, the formal development structure had been doomed to failure.

The participant group was surprised by its own map of the problem. The pieces of that map—the stories of development ventures—were not new. But they had never before been assembled and considered together. Although the resulting picture was disconcerting, participants found it convincing. It seemed to them to account for their experiences in the corporation and to make understandable the frustrations they had been experiencing. The Vice President for Technology, who had been a party to some of the client group meetings, also found the map of the problem convincing.

In constructing such a map of the problem, the client group had taken a major step in the direction of good dialectic. In surfacing some of what the organization knew about development (that it had been unable to say) the group had revealed the incongruity of espoused theory for the development of new businesses with the corporate theory-in-use for that process. For many years, NBD had been operating on the espoused theory and had been failing. Errors had been attributed to tactical mistakes or to management resistance. Now that "resistance" had been made a part of the map of the problem, it revealed fundamental incompatibility in the requirements for decentralized management, on the one hand, and for development, on the other.

As the participants sought to invent solutions to the problem they had mapped, they encountered yet another difficulty. They were strongly tempted to invent solutions acceptable to the present system. But these were the ones least likely to resolve the underlying dilemma.

In this process, the consultant took the role of publicly testing proposed solutions, helping the participants to identify in them the potential for unintended consequences. The clients' norms of rationality made them sensitive to the possibility that they might produce consequences they did not intend, and suggested that the problem might not be truly solved unless they confronted the dilemma fundamental to it.

In the course of this inquiry, the client group came up with five principles for the redesign of the corporate development process:

1. Find better ways of mobilizing and managing the allocation of existing commercial and technological competences throughout the corporation,—instead of setting up parallel structures and resources.

2. The corporate development function must: create and manage networks of dispersed corporate competences; oversee the budgeting and management of resources for development; and integrate these functions with ongoing technology planning.

3. The process should start from early top-management commitment to business and technological targets, rather than generate many balls in the air for top-management review.

4. There should be a new charter for corporate development which reflects these considerations.

5. It is important that divisional managers understand the conflicting requirements which they experience, and that they and top

management design incentives and sanctions which would encourage divisional managers to "play the current game well," and to function from time to time as a "good piece of the larger puzzle."

The client group recognized that these principles could not be realized unless top management and divisional managers entered into a dialogue with those presently responsible for corporate development, a dialogue which would begin with the problem mapping the group had undertaken and with the dilemma of development that had been surfaced.

The prospects for such a dialogue seemed uncertain. Some members of the group worried that, "Should you ever formalize this process, people might reject it." The Vice President for Technology felt that such a dialogue was necessary but would have to be approached with care.

Whenever such shifts are made in the maps, the invention process becomes more difficult because the solutions now will violate or deviate from accepted policy. Under these conditions, it is not unlikely that the clients will revert to previous maps and inventions. The hope is to find a way to solve the problem without having to make basic shifts in policies and in the nature of the organizational practice.

Again, the task of the interventionist is to confront through inquiry—inquiry that surfaces the inconsistencies, incongruities, and unintended consequences. Soon the clients will have to face reality. Effective change will not occur until changes are made in the ecological system and in the policies and practices.

In our experience, it is very difficult to face this reality, and facing it does not necessarily lead to progress. For example, to make such changes means that the clients are making the hard decision to find ways to change their system, which they consider brittle and unchangeable. Moreover, it means that they run the risk of experiencing the negative results of the double binds described in O-I systems.

The most frequent response is for the clients to select some relatively skin-surface solution to implement. Another very frequent response is to accept that a fundamental restructuring of organizational theory of rebirth is necessary, but to call a halt to further activities until they can sound out how the top of the organization will react. Still another response is for the clients to espouse the need for restructuring, to keep holding periodic meetings (with increasing time lapses between meetings) to assert the importance of change, to keep inviting the interventionist to return yet to have very little for him or her to do while there, and to translate the problem into a lower-level issue and ask the subordinates to deal with it.

Yet another alternative is for the interventionist to invent ways to produce the solutions that the clients do not think they can produce by themselves. We see this as a temporary solution, one which may be necessary but hardly to be recommended. A frequent invention is a one- or two-day confrontation session which the interventionists manage in order to minimize the dysfunctional impact of the primary and secondary loops. But, as we have stated previously and will elaborate on in the next part of this book, such strategies rarely solve the problems effectively. If the people are candid and the interventionists skillful, much important valid information is surfaced and action plans are made. Some changes do occur when people return home. However, once in the back-home situation, the clients are under the influence of their O-I system. Consequently, the candor and risk taking are lost, the validity of the information is reduced, and the actions designed remain within the existing constraints of the O-I system.

If the clients do decide to move toward double-loop learning, then several alternatives must be explored along the lines described in the previous chapter. The first is to design a learning environment and a program which could help them to learn Model II theories-in-use.

Second, in preparation for learning how to move toward an O-II learning system, a diagnosis of the organization's learning system may be commissioned.

A SUMMARY OF THE PHASES OF THE INTERVENTION

The intervention process begins with the mapping of the problem as the clients perceive it. The map includes the factors and their interrelationships that together define the problem, together with the relationships of this problem with the living system of the organization. These aspects represent the ecology of the problem. The second phase is the internalization of the map by the clients. Through confrontation and inquiry, the interventionists seek to develop a map for which the clients can accept responsibility, yet which is as comprehensive as the clients' present readiness to learn permits (e.g., it includes as much of the learning system as possible). The third phase is to test the model. One way to test the model is to "derive" testable predictions from the map. For example, predictions might be stated about conditions under which the problem would and would not arise. The next step would be to examine the existing practice and the past history to locate examples in which the problem did arise or does exist, and note whether the stipulated conditions also exist. If they do not, then further modification of the map is necessary.

The fourth phase is to invent solutions to the problem and simulate them to explore their probable impact. Inventions also serve to set the groundwork for further testing of the model because they represent a new sequence of processes and outcomes. The model should inform the clients ahead of time as to the barriers and difficulties that must be overcome, as well as the factors that will facilitate their efforts to produce the invention. The fifth phase is to produce the invention, and the sixth is to study the impact of the production in order to correct errors as well as generate knowledge for future designs. These last two phases also serve to test the model. If the production works under the conditions specified by the model, then the map is not disconfirmed. If the evaluation produces evidence that the production went wrong at the moments when it violated the recommended processes, then the model again was not disconfirmed.

The sequence of this intervention strategy is mapping (internalizing) the map-testing the map-inventing solutions, producing the solutions, and evaluating and generalizing—which leads to further mapping or inventing or producing. This is the basic intervention sequence that may be used by the interventionists to guide their design of the total intervention.

The other guideposts that the interventionists need are criteria to inform them of the behavioral strategies that they should follow in designing their interventions, big or small. Seven such criteria may be identified:

1. Whatever methods of inquiry are used, they should provide the clients with maximum control over how much they choose to reveal, the depth of their revelations as well as the timing, and the freedom to "erase" something that they have said.

2. The methods should include provisions for the clients to generate rules and norms that guarantee that no one who participates by being candid and taking risks will be punished in any way for such actions. The clients may expect that the interventionist should make these

guarantees. No interventionist either can or should make such guarantees. These requirements for safety are excellent opportunities for clients to learn to work with an important set of issues.

3. The methods used should not permit the interventionist to surface games of deception unilaterally or to break confidences unilaterally. To do either would be to place the clients in an extremely difficult, if not dangerous, situation. It would also be a powerful Model I act that would destroy both the interventionist's credibility as a professional and the applicability of Model II theory-in-use.

4. The methods should permit the clients to begin the mapping processes where they wish to begin. As we have seen, this is usually with the instrumental problems.

5. The methods used should make it increasingly possible for the clients to explore areas that have been hitherto considered undiscussable. For example, early in the relationship the interventionists may help the clients to bypass the primary and secondary inhibiting loops, but they should do it in such a way that later they may return to explore these defensive activities.

6. The methods should minimize the probability that the very methods used to collect data may significantly alter those data and/or reduce the probability that they will be publicly testable. A methodology that the clients can blame for the data can easily be used by them to resist further learning. A methodology that produces publicly untestable data may cause the clients to doubt their ability to generate testable data when the interventionists are unable to do so.

7. The methods should be so designed that they value rationality (consistency), testability, and personal causation accompanied by a sense of competence.

These seven requirements are congruent with Model II values. The first five act to enhance the probability that free and informed choice will lead to internal commitment to the choice made. They enable the clients to generate as much personal causal responsibility for their actions as they wish. The fifth requirement makes it difficult for the clients to project upon others the responsibility for the data that the clients generated. The seventh requirement, on the other hand, bridges the distance between Model I and Model II, assuring that the motivation for change will be in the hands of the clients and utilizing criteria that they understand.

PART IV

PARTIAL MODELS
OF INTERVENTION

Another way to illustrate the nature and probable value of Model O-II learning systems and intervention strategies is to explore alternative approaches to organizational (or interorganizational) analysis. We will attempt to show that because these perspectives do not differentiate between espoused theory and theory-in-use; because they do not have a model of a learning system other than ones that approximate Model O-I; because they do not differentiate between single-loop and double-loop learning; because they do not have a model that takes into account the complexity of double-loop learning; and finally, because they do not have a theory of intervention to move from the present state of affairs to a state with a different set of norms, governing variables, and assumptions, their interventions will tend to be limited. Moreover, because of such limitations, these alternative organizational analyses will tend to manifest important gaps and contradictions conducive to interventions that are counterproductive to the goals the analysts have set for themselves and to unintended, sometimes unnoticed, consequences.

Although our intent is to show that these approaches are limited, we do not imply that the work reported was in some sense shoddy or unsystematic. Quite the contrary; we have selected cases that, in our opinion, illustrate the high quality of work that is possible in each of the respective traditions. Our intention is not to criticize these scholars but to point to the limitations inherent in the paradigms of their respective approaches.

Case A represents a sophisticated action research by a Scandinavian research-consulting organization which is, in our opinion, a leader in conducting organizational analyses that focus on problems of organizational learning. That organization's approach in Case A was heavily weighted toward changing structural conditions to reduce what its members call vicious circles that inhibit organizational learning. Case B represents a different perspective. It describes a major American corporation's attempt to make massive changes in organizational structure and leadership, as well as in the organizational theory-in-use. The organizational change program was coupled with one of the most extensive educational experiences ever designed and produced by a large organization for its upper- and top-level managers.

With Case C we turn to an insightful analysis of the relationships among organizations in the public sector, such as town, city, regional, and national units. In Case D we switch from a sociological perspective to a political-science perspective and focus on the implementation process in the public sector.

In Case E we focus on the field of information sciences and management information system. There is a growing body of literature which analyzes the disappointing results of the implementation of management information systems and makes recommendations to reverse the trend. We examine these diagnoses and their recommendations in terms of our perspective. Finally, in Case F, we focus on the behavioral approach to organizational development with its focus on experiential learning as a basis for intervention and change.

CHAPTER TEN

Other approaches to intervention

CASE A: THE STRUCTURAL APPROACH

One underlying assumption of the structural approach is that changes in structural variables can, by themselves, over brief or extended periods of time, cause changes in human behavior so as to enhance organizational effectiveness. To explore these assumptions, we present first a case of a consulting relationship carried out by one of Europe's leading research-consulting organizations with a world-wide multinational organization. In the opinion of the writers, this consulting group (referred to throughout this chapter as the Institute), is one of the few that is highly sophisticated in conducting organizational diagnoses to assess, and in designing intervention activities to enhance organizational learning, especially of the double-loop variety.

Our presentation will be divided into two parts. First will be an analysis of the written document the research institute gave to the client. (Except for authors cited as references, all proper names have been disguised.) The document spells out very clearly the structural approach taken and the recommendations that followed. In the second part, we wish to explore briefly how the researcher-consultants, while diagnosing client problems, created ambiguous and inconsistent relationships among themselves. They, too, had their consulting strategy informed by a structural approach.

1. The Intergovernmental Organization

One of the key problems the Institute had found in many international organizations (both intergovernmental and private multinational firms) was the organizations' inability to learn because of "vicious circles." The intergovernmental organization to be discussed below was no exception; it was afflicted with vicious circles.

Vicious circles are complex multilevel organizational processes that are highly interdependent; they interact with and feed on each other in such a way as to prevent the identification and correction of errors. In our language, they are inhibiting loops that create cumulative ineffectiveness, resistance to change, and long-range deterioration of the capacity for organizational inquiry essential to good organizational dialectic.

The Institute's diagnosis of these vicious circles may be described by presenting the diagram included in their report (Fig. 10.1). Summarizing their insightful discussion:

1. The foundation for vicious circles is a structural one. The headquarters have different functions that require different attitudes in re-

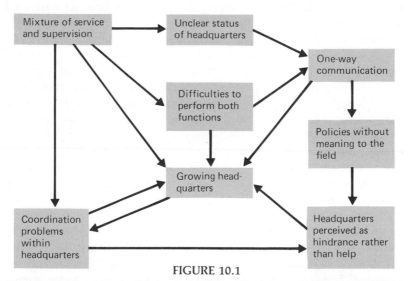

FIGURE 10.1

(Scandinavian Institutes for Administrative Research, *Management Survey of UNICEF.* Published by the Scandinavian Institutes for Administrative Research, Stockholm, Sweden, and Cambridge, Mass., USA, 1975. Reprinted by permission.)

lation to the field which are not reflected in the management methods developed. "It is thus very common that headquarters have both a supervisory role and a service role, and too often neither headquarters nor the field can made that distinction" (p. 8). The result is that all people from headquarters are regarded (and regard themselves) as superiors of a kind, with supervisory functions. Yet their crucial function is to service or help the field.

2. The mixture of supervisory and service functions makes the status of headquarters ambiguous: "People from headquarters are generally regarded in the field as more powerful than would be justified by their knowledge of the requirements of the field situation" (p. 9). Field people see headquarters people as more powerful than they are, either as supervisors or as providers of needed services to the field.

3. As a result, headquarters dominates both the language (concepts and frame of reference) for managing and the communication channels.

4. One-way communication (from headquarters down to the field) leads to policies that are without meaning to the field. That is, the field sees the policies as abstract or irrelevant. The policies become one of the most serious constraints for field efficiency.

5. As headquarters discovers that its policies and communications are not having their expected impact, they respond by developing even more detailed instructions and frequent controls, and they hire new specialists and more outside experts to prevent the erosion of headquarters influence.

6. These reactions make the relations with the field worse. Headquarters is perceived as a hindrance rather than a help. This reaction causes even more anxiety at headquarters. The response is even more communication, control, inspections, policies, and meetings that appear to the field as counterproductive.

The result of these conditions is a set of vicious circles or self-sealing processes that decrease effectiveness and prevent the system from correcting itself.

Where and how to intervene to reduce—if not eliminate—these vicious circles so that organizational learning can be enhanced? It is in the nature of vicious circles that an intervention can occur anywhere, because a change in one factor will lead to changes in the other factors. A theory about effective intervention is needed to help one to select the appropriate point for intervention.

Unlike many consulting firms, the Institute does have a theory; it makes it explicit; and it designs its recommendations and actions on the basis of the theory. Briefly, the theory defines one key point for intervention as being in the relationship between headquarters and the field. The relationship contains, as has been stated above, a mixture of service and supervision, a mixture that neither the field nor the headquarters people are capable of differentiating.

The second key point in the theory is that human behavior is informed and controlled by frames of reference, by concepts, and by the language for expressing meanings. Whatever unit controls these factors controls the vicious circles.

It is not surprising to learn, therefore, that some of the key recommendations of the Institute include:

1. The relationship between headquarters and the field should be altered. For example, if the country A team develops a new idea, it now takes it to Headquarters for at least three reasons. First, to get approval; second, to show Headquarters that the team is innovative; third, to communicate it to other country teams. This creates a center/periphery model which assumes that resources for policy making should be concentrated in headquarters.

2. The Institute recommends a multicenter organization. If country A people develop an idea, the Headquarters should encourage country A to become the center of the knowledge network. The other countries would interact directly with country A; hence, A becomes the center of a knowledge network.

3. The organization should be decentralized into a two-tier structure. The central responsibility for formulating concepts, framework, and language to be used in each country should be at the country level. The countries should come to perceive Headquarters as professional advisers to whom they turn for guidance and logistical support. This would result eventually in the organization moving from a traditional pyramid to a matrix organization.*

---

*   There are many specific suggestions including personnel, budgetary, financial, and executive training activities that flow from the basic recommendations above that are not included in our presentation.

A theory-of-action perspective   There are some basic similarities between the diagnosis that our approach would make and the diagnosis
described above. We, too, see vicious circles or self-sealing processes
as basic problems in all organizations. We, too, believe that a primary
task of the interventionist is to help the organization to overcome
these vicious circles and thereby become a double-loop learning organization. We, too, would agree that a mixture of service and authority
is fraught with difficulties. And we, too, would agree that the unit that
controls the cognitive maps and frames of reference controls the organization.

However, there are some basic differences that are related: (a) to
what is omitted in the diagnosis, and therefore (b) to what is recommended, and (c) to the proper sequences for carrying out those recommendations. In order to illustrate these differences, we have taken the
original diagram and reconstructed it from a theory of action perspective (Fig. 10.2). The factors that are starred were included in the original diagram. The factors not starred are additional ones.

The first three factors are the same: (1) the inability of the headquarters and field people to make the distinction between supervisory
and service functions; (2) the predisposition of the field to regard all
people from headquarters as superior; and (3) the predisposition of
headquarters people to regard themselves as superiors.

The first difference is that we would not claim that these factors
are what makes it difficult to deal with the conflict of service and
supervisory functions. There are two factors that are missing.

Since the employees (at headquarters and in the field) report these
factors to the researchers, it means that they are aware of them. And
since these factors are not subject to discussion within the firm, we
would infer that people are programmed with theories-in-use not to
discuss these phenomena. A high degree of agreement among individual theories-in-use would make it an organizational norm not to discuss the factors. Hence the factors become undiscussable within the
organization (primary loop that inhibits deutero-learning).

If people know that the factors exist, if they know that they are
undiscussable, and if their undiscussability is also undiscussable, then
there exists a condition of open deception. The open deception is
caused by people acting as if these factors do not exist and/or as if
they are discussable (organizational games leading again to primary
loops that inhibit deutero-learning).

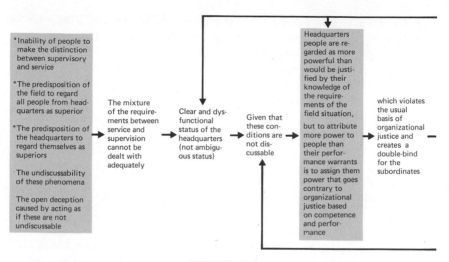

FIGURE 10.2

These two factors, combined with the first three, make the mixture of service and supervision requirements difficult to deal with adequately. Note the differences in emphasis about where responsibility lies. The Institute planted the responsibility squarely on the nature of the structure of the headquarters/field relationship. In effect, their causal microtheory was that: If headquarters is structured to perform service and supervisory functions, then there will be a conflict of the two that cannot be dealt with adequately (because headquarters people will have more power, etc.).

Our view is that this causal analysis may or may not be accurate. The question is whether the causal relationship would operate as predicted even after people were able to discuss it. If the factors become discussable, and if this results in effective organizational inquiry, then the cause cannot be structural because the structure will not have changed. That is, organizational inquiry into a discussable problem will now operate to alleviate the problem.

Our analysis does not imply that service and supervisory functions cannot conflict with one another. We accept that the structure can produce such a conflict. Our point is that people do not know how, or are unable, to deal with such conflicts.

The Institute recommended that the organization move from a center/periphery to a multicenter structure. Under these conditions, it

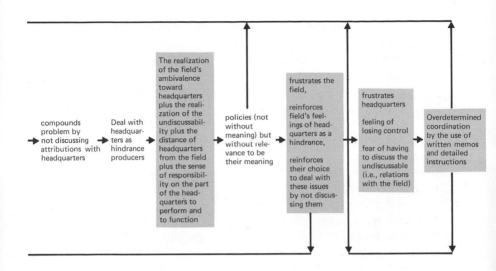

may be recalled, country A would become the center for one particular innovation and country B for another. Our analysis would now yield the prediction that country A would have the service/supervision conflict with other nations, since it would be at the center and they at the periphery. Moreover, our analysis would predict that a matrix organization would tend to increase the interdependencies by several quanta. Under these conditions, communication, especially of difficult and threatening issues, would become very important. But the present organization has norms that inhibit the open discussion of difficult issues and make open deception part of the technology of survival.

The Institute explained the perception of headquarters people as more powerful than they are, in terms of structure. Headquarters people, by being at the center, know more about internal functioning and politics. "This makes them look powerful to the people in the field who are often feeling very isolated from the rest of the organization" (p. 9).

Our explanation would be somewhat different. We believe it would be possible to cite as many if not more, data that field people interpret their isolation from headquarters as a sign of their power to keep the headquarters monkey off their back. Indeed, part of this game requires the field to know the internal politics of the headquarters in order to predict future actions and protect themselves from present ones.

The power of the headquarters, we would suggest, comes from being the gatekeeper between the field and the source of money and other scarce resources, plus the necessity for the field to clear with headquarters even for those country-oriented moves that may not require new funds. Compounding this is the fact that once the subordinates have colluded to deceive, given the power structure, they run the risk of being punished if caught, whereas the top may be immune from such punishment even though they have also colluded in the open deception.

Our analysis would take this logic one step further. We suggest that since the espoused theory of organizational justice is that power should be given to the competent, for the subordinates to find themselves assigning more power to the headquarters people than they believe they deserve (based upon performance) creates a situation of injustice in which they lose and the top gains. The subordinates are now in a double bind. If they assign more power to the superiors than they deserve, then they are colluding in self-inflicted acts of injustice against themselves. If they do not assign the superiors the power they appear to expect, the superiors may react with even more controls—which would also lead to greater injustice.

This condition does not lead to meaningless policies from headquarters (as the Institute's diagnosis stated) for headquarters espouses that all policies should have meaning; but their theory-in-use involves them in the design of policies that are abstract and irrelevant.

Since these consequences are also not discussable, the frustrations of the field will tend to increase, and resistance to headquarters will deepen. In order to counteract the expected defensive reaction from headquarters (more visits and controls), the resistance of the field may go underground. To the extent that it goes underground, subordinates are colluding to create a new layer of deception which, in turn, must be hidden lest the top discover it and react negatively.

To the extent that the top senses that it is becoming impotent, it will react, not in an uncoordinated manner (as the Institute's diagnosis would suggest), but in an over-determined and over-coordinated manner. This will feed back to reinforce the fears and defenses of the subordinates and the final loop of self-sealing is made.

To recapitulate, the original diagram focused on vicious circles that inhibit organizational double-loop learning. It placed the initial responsibility on structural factors. We agree that the key problems on which to focus were the vicious circles and the inability to engage in good dialectic. However, we would place the primary responsibility on the members' theories-in-use that prevent them from discussing the difficult issues without creating polarization and projecting blame. If the theories-in-use could be altered so that these issues could be discussed, that would be the first action step toward severing the vicious circularity of the vicious circles.

The second action step would be to create formal policies that reward people for discussing the undiscussable. Moreover, these policies should be supported by the everyday behavior of the superiors. Hence, we would recommend first the reeducation of the top to learn Model II theories-in-use.

It would be our hypothesis that to the extent that these two conditions were fulfilled, the organization would be free to confront the service/supervision conflict and to design new structures and practices aimed at the resolution of this conflict. In short, the organization would be freed up to pursue good dialectic.

The second basic recommendation of the Institute was that the client should develop new concepts, frames of reference, and a new language. Our diagnosis would suggest that the client system:

1. Has concepts and language to describe the present state of affairs, but that superiors and especially subordinates suppress them.
2. Uses concepts and language that fit within the boundaries of what the present norms consider discussable.

But even if this diagnosis is incorrect, the original diagnosis assumes that if people have the correct frames of reference, concepts, and language, then their behavior will change. Given these assumptions, one of the primary tasks of the consulting team is to help generate the appropriate frames of reference, concepts, and language. These assumptions have embedded in them a theory of intervention which states, "Given the correct cognitive maps, the appropriate behavior will tend to follow."

A theory-of-action perspective would question this theory of intervention. It would maintain that if: (1) the research team were able to generate the appropriate concepts, frames of reference, and language; and (2) it transmitted these accurately; and (3) the clients accepted them, then all this would mean that learning has occurred at the level of espoused theory. The transformation of this newly learned espoused theory to the level of theory-in-use is an enormous problem which has yet to be faced. If the members of the organization could be reeducated so that they could overcome the problems mentioned above, then they would be able to use the discrepancies between organizational espoused theories and theories-in-use as a vehicle to develop a more general model of how the organization can discover when it is making errors and how to correct them; or better yet, to help the organization to discover when it is not able to discover that it is making errors. Under these conditions, consultants and clients could work productively together to generate cognitive maps more appropriate to the organization's situation.

(2) The Institute

We will now examine another case from the files of the same Institute. The difference is that the data are taken from several sessions (some of which were tape-recorded) with the senior consultants as they were thinking through how they might approach a different client. The case sheds light on what the consultant's thinking processes were before a report was written to the client. These data illustrate how the framework described previously as structure-based and cognitive-map-oriented influenced their thinking and their intervention strategy.

The client system was a leader in its field for a long period of time. The client system perceived that it had a problem because: (1) the company had not grown during the year; (2) it was developing a cash flow crisis coupled with a disproportionate increase in costs; while simultaneously (3) new organizations were being formed that competed with them. The owner reacted to these consequences by re-entering the business and administering it with tighter controls. He also invited the Institute to help him understand and overcome the long-range problem.

The Institute's diagnosis focused on identifying mismatches between the situation in which the company was embedded and the dominating ideas and concepts of the top people in the firm as they dealt with reality. The dominating themes, therefore, became a key concept in understanding the organization's problems:

The dominant themes	*Their inappropriateness*
1. Top-management thinking is based on the assumption of continued expansion.	1. The market has "matured" and expansion may be severely limited.
2. Every market is treated in the same way.	2. Different markets require different approaches.
3. The same structure is used for all businesses.	3. Different businesses require different structures.

The researchers then asked themselves, Why do these dominant themes not change? Why does top management not see that they are dysfunctional? The research team's diagnosis was that the president was a dominating leader. For his subordinates to question his dominating themes would be for them to run a risk. Part of the climate was to find scapegoats to explain the failure of the company (rather than to challenge the dominant themes). Hence there was a tendency for the top to hide the real explanation of the difficulties and to hide the fact that they were hiding their facts.

The Institute team recommended that the subordinates develop a report with a diagnosis that included enough of the president's views so that conflict and polarization between them and the president will be minimized. The team also recommended that the subordinates develop a new set of organizing ideas for the top to conceptualize reality. For example, the team concluded that if they could give the president new concepts and help him to diagnose himself validly, then he could use these ideas to move forward. As one consultant said, if they gave the president new and appropriate concepts, "We can trust him to take the right steps." Another consultant added, "I think you are right. But we also need to help others to see the situation . . . (we must) push them to see the new ideas . . . (we must) give them new insights." The first consultant agreed, but wondered if such a strategy might not create more internal top-management problems between the president and his subordinates.

Examining the processes of thinking suggested by these notes, it appears that the Institute members acted congruently with their espoused theories. They analyzed the dominant ideas, identified their dysfunctionality, and suggested new ones. However, they were faced with a dominating president who they believed might resist their diagnosis. His leadership style (or his theory-in-use) was continually on their minds while developing a strategy, but it did not become part of their overt strategy. For example, the team members never chose to help the president become aware of his theory-in-use related to leading the company.

One reason that they did not do so was that it was not a part of their intervention theory (espoused or theory-in-use). If the intervention theory assumes that people are able to alter their behavior when given new maps and new languages, then the task of the interventionists is to develop those maps and languages as competently as they can and offer them to the client. As they said above, given the right information, the client "can be trusted to take the right steps."

According to our model, this will not be the case. The president's theory-in-use is Model I. Hence, he will tend to create primary inhibiting loops and be unaware that he is doing so. Whatever advice or maps are given to the president, he will perceive them through the filters of Model I and his attempts to use them will remain constrained by Model I. He will not be aware of these incongruities and limits, but his subordinates and the interventionists will be. However, both are programmed not to surface them.

The second reason that the interventionists may not have surfaced these issues with the president might be their belief that if they focused on his dominating leadership style, he might become so upset that he would not listen to their diagnosis. In our opinion, the interventionists would probably be correct that the client could become defensive. But, with Model II skills, they should be able to help him deal constructively with the defenses and make progress in solving the important issues.

But what if the client chose to fire the interventionists? This is a risk the interventionists should take. If the client isn't able to deal with them in such a way that he will learn, there is doubt in our minds about the quality of the relationship that he will create with his subordinates. The latter have been the recipients of the president's leadership style and for many years have been suppressing their reactions. They know that they have been withholding information from the client and deceiving themselves. It is doubtful that, under these conditions, insight into the dominant business themes will lead to the progress that is necessary.

In making the president's theory-in-use undiscussable, the consultant team began to act toward the president in the same way his subordinates acted toward him. Moreover, their strategy of "creating," "giving," and "pushing" the client to see the new concepts would place the consultants in a dominant relationship with the president. They would then be in the difficult position of recommending to the president not to be dominating while, at the very same time, they were dominating both him and the top management group. In other words, while the clients' espoused theories differed significantly from those of the consultants, their theories-in-use were similar (i.e., Model I).

What would lead the consultants to utilize a Model I intervention strategy when they espoused a Model II strategy? One answer is that the consultants were unaware that they were doing so. A second answer is that although the Institute espoused a Model II strategy, its theory-in-use was Model I and its members were unaware of the discrepancy.

Some anecdotal evidence that lended credence to both of these hypotheses was gathered and was fed back to the members of the Institute. Two members involved in the first case agreed immediately that the additional factors were key factors. They wondered why, if they knew these factors, they did not include them. One response was that they did not know how to cope with these factors. They knew how to define appropriate dominant themes, but they did not know how to help people to discuss the undiscussable.

This suggested the hypothesis that if there were threatening issues within the Institute, the subordinate researchers would not surface them candidly. They would either describe them in abstract or oblique terms or they would suppress them. During an all-day discussion among members of the Institute, the younger professional researchers confirmed the hypothesis and gave many examples to illustrate their point. At another meeting, the younger members brought up several other cases of serious communication problems among the professionals. The underlying theory-in-use in dealing with these issues was to hide the potentially threatening information from the superiors. The superiors, not knowing the true situation, continued to act as they did before. This closed the loop and drove the issues even further underground. Hence the Institute had its own vicious circles.

One way the younger professionals dealt with these unresolved issues was to hold private discussions among themselves (in groups of two or three). During these sessions they discovered that each had similar feelings but no one had more information. Consequently, one of the dominant themes of such discussion was to attempt to analyze and second-guess the motives of the senior professionals. One such theme that began to be developed was that the seniors wanted the junior professionals to develop in their image. These dominant themes, under the conditions described above, tended to become self-sealing. This meant that whenever the seniors behaved in ways that were perceived as ambiguous, unclear or inconsistent, the juniors tended to read into the behavior whatever would follow from the dominant themes.

One of the writers had an opportunity to interview the senior members, and they espoused motivations that were the opposite of those described above. Indeed, there were many instances in which the seniors behaved in ways that the observer inferred were consistent with providing the juniors more autonomy. Yet the juniors were misinterpreting these actions.

Some of the key senior members were so intent on encouraging autonomy that they consciously withdrew from everyday management of client relationships. The juniors were concerned about the withdrawal partly because they did not feel as competent to deal with clients as they felt they should be. Given the lack of confidence and the increased sense of aloneness, they turned to learning, as quickly as possible, the perspectives and skills of the senior members. Thus the juniors were striving to become like the seniors.

The notion that withdrawal leads to autonomy, it has been shown, is commonly held by power people with a Model I theory-in-use. The logic is: If I am controlling then I will withdraw and leave the other more free. The assumption is that one alternative to Model I is the opposite of Model I. But, as we have seen, this does not work. The alternative strategy that we recommend is the open confrontation of the issues by the senior and junior members. The end result will be to help people develop such relationships that the seniors can remain involved without reducing the juniors' autonomy. Such involvement makes it possible for the firm to utilize the expertise of the seniors. Moreover, it reduces the probability that the juniors will make major errors. Now, when errors are made, the clients call the senior members, who respond immediately—thereby introducing themselves into the client/junior-interventionist relationship at the most difficult time and under the most difficult conditions. In many cases, the senior members, being aware of the potential threat to the junior members, strive to make their reentry appear as nonchalant as possible, or they reenter in a dramatic take-over fashion. Either way creates an unproductive polarization—conditions which neither the junior members nor the senior members can handle competently.

To summarize, organizations whose members use primarily Model I theories-in-use and whose living system is congruent with the model of error making described previously, create primary inhibiting loops; and once the loops are created, the organizations cannot cope with them. These conditions will tend to create taboo areas and develop limited, poorly-diffused organizational memory and consciousness. Moreover, the organization will be seen, by its members, as having a living system that is brittle and difficult to change.

These consequences will hold for client systems and research-consulting systems if their espoused theory and theory-in-use are limited to the structural approach.

CASE B: A STRUCTURAL-EDUCATIONAL APPROACH

The next case is taken from the work of James Baughman (1974), who has analyzed the attempt of one of America's largest corporations to transform itself.

Our presentation will be divided into three parts. First, there will be a short description of the Company before Mr. Cordiner became the chief executive officer (CEO). Second, there will be a description of how Cordiner attempted to change the Company and of the consequences of his efforts. In part three, we will present our own analysis which will build upon Baughman's.

The pre-Cordiner era

For nearly 60 years before Cordiner, the Company represented an example of what one of the authors has labeled "dynamic conservatism."

A dynamically conservative organization's primary activity is to work hard at remaining within its presently defined goals, policies, practices, and related living system. It consumes a lot of energy, it is true, but most of that energy is expended on maintaining the status quo.

According to Baughman, the Company could be described as focusing on seven major strategic goals: (1) internal growth, (2) constrained diversity, (3) oligopolistic competition, (4) diversification within established company strengths, (5) emphasis on domestic saturation of the market, (6) expansion internationally only as it helps to protect the domestic market, and (7) high liquidity.

Internal growth meant that acquisitions and mergers were minimized. Expansion was to be produced by Company employees and Company resources. The Company generated its own capital, its own technology, and its own management. Earnings were therefore reinvested in the Company and debt was unthinkable. Growth occurred in areas in which the Company was already strong. Thus, if the Company was a leader in manufacturing product X, its technologists found ways to develop new products from the primary technology used to make product X.

The Company minimized competition and allocated markets by region, product, and function. It minimized competition by using its financial resources to drive less efficient competitors out of the market and then developing agreements with the remaining competitors to live and let live. Growth for the remaining organizations occurred as the market expanded, and the Company aspired only to its fair share of that growth.

Baughman documents carefully how the Company was able to accomplish these objectives and never run afoul of the anti-trust laws because of its very strong patent position. Indeed, for a long time, the Company was able to prove that its policy was supportive of healthy competition.

Although the Company was a giant in its industry, before Cordiner entered as CEO it was administered as one big plant. The emphasis was first on manufacturing and second on engineering and marketing. The top management clearly and tightly controlled the entire organization through carefully articulated strategic plans that were defined in such a way that they produced clear guidelines for decisions made at the lowest levels. The structure, which was highly centralized, evolved out of the articulation of these strategic plans.

The climate within the existing subunits included a sense of ingrownness, pride in internal abilities, minimal risk taking at all major levels of management, expansion in territories already known, slow but steady growth, and a dependence on the top to provide the important initiatives.

The Cordiner era and the big change

When Cordiner became chief executive officer (shortly after World War II), he decided that the Company was to grow and grow fast. If the Company had been a prime example of dynamic conservatism, Cordiner would strive to make it an example of dynamic growth; if the Company had been highly controlled by the top, Cordiner would strive to decentralize it; and if the Company had been managed rigidly, Cordiner would appear to espouse permissiveness.

It cannot be overemphasized that Cordiner intended to sky-rocket the Company into a period of unprecedented growth, unprecedented management, and unprecedented relationships with its competitors, unions, and the government. One of the authors, who was closely involved in the transformation, recalls the sense of excitement in the air as everyone predicted that Cordiner would manage the Company in ways that would make the old management turn over in their graves, startle employees at all levels, bewilder competitors and the government, and make the Company a prime example of meteoric corporate growth.

Cordiner's theory of transformation had several key interdependent components. They were:

1. Decentralize the Company into relatively autonomous profit centers with presidents who could be counted on to accept the responsibility and take the initiatives required for growth.

2. Make decentralization a reality by leaving the division presidents alone. Monitor the results periodically and hold the presidents accountable through performance measures.

3. Change the role of the CEO to that of protector of the new decentalization and banker and chief investor of a large portfolio.

4. Let the CEO make loans to the presidents to invest in new growth opportunities, the amount of loans being limited primarily by the capacity of the presidents to pay the interest.

5. Let the office of the CEO provide an emotional (as well as intellectual) basis for the new climate by generating metaphors that convey the new messages. For example, the Company executives began to talk about themselves as people who not only *could* do, but *should* do ("We should get in now because it will

cost us more to get in later," or "It is going to cost more not to do it.")

Baughman describes what he calls a "marketing macropia" that developed which permeated the thinking and the levels of aspiration that were quantum jumps from the old goals. For example, where the Company had once produced wiring and meters (among many other things), it now produced "construction materials" and "measuring devices."

Working for the Company during those days would understandably give many people a heady feeling of growth, expansion, unlimited ceilings, and an unbeatable organization. The aim was to beat any competition and to overcome any obstacles.

As a result of all these changes, relationships with the environment and the internal climate changed dramatically. As to the former, competitors began to fight back, the government began to become more confronting, and the unions were much more strident in their posture. The internal climate changed to one of high risks and fast expansion in many directions; debt accumulated, and competition among divisions for scarce resources increased greatly. There was a continual sense of go-go-go, even though it was not clear how to organize and monitor progress or even what and where the right paths were.

Briefly, the results were positive and negative. In terms of increase in sales, percentage of market, and diversity, Company management achieved most of its objectives. In terms of profitability, it failed to reach most of its objectives. Why?

Baughman's analysis suggests that the answer is related to several major factors. First, Cordiner made decentralization almost a fetish. If goals were not achieved, Cordiner reacted by reorganizing, not by examining the strategic plans for possible gaps and inconsistencies. "There is no doubt that structure was more of a professional interest to him than strategy" (p. 49).

Second, Cordiner altered some time-honored Company practices without providing precise criteria for implementation of the new practices. For example:

1. Cordiner muted the long-standing formula of how to allocate financial resources to the three primary components of the business. He did not provide new strategic guidance as to the pre-

ferred methods to distribute resources for expansion or contrac-
tion (p. 56).

2. Cordiner asserted that the Company should grow wherever desirable, but he seldom specified the strategic rules for assessing
desirability (p. 56).

3. Cordiner set two arbitrary goals for the Company: seven percent
net earnings as a percentage of sales and 20 percent net earnings
as a percentage of shareowner's equity. He acted in ways that
suggested that these figures were in real terms (i.e., over and
above inflation) which, Baughman asserts, was "plain unrealistic" (p. 61).

4. Cordiner used a "ratio analysis" method to determine profitability. The value of ratio analysis is that ratios are precisely input-
output measures; they have numerators and denominators. They
force a mental discipline that compares outputs (numerators) to
inputs (denominators) and raises questions of efficiency. The
danger of using this procedure lies in the fact that if one forgets
about denominators (and thereby forgets efficiency, too), one
then begins to believe that a profit dollar is a profit dollar. Apparently Cordiner fell into the trap (pp. 63, 64).

But why should one of the world's leading organizations, with
some of the most sophisticated and advanced staff resources, help to
generate fuzzy, incomplete, and incorrect guidelines? Baughman suggests that the errors made may be partially accounted for by the state
of the art of financial analysis in the early 1950s. But he admits that
the fuzziness and the incompleteness baffle him.*

Baughman's explanation of why Cordiner lost sight of the
strategic plans, and hence lost control of the Company, was in Cordiner's apparent preoccupation with structure and diversity. Almost
every success or failure was translated, by Cordiner, into evidence for
the value of decentralization or the need to make decentralization
even more precise and effective. Cordiner's espoused theory was to
make competitive growth, diversification, decentralization, and the
new chief executive roles means to the end of increased profitability.
However, Cordiner's theory-in-use was " . . . to allow (or cause)

---

*   Personal communication.

decentralization, competitive growth, and diversification to feed upon one another with little corporate benefit" (p. 50). There was a logical flaw or a behavioral permissiveness in the chief executive officer's theory-in-use of which he apparently was unaware.

Was this a logical flaw? Why the behavioral permissiveness? We believe that a theory of action perspective would include factors that would suggest that Cordiner did not behave illogically and that his permissiveness was necessary, given his view of what the Company needed if it were to grow and maintain profitability. Yet, we will also show that, given the Company's learning system, Cordiner's logical behavior became illogical and permissive in the sense that the former created unanticipated and undesirable consequences while the latter was used to hide error.

A theory-of-action perspective. Cordiner knew the internal workings of the Company. During the second World War, he observed the enormous potential of the Company when some of the old rules were suspended and the managers were given greater latitude and discretion (in the name of patriotism and winning the war). Cordiner also knew, as Baughman documents, that to make the Company grow at the rate he had planned—without mergers and acquisitions—he would have to rely on the top management of his Company. Cordiner also realized that he could never know all that he needed to know to produce and manage the growth personally. He concluded that, while this was the propitious moment for change, his lofty goals would never be achieved—nor would his strategy seem credible—unless he gave the presidents as much authority and autonomy as they needed.

Decentralization was the only way he could conceive of to achieve these conditions. Thus decentralization was not primary, but secondary—a means to an end. But this means had rarely been utilized in the Company during the preceding six decades. Thus, Cordiner was faced with management and employees, embedded in the living systems, who had never experienced the freedom and the responsibility that they were about to be given.

It is understandable that the top management under Cordiner would begin with some degree of skepticism about the new concepts. They had worked in a learning system that rarely sanctioned what Cordiner was recommending. This meant that the management did not hold either the attitudes or skills required for the new era. Hence, they were being asked to manage units populated with people who, in turn, were supposed to perform in ways in which they had rarely performed before. The presidents knew that the living system of the Company was not ready to support the new policies. Worse yet, they feared that the organization's learning system could help bring about the demise of the new policies as a self-fulfilling action. For example, the lower-level management tended to be somewhat bewildered by the autonomy, risk taking, and initiative being recommended. They doubted that the employees could respond appropriately. These doubts were communicated to employees in many subtle ways and a few more that were more overt. (E.g., "Let's not have these new policies go to your heads; we still run the show.") The lower-level managers and employees reacted by playing it safe and inhibiting their initiative. The middle- and upper-level managers, who were more imbued with the idea of fast growth, reacted by controlling the lower levels even more, in order to push them into the new era. The increased control led to an increase in subordination and dependency, which simultaneously violated the new philosophy and made the living system closer to the one the employees had known for years.

To compound the problem, the new presidents became more visible and more vulnerable. Before, the top executives were covered by the paternalistic blanket of the top. Now, not only was the blanket taken away, but the competitors, unions, and government were becoming more militant. Moreover, the Company's internal units also became competitors, each vying for the scarce financial resources to achieve the targets set by the top.

The new presidents felt a sense of ambivalence. On the one hand, they wanted to run their own show, as some of them had done when central controls were relaxed during the second World War. On the other hand, they had never before been in such a vulnerable and exposed position.

How did the presidents respond to these new pressures? First, they paid strict attention to the measurement criteria for success and strove to achieve them as best they could. But the measurements used encouraged the presidents to concentrate on improvement of ratios rather than improvement of dollar profits. Hence, many presidents interpreted their task as ". . .merely seeing to it that their department's current net earnings on current sales approximated the corporate median (at best), or mean (at worst)" (p. 63).

Second, the presidents became oriented inwardly to the survival of their own units. Now, units within the Company were competitors for scarce resources. Hence, the presidents interpreted their task as keeping their ship afloat and letting the others worry about doing the same for their departments. The result was an increasing sense of interdepartmental rivalries that reduced the probability that the presidents would think in terms of the good of the company as a whole. That became the task of the chief executive officer.

Third, the presidents realized that they were governing systems that had never known the degree of autonomy and self-responsibility that was being offered to them. They knew that it was highly unlikely that they could reeducate all their employees and change the learning system and, at the same time, achieve the goals set by the top. Hence, the relationships within the units remained as centralized as they had been during the past. The learning systems were not to be changed; they were to be galvanized to relate to their respective presidents, the way everyone related to the top in the pre-Cordiner era.

Cordiner had created a dilemma. He believed that autonomy and support had to be given to the individual units. He also believed that the innovation and growth had to come from within the units. Yet the presidents were responding to their new roles by making their units adhere to the conditions that Cordiner assumed were contrary to innovation and risk taking.

Cordiner's behavior related to change permits us to infer that he probably realized that the 60-year-old learning systems were not going to be changed within the time he had in mind. He had to depend, therefore, on a strategy that, in practice, ignored the learning system. First, he communicated in as many ways as he could that decentralization was not a fad but a genuine change. The repetition of this message had to be frequent, because the presidents and those below were understandably skeptical. They looked for every possible chance to say to Cordiner, "There, you see, you do not really mean to give us our freedom." Many did so, in our opinion, not so much because they craved the freedom and responsibility, but because they feared it. They, too, grew up under the old centralized management, and the new style—now that it was a reality—was threatening. If they could prove to themselves that decentralization was a fad, they could relax and wait for the top to eventually take over.

It may have been this need to reconfirm the genuineness of decentralization that made Cordiner appear to focus on it to the exclusion of other issues. Cordiner could hold the presidents accountable if he were certain they had the conditions and the resources to be presidents. They, in turn, had to have their position continually reconfirmed—partly because of the newness of the decentralization policy, but largely because of the continual danger, as they saw it, that decentralization might fail, given the living systems of their respective units.

Cordiner's second response was to institute the most massive reeducation program in the history of private enterprise. A beautiful college campus was built and full-time faculty were hired (who in turn brought in visiting faculty). All the top management within the divisions who would play key roles were to be educated in a three-month program. The heart of the program was described in a set of ten volumes, written by the Company faculty, which described the new decentralization program. The Company's new ideas about management and structure were described in detail. Moreover, key top executives from the central headquarters taught at each class, repeating and repeating and repeating that Cordiner really meant decentralization. Thus, the core of the program was indoctrination. Its assumption was that the good executives could be persuaded to take on the new roles; all they lacked were the maps, and the school would provide those.

The educational program mirrored in its curriculum the same myopia manifested by Cordiner. The curriculum assumed that change could be brought about by implanting the new concepts, changing the structure, and educating the people to both. The program also assumed that top management could change the living system regardless of the involvement and skills of the people who created that system. In short, the program assumed that the impact of decades of working within a particular kind of living system could be ignored and overcome by top management who clearly understood the new policies. To make certain that decentralization was understood, ten volumes were written by Cordiner and a select group of top executives. These "blue books" represented both the bible and the handbook for decentralization. The assumption was that if the top executives learned what was in those books, then effective implementation would not be a problem.

But the people who read the books saw them, to use our language, as containing espoused theory. The difficulty that they were facing was at the level of theory-in-use. They knew that few, if any, of the living systems would encourage and support the behavior recommended in the blue books. They also knew that few people had the skills to make these new policies part of the organizational theory-in-use. They repeatedly asked their superiors about how the rigid, old-line qualities of their units were to be changed. They were told that Cordiner was confident that they, with their respective management teams, could produce these changes. Cordiner was counting on them and he would back them up.

Many of the faculty were aware that the ten volumes virtually ignored the learning system. They knew changes were not going to occur, even if every top executive was somehow transformed within the three months of the educative period. Therefore, they hired outside faculty to fill in the gaps. The outside faculty attempted to fill in the gaps by pointing out such issues as resistance to change, the rigidity of organizations like the Company, etc. The executives felt confirmed in their fears and then lashed out at the visiting faculty for answers. The visiting faculty understandably said that they could not provide answers without working in depth with the units and their executives. They left the executives, therefore, with confirmed fears and espoused theories but no theories-in-use about how to deal with the change. Incidentally, the visiting faculty were also the lightning rods for the aggression and fear that the executives generated as they began to understand more clearly the gap between what was being expected of them and the learning system of the units that they were administering. It was not by accident that the lecture halls in which most of the faculty taught were dubbed "the snake pits."

From a theory-of-action perspective, therefore, Cordiner does not appear to have lacked a strategy, nor does he appear to have defined criteria ambiguously because he (or his staff) may have been careless in their thinking and sloppy in their strategic specifications. If Cordiner defined the strategic criteria as clearly and as unambiguously as Baughman suggests was necessary, then it is highly likely that such a step would have raised, in the eyes of the presidents, the credibility of the decentralization. They would have seen such specificity as evidence that decentralization was just a trick or gimmick.

Hence the dilemma: Without strategic guidelines of the specificity that Baughman proposes, growth occurred at disproportionately high costs. With the guidelines, the strategy proposed for growth would fail.

But why couldn't they be combined? Why did the presidents interpret clearcut strategic guidelines as evidence that decentralization was a sham?

First, the theory-in-use in Cordiner's actions was the one we have found in most cases in which superiors decide to provide autonomy to subordinates. Being programmed with Model I theories-in-use, both view autonomy as being created by conditions that are the opposite to Model I. Hence, if a superior or an organization has been overcontrolling and dominating, the answer is to withdraw the control and the domination and give managers their head. Moreoever, subordinates programmed with Model I theories-in-use, working in a living system characterized by Model I conditions, also see autonomy as being credible when they, too, are left alone. Hence, we suggest that Cordiner saw his strategy to be permissive (as Baughman described it) as necessary.

The consequences of such withdrawal—namely, less effective monitoring and correction of errors—are also found in other cases. When the superiors withdraw, they take with them years of knowledge and experience that could be helpful to the subordinates to alert them when they may be getting into trouble. To compound the problem, if the subordinates consider their being left alone as evidence for genuine decentralization, then they will tend to see going to the superiors for help as a sign of weakness. Hence, the subordinates hesitate to discuss their difficulties with the top during the early stages. They usually wait until the results *must* go to the top. Then they spend much time developing a case to explain why they did not seek help earlier.

Second, if specific strategic policies, as recommended by Baughman, are to be introduced without destroying the credibility of decentralization, it would be necessary for those involved to participate in defining these criteria and in monitoring their performance to see how well they are being achieved. Moreover, if the monitoring is to have teeth, there must be mechanisms by which resources can be reshuffled in order to correct poor performance. In order for these conditions to have existed in the Company, the presidents would have to have been in an interdependent, cooperative relationship with each other, where they were responsible for the profitability of the organization as a whole.

As we have seen, Cordiner's scheme created the opposite conditions. The different departments were pitted against each other, vying for scarce resources. The presidents learned that personal survival or success meant that their respective units must achieve their goals. Hence, the presidents became unit-centered rather than concerned about the organization as a whole. Finally, the presidents were under significantly increased pressure from units within the Company, as well as from private and public institutions outside the Company. Therefore, the new policies, plus their consequences, made it highly unlikely that the presidents would operate effectively as a cooperative group to define strategic plans. But this consequence is a self-fulfilling prophecy, and not a logical necessity.

There is no logical reason why Cordiner could not have attempted to develop the presidents into a team who jointly evolved strategic plans and decision rules. Instead of an arrangement by which each president was rewarded for being unit-centered, a structure and reward system could have been developed that encouraged cooperation among the presidents for strategic planning purposes. Such an effort might have made it easier for the presidents, who were skeptical about the pace of expansion and the expansionist metaphors, to raise these issues. Such questioning might have made it easier for the Company to reexamine at least five of the major new businesses that it developed that never became profitable and had to be dropped. One of the authors recalls having a discussion with skeptical top-line and staff people about some of the directions of expansion. They all hesitated to raise these questions for fear they would be misunderstood by the top as well as by their fellow presidents.

This leads to another consideration; namely, that none of the presidents (or anyone else) could change their theories-in-use by simply being given the opportunity from above. Such freedom is a necessary condition, but not sufficient in itself. In order for changes in theory-in-use to occur, the learning system must reward and sanction these changes. Moreover, our research suggests that changing theories-in-use is very difficult even when the opportunities are there and the learning system ranges from benign to cooperative with respect to the new program. The difficulty lies in the fact that people programmed with Model I do not have the skills to help themselves and each other to alter their theories-in-use, even though they *are* able to alter their espoused theories. Further, they tend to be unaware that this is the case.

To summarize, Cordiner attempted to promote unprecedented growth by changing the CEO's relationship with the people immediately below him from Model I to the opposite of Model I. This, in turn, placed the presidents in a visible and vulnerable position with increased pressures from within and without. The presidents, who held primarily Model I theories-in-use (a fact made painfully clear in their interactions with the faculty during the three-month courses), did not have the skills to help create a new learning system that would reward and reinforce risk taking, initiative, flexibility, and growth. Nor did the other participants have these skills.

The educational program designed to reeducate the top was inadequate because it remained at the espoused level and rarely dealt with the theory-in-use. It focused on structural changes and ignored the learning system, and it produced learning environments whose internal characteristics were closer to the conditions existing during the pre-Cordiner era (i.e., conformity to a company-line, centralized definition of major concepts, specification of what to think and what to tell others to think, etc.).

Baughman's suggestion that the situation would have been better if Cordiner had defined adequate and precise strategic plans and criteria seems to us valid, but incomplete. Our view is that if Cordiner had unilaterally defined specific strategic goals, the presidents would have questioned the concept of decentralization and Cordiner would have been placed in the position of managing a colossus he believed could not be managed effectively from the top.

Cordiner, who sensed these issues, responded by making decentralization a fetish (as others saw it), and kept strategic plans and criteria less structured than might have been desirable in order to convince his subordinates that he meant to give them autonomy. His ambitious reeducation program, meanwhile, reeducated at the espoused level, not at the level of theory-in-use; it focused on selling and persuading rather than reeducating, and appeared to ignore the learning system of the corporation.

Under these conditions, it was predictable that the organization would move from Model I to the opposite of Model I, then back to Model I—hence, a new phase of oscillating Model I. Apparently this is what is now occurring. The two CEO's who have followed Cordiner have increasingly centralized the Company through the use of strategic plans and criteria, and have developed more sophisticated management-information systems to monitor the execution of those plans and the achievement of the criteria.

CASE C: STRUCTURAL-INTERORGANIZATIONAL APPROACH: A SOCIOLOGICAL PERSPECTIVE

A study of interorganizational relationships written by Michael Crozier and Jean-Claude Thoenig (1976) presents an insightful case analysis that goes beyond the rhetoric of "interorganizational networks" so common in the study of interorganizational relations. They intend to study these relationships as a system. They take the concept "system" seriously and focus on the systemic processes of regulation, integration, and homeostasis. They ask to be held accountable for evidence that the organizational units are part of a system in which the sum is more than the parts and in which systemic activities exist independent of the activities of the parts (pp. 2, 3).

The analysis of the system is tight, and it leads to some conclusions that are not so obvious (some of which we will discuss below). It appears to us that Crozier and Thoenig have presented a case study that illustrates the value of such studies when they are done well.

The focus of the case study is on collective decision making in France. The authors show that public affairs at the local level are, in fact, managed by a complex but stable and organized system of institutions and groups (p. 3). Thirty-four thousand communes and 96 departments comprise the system.

Our description of their analysis is necessarily abbreviated and incomplete. The objective is to describe enough of the Crozier-Thoenig analysis to suggest how a theory-of-action approach may add to their perspective and, in a few cases, surface some gaps and inconsistencies embedded in it.

The authors point out that all the subunits at all levels of hierarchy are involved in the same game, a game of noncommunication and defense of protection. The game unites all the players. "If there is steady resistance to coordination and formal adjustments, it is not because the players do not know one another, nor because they are far from one another, but because they belong to an informal but complex stable system which has other forms of regulation which may be only half-conscious but are nevertheless all the more efficient" (p. 5).

One example cited is the relationship between the mayors and prefects of middle-sized cities. They play a game which includes apparent hostility and criticism toward each other. The games conceal a deep complicity; an efficient mayor knows how to listen to his prefect and is naturally attentive to him (p. 6). Although the mayor must take the initiative, he allows himself to be influenced by the prefect provided the prefect agrees to be sensitive to the mayor's requirements (p. 6). Crozier and Thoenig admit that the subtlety of the relation may lead to misunderstandings that, in turn, do not facilitate rational and formal coordination. Indeed, they imply that the functioning of this complex game system may take priority over the preferences of the decision makers who, we recall, are representing French citizens. The priority may be so potent that communication between State officials and local political and economic elites (even if formally they are independent and their respective institutions are rival) is easier than it is for each of them within their respective institutions (p. 7).

One of the most important rules of the system is that a compromise cannot be negotiated directly between the parties directly involved. Compromise is brought about by the intervention of a third party. "Often the coordinator imposes a preconceived solution which takes into account the different interests but is imposed on them without open negotiation" (p. 8). Such a solution is reinforced and made unchangeable by rationalizing it in terms of technical imperatives, legal constraints, and the general interest.

It appears that within this system there exist political and technical interdependencies that make it difficult for any one actor to dominate the others, but, if we have understood the complex system correctly, it also makes it likely that all actors will shun responsibility and cover themselves in order not to get into trouble. Thus the mayor is the sole person who coordinates the disparate elements of the village who are hardly capable of reaching compromises among themselves. The mayor gains his power from this role and from the fact that he selects his municipal councilmen much more so than the municipal councilmen elect him. But in order for the powerful mayor to take positive action, he must cooperate with the relevant field officers of state bureaucracies who can block the appropriation of needed funds until they are satisfied that the mayor and the village are concurring with regulations. Crozier and Thoenig show how the mayor is largely dependent on the state bureaucrats and how the latter are dependent upon the next higher level. Hence, the process of power and decision making is neither hierarchical nor democratic nor contractual. "It is an intersecting or zig-zagging process *particularly well adapted to a model of shunning responsibilities*" (p. 11, emphasis ours).

The networks of local-level units regulate each other in an indirect manner. Each unit is sustained and maintained by the pressures from the system. It is advantageous for each unit to communicate as little as possible with other units, which are potential competitors or rivals. Face-to-face relationships are avoided. "The result is isolation or atomization of the political fabric" (p. 15). The relationships are easy and friendly but the game is closed and secret. The system constantly produces exclusions. The members fear public opinion and hide from the sanction of electoral suffrage. Moreover, the politicians tend to perceive the citizenry as unable to be self-responsible, as being self-centered toward parochial interests, and as reluctant to participate more in public affairs. "All they can do is to be demagogic and self-destructive" (p. 15).

Under these conditions, the best mayor is not the one who achieves most, nor the one who is the most attractive politically. The best mayor is the one who has the best access to the people who make decisions at the higher levels.

The French system of collective decision making causes considerable frustration and strong criticism among its members as well as among the citizenry. Yet nobody really works to overthrow it and it continues to be rather well accepted (p. 18). Crozier and Thoenig explain this apparent paradox by noting that the oppression is anonymous and the authority is impersonal. As a result, one or two particular individuals cannot dominate others. Oppression is impersonal and diffused, and in consequence, tolerable. A friendly relationship can exist because the conflict is one between roles, and thus does not hinder individuals communicating on other grounds (p. 19). "(Also) the system produces exclusion and privileges, thus creating discontent and uneasiness; but it does it in a sufficiently well-balanced manner, so that the complaints against it do not go beyond the acceptable threshold and do not balance the personal benefits every member is expected to get in return" (p. 20).

The system is ultrastable and hardly adapts. It pressures all the parts to remain the same. For example, even though the population of France has expressed forceful demands for participation in public affairs, the system has become more closed. "Rather than stimulating more initiative from the periphery and broadening its base, it has sought to preserve its secretive and restrictive practices" (p. 22). No solutions other than the traditional ones can move them.

However, the socio-economic pressures from the population have continued. The result is that the local politicians' influence has decreased. As a result, there are two different administrative networks of public management: one for rural France, and the other one for the metropolitan areas (p. 24). Moreover, the system tends to concentrate on the problems it is capable of dealing with (p. 24).

A theory-of-action perspective Crozier and Thoenig have provided an insightful analysis of an ecological system. The first difference from our approach is that they show little interest in reflecting on their model of the system to present a model of what factors facilitate or inhibit systemic learning. If we may infer from the rich accounts of the games of deception, open secrets, win/lose, polarizing issues, unilateral decision making, and camouflage, it appears likely that the system they describe approximates an O-I learning system.

What is gained by connecting their analysis to the O-I model? The first advantage is that it connects an empirical case to a model. The connection makes it possible for the case-study results to be generalizable to other systems. As Crozier and Thoenig point out, their analysis is not generalized beyond their universe. Yet if their empirical work is validly connectable to O-I, then we may see that the French collective decision-making activities have learning systems whose properties are common to many other types of organized unities.

Another value of connecting the empirical data to the O-I learning-system model is that it provides a map of the primary and secondary loops that inhibit learning. The map, in turn, provides an explanation of why the French system is not able to engage in the double-loop learning essential to good dialectic, and why it will always tend to focus on single-loop learning, even when, according to

Crozier and Thoenig, an increasing proportion of the population is asking for changes that go beyond the present capacity of the system.

This raises questions about the capacity of the system to change and to be effective. Crozier and Thoenig state at several points that the system is efficient and inefficient, humane and inhumane. The system is efficient because it accomplishes certain goals without permitting any one component (e.g., mayors, prefects, regional and state bureaucrats) to obtain all the power. It is inefficient to the extent that it cannot represent and fulfill the needs of the citizenry, especially in the cities. The system is humane because some needs are fulfilled, and it is inhumane because it can be distant, secretive, manipulative, unilateral, and rigid. And, if we may add, the deepest aspect of its inhumaneness may be the fact that it necessarily couples these characteristics with its getting things done. The system informs its citizens that if it is to work at all, they cannot challenge the secretiveness and manipulation.

Although Crozier and Thoenig present both sides of the efficiency-humaneness picture, they decide that the system is more efficient and humane than vice versa. First, they state that the reader should think carefully before tampering with the system. Second, when it comes to change, the energy they see for progress and change must come from outside the system. For example, they assert that ". . . charismatic figures will certainly emerge and offer intuitive solutions to the problem of change and adaptation" (p. 40). However, they do not concern themselves with how to generate these charismatic figures, how they will be introduced into the system, how they will obtain power, nor how they will refrain from being neutralized by the system.

Indeed, the paradox is that Crozier and Thoenig recommend that the change agents (whoever they are) work within the system. For example, they state that if the ". . . participants are not able to play the new games imposed by these transformations, it is preferable to reinforce an integrating centralization mechanism around individuals and groups capable of rapid adaptation, rather than to transform the whole structure so that it fits the nature of the problem" (p. 40).

One difficulty with this analysis is that it makes assertions about effectiveness and change not only without testing them, but without making them testable. If the French O-I learning system is to have its effectiveness genuinely tested, it must not be compared only with states of affairs that remain within its governing variables and behavioral strategies. Tests of effectiveness require that the system be compared with systems that have different governing variables and behavioral strategies. Otherwise, the most the Crozier-Thoenig approach can offer is assessments of effectiveness which are single-loop. Assessments that focus on double-loop criteria will not be possible. However, in order to focus on the latter, Crozier and Thoenig would require another model, the equivalent of our O-II, which may be used as the basis for the good organizational dialectic that includes double-loop learning. Without this, the knowledge that they produce may range widely, but it will do so within the constraints of O-I governing variables and behavioral strategies.

Why should Crozier and Thoenig be interested in double-loop learning? There are several reasons—some to do with the "game of science" and some to do with the applicability of scientific knowledge.

As to the game of science, the development of a model that indicates how intergroup relations, regulations, and multilayered interdependencies create a system is not adequate evidence that this is the way the system actually exists. The next step is to vary the factors of the system and see if the predicted consequences occur. For example, if Crozier and Thoenig's theory of informal relations is correct, then an alteration of the formal structure should produce little systemic change. Or, a change in the hierarchic relationships will be less powerful than a change in the games that the actors play to get their share of the benefits permitted by the system.

Crozier and Thoenig assert that the system is humane and effective. This implies that for them, humaneness and effectiveness are criteria that their theories value. If so, then they are responsible to present models of how humaneness and effectiveness may be increased. If they present such models, and if they or others show through empirical research that the models are not disconfirmed, then they will have added greatly to the empirical validity of their perspective.

As we have mentioned above, although Crozier and Thoenig probably did not intend it, their perspective in this paper was single-loop and not double-loop. Not only does this limit the scientific testing of the perspective, it also limits the options that social science may offer to the population that supports it.

For example, let us note some of the properties of the French system as experienced by the population. The analysis suggests that the system is one which:

1. Is efficient by being managed half-consciously by the actors (i.e., mayors, prefects, regional and state bureaucrats).

2. Is ultrastable and not able to learn in ways to transform itself in order to double-loop learn.

3. Is more concerned about its own functioning than the interests and needs of the citizenry.

4. Imposes preconceived solutions which may take into account the different interests, but permit no open negotiation.

5. Encourages the political actors to shun their responsibilities.

6. Unilaterally produces exclusion of persons and groups.

7. Induces the actors to perceive the citizenry as nonresponsible, demagogic, and self-destructive.

Let us suppose that there are French citizens (or citizens in other countries where similar systems exist) who wish to change these properties of their collective decision-making system without destroying its capacity to produce results. What kind of help would Crozier and Thoenig's perspective offer? If we have understood them correctly, the answer is help that conserves the present ecological arrangements. One reason for their focus on conserving the present ecological arrangements may be their fear that practitioners would too quickly jump to inventing more mechanistic solutions that would destroy the ecological balance. We would also predict that such single-loop help will soon reach its limits because it remains constrained by the existing governing variables and the behavioral strategies. We would also predict that if the citizenry wished to support research and experimentation of different systems, then they would have to explore Model O-II learning systems.

As our book went to the publisher a paper appeared by Turner (1976) that illustrates graphically the constraints involved when interorganizational units are required to learn in order to solve a complex social problem. Turner analyzed three disasters that were a long time in coming; that is, their incubation period in each case was several years (e.g., the British coal-mining town of Aberfan, where a landslide killed many children). The actors in the case represent several different social units (e.g. town citizens, town officials, Coal Board officials, etc.). There were, in other words, a number of groups and individuals usually operating in separate organizations and separate departments within organizations.

Turner identified key factors that were associated with the failure of foresight. First, there existed culturally accepted beliefs and norms, as well as rules and practices as to how to remain within the beliefs and norms. These beliefs and norms formed a system that we may infer to have had O-I characteristics. For example, tips about potential danger were rarely explored. The learning system encouraged the solution of well-structured problems and discouraged the solution of ill-structured problems. It also appears that the learning system did not encourage people to reflect on the fact that their learning system inhibited double-loop learning.

When representatives of these systems met they tended to have discussions that ignored the ill-structured problems. For example, in one of the tragedies, ". . . the police escort and the transportation crew stopped to discuss the problem (the hazard of arcing onto the overhead electric wire) as well as the problem of negotiating an uneven section of the crossing. But none of these parties considered the particular danger to which a long, slow road might be exposed" (Turner, p. 388). The first two problems were known, while the third was an ill-structured problem.

Also, in two cases, individuals outside the principal organizations concerned had foreseen the danger that led to the disaster, ". . . only to meet with a high-handed or dismissive response . . ." (Turner, p. 388). In all cases, unresolved ambiguities about warning signs, orders, procedures, and responsibilities were found: "Wrong or misleading information was sent from one party to another, sometimes because of interpersonal difficulties between two particular individuals, and information was unintentionally distorted" (p. 389).

There were many examples in which individuals ignored, discounted, misperceived, or distorted information, but when they were doing so, they were acting in accordance with their respective O-I learning systems. As Turner writes, "Disaster-provoking events tend to accumulate because they have been overlooked or misinterpreted as a result of false assumptions, poor communications, cultural lag, and misplaced optimism (p. 395). If we may hypothesize that most of these "failures" in error detection and correction occurred because the participants were following the dictates of the learning system in which they were embedded, we would predict that such a learning system would have characteristics that approximated Model O-I, and not those of Model O-II.

CASE D: STRUCTURAL-INTERORGANIZATIONAL APPROACH: A POLITICAL SCIENCE PERSPECTIVE

In addition to the sociological perspective illustrated by the previous case, there is another perspective that may be called the conflict-resolution (coalition-bargaining) model. Organizations are seen as consisting of rational individuals and subgroups with different interests, perceptions, demands, and resources. Participants engage in conflict which they then attempt to resolve through bargaining processes, using threats, bribes, trades, and compromises (Olsen 1976, p. 83). As in the previous perspective, we were unable to find cases in which researchers designed their research to include an intervention which was designed to help a client system and simultaneously to provide a test for aspects of the researchers' theories.

In an analysis of the implementation game, Bardach (1977) came closest to approximating such a study. He studied politicians and bureaucrats as they tried to implement programs. Moreover, he developed recommendations for more effective implementation and illustrated these with actual cases.

Bardach's inquiry is primarily focused on the implementation process. How do laws or programs become implemented? What are the implications of the answer to this question for making implementation more effective and for the kinds of programs government should design and fund?

Bardach sees the implementation process as complex. It is composed of several multilevel processes that coexist and feed upon each other. The implementation process includes the activities required to assemble numerous and diverse program elements such as administrative and financial accountability mechanisms, clearances, funds, political support, and trouble shooters. People are persuaded to participate through the use of "implementation politics," which are, at their core, a complex set of interrelated games that have specified players, roles, stakes, tactics, and rules. These games form a system of activities that are at the heart of the implementation process.

To begin with, there are three sets of games related to three objectives: the diversion of funds, influence over goals, and influence over administrative actions. Games to divert resources include: *Easy Money* (making off with funds in exchange for program elements of significantly less value); *Budget Games* (moving money, making certain that all of it is spent even at the risk of failure of a quickly funded project, and intergovernmental "revenue sharing"); *Easy Life* (compensating for low salaries by designing the work environment to suit oneself), and *Pork Barrel*.

The second set of games is used to deflect the goals of policies. For example: *Piling on* (adding a large number of objectives to a successful program); *Up for Grabs* (defining programs with minimal bureaucracy and modest budget, which encourages bureaucrats or others to convert the ambiguous elements into political resources); and *Keeping the Peace* (defining programs to keep the peace between extremists or zealots and the conservatives who scrutinize the former—and who could terrorize agencies charged with administering the programs.)

The third set of games arises from the dilemmas of administering programs. Tokenism is an attempt to appear to be contributing to a program while privately conceding only a small contribution. This leads the agency to develop monopoly power which, in turn, produces a new set of games on the part of other agencies or the clients for whose assistance the legislation was designed. These include such games as: *Do Without; Create a New Monopoly; Foster Competition; Buy the Agency Off; Co-opt the Agency; and Build Institutions with Countervailing Power.*

Massive Resistance is another major game played by agencies. The actions that may be developed to counteract massive resistance include *Prescriptions* (orders), *Enabling* (give added resources), *Incentives* (for cooperation), and regulations which make deterrence unlikely.

All of these multilevel games exist in, and help to reinforce, social entropy, which is a state of slow social deterioration. Social entropy not only is encouraged by these games and reinforcing of them, but is itself doubly reinforced by the incompetency of the civil service (especially at the higher levels), variability in the objects the legislation requires bureaucrats to control, and the quality of coordination among various agencies (which, as one might surmise, tends to be low.)

These games produce a good deal of defensive reaction. Individuals, groups, and organizations consume much time and energy avoiding responsibility, defending themselves against maneuvers by other game-players, and setting up situations advantageous to their own game-playing strategies. These defensive reactions in turn produce a new set of games which reinforce the original games, the defensive reactions, and the games themselves. They include *Tenacity* (stymie progress), *Territory* (staking out one's action space), *Not Our Problem, Old Man Out,* and generating a particular *Reputation.*

These games form a system of rules and norms for effective behavior. Actors must play within these constraints if they are to succeed. The system of games is, in turn, the context within which decision processes occur. A decision process is one in which two or more different parties decide, through negotiations or through a sequence of maneuvers and countermaneuvers, to contribute or withhold certain contributions from the collective enterprise.

The decision process is incremental and iterative. A first step is taken, information is obtained, learning occurs, new actions are designed, the new actions are produced, and so on. The decision process is also guided by the future as it emerges after every play. The map of the "emergent future" is critical to the designing and testing of new ideas about subsequent steps.

At the heart of the decision process is negotiation. The negotiations are win/lose oriented with each side trying to maximize their gains and minimize their losses. The negotiations may also be characterized as a set of interrelated games. For example, one side asks for more than it is willing to settle for and the other side cuts the amount down. In the process, the level of mistrust and the feeling of vulnerability both increase. The result is poor communication and delays. The delays feed back and reinforce the games, the mistrust, the poor communication, and the delays themselves. The result is a set of self-sealing processes whereby the game is never questioned even though the results may be less than what is desired by all parties.

The description of these games appears to us to approximate a Model O-I system. For example, there are win/lose dynamics, unilateral control over others in order to advocate one's position, emphasis on keeping the peace as well as the covert games of *Easy Money*, *Agency Revenue-Sharing*, and *Easy Life*. Also, there are games to camouflage other games, such as *Tokenism, Do Without, Co-opting the Agency*, and building institutions with countervailing powers. Neither the games, nor the camouflage of them, are discussable. All sides play the games and abide by the rules, including the rule not to discuss the games.

If Bardach's analysis may be understood in terms of Model O-I, then it is possible to make certain predictions. For example, the actors should report the system of games as almost impossible to change; they should see them as part of the fabric of life and despair about anyone changing them. They should also experience the double bind of being ineffective if they confront the games, and being exhausted as well as ineffective if they ignore them. Bardach provides rich anecdotal data that players do have these feelings and views. We may also predict that double-loop learning should not occur under these conditions. Again, anecdotal data are provided to illustrate that learning, if it occurred, was single-loop (i.e., it remained within the existing constraints of the system).

There is another prediction we can make: To the extent Bardach does not provide another model, with different governing variables and behavioral strategies, he will not be able to create the conditions of good dialectic. Without the good dialectic, Bardach will be unlikely to suggest actions to overcome the problems that confront and overwhelm the implementation system he has described.

As we understand Bardach's recommendations, our predictions are not disconfirmed. His first recommendation is the equivalent of going in the direction opposite to Models I and O-I. Bardach advises the design of simple, straightforward programs that require as little management as possible. If the games are a losing proposition, then avoid playing them. The best action is to implement programs through manipulating prices and markets rather than by attempting to enforce programs through rules and regulations.

If we follow Bardach's own analysis, there are several problems with this advice. First, if the implementation process is what Bardach claims it to be, and if it is as powerful as he illustrates it to be, then such a strategy will threaten all the game players and their organizations. Consequently, one runs the risk of uniting players to cooperate in ways that should reinforce and strengthen the games. Second, our perspective suggests that people at the local level, even if reached through market mechanisms, will tend to form their own O-I systems. Thus, if a city like Oakland distributed funds to building contractors through a market mechanism, that would not prevent the builders and the contractors—or the builders and city hall—to develop their own O-I systems.

Bardach's second major suggestion is for the actors to write scenarios that attempt to surface unanticipated costs and to define the stresses and strains that may be developed if the program is to be implemented. A detailed list of questions is included so that the actors can be guided in their information seeking. But even if the actors were willing to write the scenarios, where would they get the information? If they ask only their own group, they run the risk of creating self-sealing processes. If they were to involve the agencies and institutions that would eventually have to participate, why would these agencies participate in an inquiry that could harm their power position, or could even kill a program in the first place? Or, more likely, assuming it participated in the inquiry, why would it not instruct its members to begin to play games in terms of the data that they gave?

Bardach's third suggestion is for individuals or coalitions to act as "fixers." Their task is to repair the process or to adjust elements of the game in order for a particular side to win. Fixing, Bardach admits, carries a connotation of covertness which is appropriate because it does go on behind the scenes and out of the public view. The fixers attempt to rig the game to increase their own winning and minimize their losing. Hence, effective fixing depends on effective deception, secrecy, and manipulation.

There is another difficulty with the second and third suggestions. The second assumes that the planning process is not subject to dysfunctional activities of the sort Bardach has been describing. The third assumes that it is possible to bypass the implementation games. Our hypothesis is that neither assumption is realistic. The policy-making process is subject to O-I learning-system difficulties. The games of "fixing" would also be subject to counter-games.

To summarize, Bardach's implementation process approximates very closely a Model O-I learning system. As one might predict, the actors in it report little probability that it can be confronted effectively and altered significantly. Bardach does not generate an O-II learning system, hence he does not envisage an opportunity for the good dialectic. The result is that all of Bardach's action recommendations remain within the O-I learning system. As such, the recommendations unintentionally reinforce the status quo.

It is interesting to note that Bardach himself concludes his analysis with a note of despair about working within the O-I implementation system, a note of despair illustrative of dealing with the double bind that exists for the actors within the system:

"The longer I watch the evolution of public policies and programs, and the closer I get to the process, the more attached I become to the first two heresies, described in the Introduction, which currently threatens the ideology of liberal reform: government *ought* not to do many of the things which liberal reform has traditionally asked of it; and even when, in some abstract sense, government does pursue appropriate goals, it is not very well suited to achieving them. Markets and mores are sturdier and more sensible, and government is probably less sensible and less reliable, than liberal reformers have been willing to admit." (Bardach 1976, pp. 11–22)

The question we would ask is, How good are markets in producing O-II learning systems or, at least, counteracting O-I learning systems? As we understand the current dialogue regarding the implementation effectiveness of market-type programs (e.g., school vouchers, negative income tax), the O-I type games surface when administrators and researchers attempt to understand what pilot projects and "experiments" have proven and what is to be learned from these.*

A closing concern about three omissions that we found in the published material during our search for cases in the field of political science:

The first was that an overwhelming number of studies lacked the minimum characteristics required to generate possible solutions that did not reinforce the status quo. Few scholars concerned themselves with developing models of systems that differed significantly from the status quo in terms of governing variables and behavioral strategies.

---

*   Alexander George has developed a model that is congruent with a Model O-II learning system. It was not included because the only description we could find was at the espoused level. For details of George's model, as well as the literature reviewed, see Chris Argyris "Double-Loop Learning and Decision-Making," *Administrative Science Quarterly*, September 1976.

As we have suggested, without alternative models it is not possible to create the conditions of the good dialectic which are required for double-loop learning.

Also, without a model it is not possible to help others change the system so that they may begin to correct the underlying causes of their errors. Bardach, not having an alternative model, is led to make recommendations that are consistent with Models I and O-I. If our perspective is valid, then such recommendations would reinforce the system of games, not correct them. Indeed, it would be instructive if Bardach developed a scenario of the kind that he recommends about his own solution so that he could project what the future might look like if his suggestions were implemented.

The second omission we found in the literature was a lack of research designed to generate knowledge by intervening in on-going reality. The overwhelming majority of the researchers in this field consciously ignore intervention. Their rationale appears to be that reality must first be understood; only after adequate knowledge has been developed should we begin to experiment with intervention.

We believe that this logic is incorrect for two reasons. First, one of the best ways to understand reality is to attempt to change it. As we are beginning to learn, there are, in most human organizational systems, inner contradictions that do not surface until late in their history. These inner contradictions surface much more quickly if double-loop changes are attempted because the changes cannot be successful if the inner contradictions remain. Bardach's study is an excellent example of how the study of the implementation process (which is an intervention process) tells us much about the nature of the steady state of the system. We would suggest that if Bardach or others attempted to design and implement a study to intervene in an implementation process, they would generate knowledge about that process that hitherto had not been surfaced. But in order for social scientists to design such studies, they require as a minimum a map of what state of the universe they wish to go toward.

The third omission we found in the literature was a lack of emphasis on discovering the theories-in-use (be they individual or organizational). If there was a more determined emphasis on understanding theories-in-use, the type of instrumentation used and analysis made would alter significantly.

It is not possible to infer the theory-in-use of an individual or an organization without obtaining relatively directly observable data such as tape recordings or reconstructed scenarios. Obtaining such data is not easy. Analyzing it is even more difficult. Tape recordings of one day's activities of one group of executives can produce nearly 500 pages of transcript. Extrapolating to the hundreds of groups that exist in one organization makes the problem of data collection seem insurmountable.

This may not be the case if the ultimate objective of the research is to generalize about theories-in-use and not behavior. We have found that, to date, there are only a few different types of theories-in-use. We have also found that although people may conceal or distort their behavior, these concealments do not go beyond the boundaries of their theory-in-use. Hence a five-page scenario may provide adequate data to understand the theory-in-use of an individual throughout all of his or her working life. Or a day's transcription of a particular group may be adequate to infer the group's theory-in-use.

If an intervention component is designed into the research, then the inferences made about theories-in-use from such data will be put to experimental test. Recall our description of testing the analysis of an organization. The feedback session provides a test; the design (with the clients) of change activity provides another test; the implementation of the change activity, still a third test.

There are two advantages in focusing on theories-in-use and in collecting relatively directly observable data. First, the data base may be used by scholars of many different persuasions to see more clearly how certain inferences were made and how certain conclusions were reached. Second, the same scholars have a better opportunity to impose their conceptual template on the data and hence to provide alternative explanations. (For example, in Argyris's reexamination of the data collected by Burns and Stalker regarding mechanistic and organic groups, it appears that both types are versions of Models I and O-I. Such a conclusion would not have been possible without the directly observable data periodically included by the authors or without the concept of theory-in-use and Models II and O-II.)

Finally, there is another encouraging prospect surfaced by relating Bardach's findings to our theoretical scheme. We would suggest that the reeducation necessary for people to learn Model II and create O-II learning systems may also assist in solving the problems that exist among organizations. If this turns out to be the case, then the intervention theory we propose may also be used to cope with interorganizational problems. The assumption is that whenever organizations interact, it is through their agents; these agents form a temporary organization in order to manage their interactions; and these agents can help their temporary organization to be more effective by using the same values, knowledge, and competences required to maintain effective internal environments in the respective organizations.

We do not maintain that Model II people together with Model O-II learning systems will be sufficient for all organizational and interorganizational problem setting nil solving. But they are necessary ingredients if individuals and organizations are to detect and correct error, learn when they cannot do so, and hence design the assistance they may need.

CASE E: THE MANAGEMENT-INFORMATION-SYSTEM APPROACH

Another major intervention approach used in organizations today is the application of information science technology to design management information systems (MIS). An underlying purpose of the MIS is to generate valid and usable information that will help organizations to detect and correct error and to plan future activities.

In a review of the literature, we found that the MIS experts were becoming increasingly disenchanted and disappointed with the implementation record of MIS. We were able to identify seven major factors hypothesized to cause the implementation ineffectiveness:

1. MIS systems (especially their underlying assumptions) are not well understood by line management.
2. Top management is not involved in persuading and selling the use of MIS.
3. MIS are not as fool-proof as they could be.
4. MIS are technically too complex and thus too costly to create and utilize.
5. MIS specialists and line managers do not understand each other's roles, job requirements, and job pressures.

6. MIS ignore line managers' cognitive styles.

7. The implementation of MIS is too narrowly conceived.

These diagnoses (with the possible exception of the last one) were generated by examining practice. The strength of these conclusions therefore, lies in the fact that they are firmly rooted in actual experience. However, this rootedness may also cause problems. It may be, for example, that there are other causes of ineffective implementation that are not easily observable and would require a theory to alert the researchers to their existence. We believe that our living system model of error making and error correction provides a useful perspective with which to examine the implementation crisis of MIS.

MIS may be conceived as an attempt to construct patterns of information from the history of the system. The purpose for creating the patterns would be to develop maps that would minimize unclarity, ambiguity, or inconsistency of the present or the future. This will reduce error and increase predictability, and thereby make the system more manageable for the agent.

In order to construct valid maps from the past, one must produce valid information by reflecting on and making inquiries into the past. Reflecting on the organization requires that the organization use and make explicit its learning system, and this requirement creates a dilemma. One of the underlying rules of the game within the learning system is to keep the games and the map secret. To surface the map would be to violate the rules. To surface the fact that rules were being violated would also raise the question with management as to why they were not aware of the learning-system rules, the violations, and the errors that were hidden by the rules. This, in turn, would lead to the exposure of the camouflage of the camouflage.

This dilemma would not exist for information that was discussable and errors that were correctable, but for issues that were not discussable and errors that were not correctable. To the extent that reflection and inquiry will tend to focus on the latter, such activity places the employees in a double bind. If they do not expose these issues, they run the risk of being caught for violating formal rules and regulations. Dilemmas and double binds are especially powerful error-producing conditions, and therefore the inhibiting loops will probably be operating at peak capacity.

To compound the problem, although the MIS specialists and the line executives manifest the same Model I theories-in-use, neither believes this to be the case. They tend to create their own in-groups which cause them to believe that the other groups are different and do not really understand them (Argyris 1971). Such in-group dynamics lead to intergroup rivalries, which, in turn, compound and reinforce the inhibiting loops.

There is another set of factors that could prevent the effective use of MIS. Ironically, that set is embedded in the very nature of the present conceptions of effective management information systems. For example, an intended use of MIS is to make the management of the organization more rational. By more rational, we mean to include such activities as defining objectives and goals as clearly as possible, defining paths to (procedures for) achieving the goals, and defining acceptable levels of aspiration of—and criteria for—effective performance. Once the objectives, paths, levels of aspiration, and criteria for performance for every subunit and the whole are defined, the organization assumes that these factors will guide and inform behavior within predefined limits of variance. In order for this condition to be met, another is required; namely, that objectives, paths, and performance criteria must be made public. Thus we have MIS producing public procedures to define and control, within acceptable variance limits, human performance in the organization.

The more these conditions are created and adhered to, the less the probability that the actors can vary their behavior according to their personal-intuitive criteria. Their degree of discretion, therefore, is reduced. The degree of discretion may be equated to the concept of space of free movement (Lewin 1951). We are predicting, therefore, that people will experience a reduction in their space of free movement.

For example, Wagner (1974, pp. 280–281) has suggested a list of nine questions that must be answered to begin to design effective production and inventory planning systems:

1. How much of each product is to be manufactured over the entire planning used by the company?

2. When is the plant to produce each individual item, on what facility or equipment, and in what amount?

3. What are the raw materials to be ordered and in what quantities?

4. How much inventory buildup of each item is planned in anticipation of future peak sales?

5. During each time interval, what are the target inventory levels for all the items at every stocking point within the system?

6. If customer orders exceed stock availability at any time, who is allocated the available supply?

7. What record-keeping, status-reporting, and cost-gathering information systems are required?

8. When and under what circumstances are the plans subject to revision?

9. Who in the organization is responsible for setting management policy governing the answer to all the preceding questions . . . for carrying out the planning processes and daily decisions . . . for monitoring the system . . . ?

Once the answers to these questions become public and relatively fixed—once they become procedures informing behavior—then those performing the actions must not only follow the procedures, they must also be subject to having the effectiveness of their performance monitored and challenged by superiors and peers. Moreover, once the procedures are established, the probability diminishes that actors may be able to extract or give help or favors by modifying unilaterally and privately the procedures presently in existence. Finally, there is a lower probability that actions to cover up error could be kept secret from superiors and peers. All these conditions indicate a reduction of the space of free movement—and this is accompanied by feelings of tension, fear, dependence, low personal responsibility, and high risk (Lewin 1951).

We may hypothesize further that these feelings should be especially strong with regard to issues that have been covered up or camouflaged, and where the covering up has been supported by games of the learning system (such as described in column 9 of the O-I model shown in Fig. 5.2).

The less space employees have for free movement, the less able they will be to define the goals of their work, the paths to reach those goals, or the levels of aspiration involved. And the less able they will be to relate the goals to their needs. These conditions lead to psychological failure (Lewin, Dembo, Festinger, and Sears 1944), which means that the persons affected do not experience themselves as personally and causally responsible for their actions. Hence, even if they succeed in performing the expected tasks, psychological failure will still exist.

The stronger the employees feel that the effective implementation of MIS will lead to increasing psychological failure, the more likely they are to resist it. To the extent that individuals have internalized as part of working life that space of free movement will be low, the hypotheses of MIS will be invalid and psychological failure inevitable. These people will rarely resist MIS on the basis of what it might do to them once implemented. If they resist MIS, it will be for reasons that it may surface the defensive, cover-up activities they have created to protect them and their withdrawal from top management. Moreover, people who have accepted low space of free movement and high degree of psychological failure as inevitable and natural will also have low investment in monitoring and correcting system errors.

The argument above has been based on the consequences that are hypothesized to result when a certain model of rationality is used to manage organizations whose learning activities approximate the Model O-I. There is another set of consequences that compounds the consequences above. This set is related to the fact that many MIS are designed in such a way that their procedure and performance are required to be publicly examinable and disconfirmable or confirmable, and that they make it possible to minimize intended or unintended deception.

But as we have seen above, these conditions are not encouraged in Model I organizations and will be resisted by individuals with Model I theories-in-use. Thus the characteristics of MIS that are valued as good by their designers will tend to be experienced as threatening by their users. To discuss such issues openly, however, would also violate the model described above. Discrepancies about what are valid, worthwhile, and useful MIS are not likely to be discussed effectively by line and MIS specialists. If discrepancies are discussed, the underlying ones (as defined by the actors) will be suppressed and the more superficial ones surfaced. Both sides will report that this censorship is going on (or independent evidence will be obtained that neither side will deny), and both sides will report (or agree) that discussion about the censorship is itself censored.

We may now return to the diagnoses made by MIS specialists regarding the problems of implementation of MIS. Let us reexamine them in terms of the recommendations that flow from those diagnoses. The purpose is not to show that the recommendations implicit in the diagnoses are wrong, but that they are incomplete, and would inadvertently lead to a state of affairs in which cover-up and deception are reinforced.

Moreover, we would suggest that the recommendations will not solve the basic problem of MIS implementation. Consequently, both specialists and line officers may become disenchanted and the entire success of MIS may deteriorate even further.

Recommendation I: Make MIS more understandable to the line executives. In the literature, "more understandable" had a wide variance of meaning. It ranged from packaging in readable form (that is, an emphasis on cosmetics) to emphasis on making explicit and clear the underlying assumption of the MIS. These suggestions would appear to make sense.

However, they may contain some unanticipated consequences. For example, as the underlying assumptions are made clear; as the impact of MIS is made explicit; as its potential for managing behavior becomes clear; the users of the MIS (especially at the lower levels) will also become more clear about the potential of MIS to reduce their space of free movement, to increase psychological failure, and to reduce their feelings of being essential to the organization.

Given the Model I theories-in-use and the defensive behavioral world, these consequences will tend not to be discussed. An employee discussing them would run the risk of being seen as a deviant or trouble-maker. Moreover, if these undiscussables were surfaced, the risk of surfacing the games of deception and camouflage would also be increased greatly. Bureaucracies have ways of punishing people who are responsible for such consequences.

Recommendation II: Involve management more, so that they can persuade others to value and use MIS. Again, such a recommendation appears to make sense, especially to a war-weary exhausted MIS specialist. But there are unanticipated consequences that should be surfaced. Research has shown that the predominant philosophy of management (in both public and private sectors) may be described briefly as unilaterally controlling others in order to get them to do what the organization requires while at the same time controlling possible confrontations of management authority (Argyris 1970; Ghiselle, Haire, and Porter 1966; Likert 1967).

It is this theory of action that reinforces Model I theories-in-use, which in turn produce primary inhibiting loops. Hence, the recommendation could increase the potency and scope of the very factors that make effective implementation of MIS more difficult.

Recommendation III: Make MIS as foolproof as possible. The emphasis of this recommendation is on better ways of detecting error and the potential for error while simultaneously reducing the flexibility at the local level to edit, forgive, and correct errors privately. This recommendation appeals to top-line management because it responds to one of their greatest anxieties, namely, their concern over control. As one may hear at management levels, "Nothing gets done unless I check on it"; "People respect what you inspect"; "Management must be on top of things."

There may be several unanticipated consequences. First, an MIS that aspires to be foolproof also indicates lack of trust of the user and sanctions unilateral control by the top. These messages are heard clearly by subordinates. In the world we just described, the subordinates' reaction will tend to be to make management's assertion that management must be monitoring and controlling continuously a self-fulfilling prophecy. The employees may also reduce their sense of responsibility for monitoring and produce at the safest minimum level. There are cases on record in which employees have watched an MIS produce errors, permitted the errors to get into the management process, and watched while the financial and human costs escalated.

Recommendation IV: Simplify the models and data needed to make them work so that costs are reduced and usability may be increased. Serious MIS specialists recommend less elegant models and a reduction of required statistical information in order to speed up the construction and to increase the use of the model (Wagner 1972). Again, this recommendation appears to be useful. However, our perspective alerts us to the possibility that such simplifications may leave untouched the problems described above.

Recommendation V: Have line and staff (especially staff) better educated about each other's problems. Again, education is a laudatory response. But in none of the discussion could one find any awareness of the primary inhibiting loops with which people are programmed. These loops do not impair the staff from hearing, let us say, about the pressures on line management. Indeed, it has been found that staff specialists understood these pressures and sympathized with the line managers. But they also felt that some of these pressures were self-inflicted; that their MIS might help to reduce them; that they, too, were under pressure, especially pressure created by line managers.

Moreover, MIS specialists tended to be unaware when they were making their line managers defensive. Many cases were observed in which MIS individuals were making things worse by utilizing strategies that they had hoped would make things better. The phenomenon of unawareness was equally valid for line managers. Indeed, under these conditions, it appears to be valid for most of us.

Recent research suggests that even if people become aware of the views of "others"; if they become aware of new behavioral alternatives; and if they accept these new behaviors; they tend not to be able to use them in noncontrived settings. It takes unfreezing of the old values and skills and the development of new ones to behave competently.

Recommendation VI: Design MIS to take into account the cognitive styles of line executives. This recommendation is just beginning to appear in the literature. However, our model raises the possibility that the inhibiting loops may so reinforce each other that the impact of the cognitive style of thinking could be swamped by the other factors. Keen (1975), one of the researchers who has studied cognitive style, recently has raised the question of the potency of this factor under the conditions described above.

Recommendation VII: The introduction of MIS should be seen as part of a total organizational development program. This recommendation, especially emphasized by Keen (1975) and Ginzberg (1975), comes closest to grappling with the systemic problems described above. Both authors have only recently begun to develop this alternative, and their models, as they state, are primitive.

However, we may say that other studies of organizational development programs show that very few focus on theories-in-use. At best, they focus on altering attitudes and behavior. But altering these two factors without altering theories-in-use makes the changes gimmicks, temporary, and not particularly credible in the eyes of others.

Moreover, none of the organizational development programs have focused on the dysfunctional attributes that may be embedded in MIS if it is implemented effectively (by present standards).

CASE F: BEHAVIORALLY ORIENTED INTERVENTION

Behaviorally oriented interventions may be categorized into two types, comprehensive and limited.

Diagnostic-confrontation sessions

This is one of the most frequently used, limited interventions to bypass the dysfunctional loops in a one- to three-day confrontation session.* The underlying strategy is to bring together the people involved and structure the sessions in such a way that their dysfunctional loops operate with minimal impact. When they do begin to operate to distort information and prevent error correction and error detection, the intervenor facilitates the process. If the intervention succeeds adequately in terms of those two criteria, then the assumption is that the group members can use their individual memories to bring together hitherto scattered information, make more clear what is vague, and reduce the ambiguity and inconsistency in the information being used to manage the organization. Given the reduction of the conditions that tend to produce error and inhibit its correction, and given the reduction of the inhibiting loops, then problem-solving progress should be made.

There are several ways in which the intervenor attempts to structure the sessions to reduce the operation of the inhibiting loops. The intervenor may collect data about the organizational problems through the use of individual interviews. Since the interview setting can be highly influenced by the intervenor, and given that he or she is competent in Model II theories-in-use, there is an increased possibility

---

*   For a description of such sessions, see Richard Beckhard, *Organization Development: Strategies and Models* (Reading, Mass.: Addison-Wesley, 1969), and R. R. Blake and J. S. Mouton, *Corporate Excellence through Grid Organizations Development* (Houston: Gulf, 1968).

that conditions that distort information will be decreased and conditions that enhance error correction will be decreased. Also, if the respondents perceive their intervenors as being competent and trustworthy (they will not violate professional confidences), then they will feel free to be more candid. Hence, this first step does produce valuable information for the clients.

The intervenor collects the data and organizes it into a meaningful map. The map is then used as a basis for discussion. If the map is confirmed as valid and useful by the clients, then there are several important pay-offs. First, the consultant has brought together scattered information. The very fact that the information was there to be obtained could help increase the clients' confidence in the usefulness of the sessions as well as in each other. Moreover, if the map is validated, it provides a document with which the clients can organize complexity and from which they can begin to derive plans for action. Third, a map may become an efficient way for individuals in the organization to store and retrieve information in order to monitor the impact of the actions taken and to develop new plans.

A third way in which the intervenors can act to bypass dysfunctionalities is to influence the priority-setting process as to which problems should be tackled first. If this is done skillfully, the probability that the clients will select the unimportant problems or those that are too difficult is greatly reduced. Or, if there is adequate time available during these conferences, the intervenors may encourage the group to examine the priorities with a view of helping them to see where they have made errors.

This leads to the fourth way the intervenors may help: They may design how the inventions should be produced; they may manage the first several products; they may evaluate them, etc. In other words, the intervenors may take varying degrees of responsibility (depending on the clients' needs and abilities) for implementing the actions invented during the sessions. It is also common practice for the intervenors to set up timetables for the completion of each of the actions recommended.

Finally, if one examines the literature of the cases asserted to be successful, there are several conditions that are present that help to support the intervenors' activities and increase the probability that the impact of the inhibiting loops will be diminished. In all successful cases, the key individual or group of individuals with power have fully supported the idea of the confrontation sessions. Moreover, the intervenors wisely defined at the outset a contract, which amounted to a publicly made promise that no one will be directly or indirectly punished for expressing his or her views. Such conditions increase the probability that, during the confrontation sessions, the games will be reduced. Also, confrontation sessions tended to succeed when the clients involved felt a strong need to resolve the problems. The clients tended to call in behaviorally oriented consultants as a last resort, having reached the conclusion that they could no longer postpone focusing on such issues as deception, information camouflage, games, etc. Consequently, the clients tend to be highly motivated to overcome the ultrastability of their learning system.

Another important resource of the intervenor is to produce what is known as process consultation. In terms of our model, an effective process consultant focuses on surfacing inhibiting loops.

For example, if someone says something in a way that may be punishing of some people, the intervenors would surface that behavior to ascertain its impact. Typically, the producers are unaware of the impact and are grateful for being helped to become aware of what they were producing, since this "teaches" everyone that the producers' motivations were not to hurt others. This awareness, in turn, may help the receiver to become candid, and such a lesson can increase the level of trust in the group. Or, if the group members appear to be avoiding certain issues, or creating win/lose dynamics, or wandering aimlessly in their discussions, the intervenors can confront these inhibiting loops.

As the literature suggests, all of these conditions can lead to progress in resolving particular problems. However, it is also commonly known among professional intervenors (and unfortunately, less documented in the literature) that the level of progress generated during the meeting is rarely maintained. In most cases, groups find that they are not able to operate as effectively in the back-home setting as they did during the one- to three-day session. Frequently, members recollect "the spirit of . . ." (inserting the name of the location of the conference), wishing that it had continued. Or they may recall it in order to justify saying something that may be viewed as violating the rules. Moreover, the results of the second or third confrontation sessions, if they are held at all, are not as dramatic as those of the first. One reason is that the expectations of success in the first

session may be low, and hence success is a surprise to many participants. On the other hand, this very success may produce unrealis-
tically high expectation for subsequent sessions. Another reason is
that the experienced consultants may know how to select for resolution those problems that are solvable. As the confrontation sessions
continue, they must select the more difficult ones for the group to
solve.

It is at this point that the limits of the conditions that lead to
success may have been reached. There is just so much interviewing
that one can do; just so much process consultation to bypass inhibiting loops; and just so much encouragement and persuasion from the
top. The repetition of these types of interventions only serve to prove
to the clients that they are not learning to learn. Their dependence on
the intervenors may become more clear and that may lead to feelings
of discouragement and failure.

But the most important limitations revolve around the fact that
the clients are programmed with Model I theories-in-use which lead
them to produce primary inhibiting loops and to be unaware of their
inability to double-loop learn. These two conditions must be overcome if long-range progress is to be made. In other words, the success
of these sessions is due to the ability to bypass and neutralize the negative impact of first- and second-order loops, but that very bypassing
and neutralizion impose limits on the long-range success of these programs.

Longer-range, T-group-based intervention programs

The second type of organizational development program is designed
to overcome some of the built-in limits of the first type just described.
These programs are usually much more long-range, with a greater
focus on inhibiting loops, and with the use of many more resources.

To illustrate our point, we chose an example of a company where
the conditions for organizational development approximated the ideal
(Argyris 1971). The president was intellectually and emotionally committed to the program. He attended several experiential learning seminars to focus on overcoming the dysfunctional consequences of his behavior as a leader. Second, most of the top officers had also attended
such programs and they all evaluated them very highly. Third, an in-
house organizational-development capability was created with highly
trained internal consultants. Fourth, budgets were adequate to hold

almost any type of session deemed useful by the experts and accepted by the clients. Fifth, the president did not place unrealistic demands on the organizational development experts nor on the line officers to produce lasting changes quickly. He had a realistic level of aspiration.

All these conditions did produce progress. To focus on the top, the meetings of the top management group (TMG) became more open and more productive. However, after a while the progress leveled off. The members began to express dissatisfaction and disappointment with themselves and their experts.

An outside intervenor (one of the authors) was invited to help the TMG. The intervenor collected tape recordings of the group's problem-solving and decision-making meetings. Quantitative scores were developed that indicated the degree to which TMG's activities approximated Model II type behaviors (but not Model II theories-in-use). The results showed that the group's activities were close to Model I. Every time the consultant participated in the sessions, the behavior would alter toward Model II, but as soon as the consultant left, the behavior would approximate Model I. Why? (Argyris 1971, p. 104).

To use our framework, the members who had gone through T-group experiences had become aware of their inhibiting loops and had attempted to alter their behavior. But changing behavioral strategies without focusing on their theories-in-use is not adequate. Even if behavioral change is generated, it assures that the new behavior will be producible only under conditions that are similar to the laboratory—that is, where the living system tends to sanction Model II governing variables.

Whenever the intervenor visited the group, many of the executives reported that his presence symbolized the T-group norms and living system, and thus they became more open. They trusted the intervenor to help them if they behaved in ways that might upset other individuals.

Moreover, the T-group experiences could not and would not focus on their company's learning system. They could not, because the group was composed of executives from many different companies. They would not, because in T-group practice, to focus on the learning system of the organization is to focus on material external to the T-group (there-and-then material), which is discouraged.

In a recent study of a group of presidents who were moving from Model I toward Model II, using a learning theory different from T-group theory, the executives were able to invent solutions to there-and-then problems and to produce them with the help of the other members (Argyris 1976a). For example, a president invented a solution for dealing with an ineffective executive vice-president. He then practiced producing the invention in front of the other presidents before he attempted to deal with the vice-president. Data collected during the meeting showed that the vice-president responded much more mildly than the presidents expected. In other words, the president, during the role-playing in the learning environment, actually learned to deal with behavior that was much tougher than that which he faced when he dealt with the actual vice-president. This result is commonly observed. The point is that the learning environment can prepare a student to cope with behavior that is more difficult than the behavior to be faced with when returning home.

Yet, producing the solution in the back-home setting can be more difficult for reasons that are related to the learning system of that organization. For example, the presidents had developed a history of relationships with their subordinates which was dominated by Model I. Given this history of relationships, then Model II would be viewed with skepticism by the subordinates. Also, many of the presidents aspired to behave according to Model II so well that they would manifest few errors. They imposed this level of aspiration on the grounds that their vice-presidents expected them to be perfect. Moreover, the presidents felt that unless their performance was superior, it would not be credible (Argyris 1976a).

In the learning environment, it was possible to question the presidents' attribution that their vice-presidents expected them to be perfect. This surfaced the fact that the presidents were hesitant to test publicly their attribution (an action mandated by Model II). This in turn led the vice-presidents to become aware of some of their fears about being embarrassed in front of their subordinates. Subsequent data showed that the vice-presidents believed that their respective presidents were not predisposed to test publicly their attributions of their vice-presidents, and that they were uncomfortable about experimenting with their new behavior and about producing error. The point is that all these perceptions were part of the learning system, and, unless dealt with, would greatly reduce the probability of success. For example, if the vice-presidents felt that their presidents were uncomfortable with feedback that might surface error in their behavior, then they would probably not communicate such information. But, this would be the very information that the presidents would need to assess how well they were doing in experimenting with Model II theories-in-use.

In the case being discussed, the presidents worked through all those issues. The point being made, however, is that a learning environment composed of people from different systems cannot deal with the learning system of each participant. The learning environment can help each member generate a relatively high degree of behavioral competence, but that competence can be blunted and neutralized if the dysfunctional conditions of his or her learning system are not also dealt with.

In order for the learning system to be dealt with, the presidents had to become involved in learning environments with their subordinates. This was done, and the presidents found themselves as agents of change (in some cases assisted by a professional, and in some cases not). In these learning environments, it was not only possible to focus on the relationship of the president with the vice-presidents. It also was necessary (and became possible) for the vice-presidents to focus on their relationships with each other, with their peers, and especially with their subordinates. These doubts became the basis for further learning, and, in the cases described, led to important progress. As the progress began to appear as stable, the participants turned to introducing it into other aspects of the learning system, such as the redesign of organizational structure, budgets, management information systems, etc.

Consequences of ignoring theories-in-use and learning systems

In the empirical literature related to the behavioral approach, there is, as we have tried to show, a lack of differentiation between data at the espoused level and data at the level of theory-in-use. Also, there is little attention paid to conceptualizing the learning systems of organizations, as well as to the kind of evidence that is necessary to ascertain whether they approximate Model O-I or O-II.

In this section, we will focus on some of the consequences of these gaps in the empirical literature. The consequences are suggested, in a particularly vivid way, by a recent analysis of the management behavior of Albert Speer (Singer and Wooton 1976).

Briefly, the authors point out that Speer utilized administrative principles congruent with those espoused in much of the organizational development (OD) literature. For example, Speer believed in collegial forms of decision making and applied methods of what he called "democratic economic leadership" (p. 82). Speer believed in minimizing rigid structures while at the same time emphasizing decentralization, temporary systems, and matrix organizations (pp. 84–86). He encouraged his subordinates to confront him and each other. He preferred "uncomfortable associates to compliant tools," and he ordered that any top administrators who were over 55 must have a deputy no older than 40 (p. 85).

Singer and Wooton raise the following important questions: If these and other data are valid, then why did not the OD values act to lead Speer's administrators to question the values that their munitions operations (specifically) and the Third Reich (more generally) represented? Why did Speer and his people apparently compartmentalize their values and behavior? How could they produce a collegial, democratic process emphasizing openness, yet never question the basic purposes of their activities?

These questions cannot be ignored. We maintain that the reason Singer and Wooton can even raise these issues is that current OD practice ignores theories-in-use and learning systems as the primary criteria for understanding organizational reality. In order to answer Singer and Wooton's questions, as well as illustrate our points, we wish to organize our argument around two questions. First: Did Speer's group utilize administrative practices that mirrored OD values? Second: If they did, why didn't the spillover of these values cause them to question the values of the Third Reich?

In order to answer the first question, given our perspective, we would need evidence that the individual theories-in-use and the organizational learning systems were primarily Models II and O-II respectively (for "OD values," as we have seen, contain elements of these models). Moreover, that evidence would have to be in relatively observable categories, so that readers could see clearly how the inferences were made and have the opportunity to confirm or disconfirm them. No such data were presented by Speer. Thus, strictly speaking, we cannot agree with Singer and Wooton that we know whether or not Speer's group manifested OD values. However, we would agree with them that, given the criteria in good currency about how to decide whether people are utilizing OD values, Singer and Wooton could draw the conclusions that they described. This suggests that the problem may not be with Singer and Wooton, but with the current OD practice of evaluating the effective use of its OD values.

But there is a deeper problem embedded in the illustration above. The problem can be introduced by pointing out that Speer and his group would also have had to focus on directly observable data if they were to have concluded that they had democratized their organizations and overcome the problems of group-think. Since they presented no such data (and the original sources suggest that they never thought of focusing on such criteria), we infer that they were unaware of the criteria that we maintain are necessary to their position. If they were unaware of the criteria, then we can raise the question of whether the OD values had truly reached the levels of theory-in-use. We may also say that if Speer had brought in an OD specialist armed with the logic that is presently being used (as illustrated by Singer and Wooton), he would have been told that he was operating in accordance with OD values.

There is some evidence that Speer was focusing, at best, on the espoused level, and that his theory-in-use was Model I or oscillating Model I.

For example, Singer and Wooton write:

1. The "dominant social paradigm" within the Speer organization was functional effectiveness and amoral judgment. They continue: "This dominant social paradigm was not to be questioned or not to be challenged" (p. 88).

This is clearly a Model I and O–I situation. In a Model II and O–II world, all paradigms are always open to being questioned or else there would be no double-loop learning.

2. Singer and Wooton cite Speer's insistence at having around him subordinates who confronted him and each other. They relate this policy to Speer's desire to overcome group-think. They cite Janis' study in which he showed that effective decisions were characterized by group processes where the members confronted each other openly (Janis 1972). Elsewhere, one of us has shown that the Janis cases illus-

trate an oscillating Model I and not a Model II condition (Argyris 1976c).

3. The probability that the openness and free-flowing communication was not Model II is supported by Singer and Wooton's conclusion that the participants in Speer's group were not democratized. The Speer structural changes" . . . did (not) have much impact on 'democratizing' those individuals who were participants" (p. 91).

If we accept it as probable that Speer and his group operated at a level of Model I and yet created such structural phenomena as decentralization, matrix organizations, and temporary systems, then the existence of these phenomena tells us little about the theories-in-use. These structural phenomena can indicate Models I and O-I or Models II and O-II. This is important to recognize, not merely to make a point for or against a particular perspective, but because it is crucial in developing more effective practice. It suggests that interventionists and participants must learn to realize that such participative structures together with openness (an oscillating Model I) may be more effective than Model I, but they do not necessarily indicate a world that approximates Models II and O-II.

Individuals and organizations must go through an enormous amount of learning if they are to reach beyond the point that Speer and his group may have achieved. OD practitioners and clients have greatly underestimated the gap between, on the one hand, espousing Models II and O-II (or their equivalents) and creating structural arrangements congruent with these models, and, on the other hand, producing Model II theories-in-use and O-II learning systems.

It would not be difficult to cite from current practice many examples of organizations, communities, and schools in which the participants believed that they were creating Model II and O-II conditions but actually were not. The literature cited in the section on "behavioral approaches" is an example. Not one of the cases cited by Greiner (1967) as successful O-I interventions meets our criteria, but some do meet the criteria utilized by Singer and Wooton. It is not surprising that Singer and Wooton are able to show that Speer may have followed the administrative precepts embedded in Likert and Blake's OD technologies (p. 84). The measure of effectiveness of either of these two technologies does not require data at the levels of theory-in-use and learning systems. The same is true for the leadership educational programs currently being used by Fiedler and Vroom (Argyris 1976b).

The danger of this state of affairs for effective practice is that people in organizations may believe that they are moving toward Models II and O-II when actually life may merely have become less intensely Models I and O-I. In such a case, not only may the clients be deceiving themselves, but this may also increase the probability of long-run failure. For example, the people at the lower levels may hear the rhetoric of decentralization, matrix organization, anti-group-think, etc., but they also realize that the theories-in-use and the learning systems are still Models I and O-I respectively. Under these conditions, they will see the current state of affairs as a fad *and* as not to be confronted (since the top appears blind to the fact that it is a fad).

There is another important issue involved. It is related to how long and how much effort it takes to change human values in such a way that they do not wash out under zero-to-moderate stress. We are suggesting that it takes much longer than the current criteria being used. More important than that, however, is the requirement that must be met if values are to be changed at all. As we described above, the key components of the comprehensive learning experience are double-loop learning and the good dialectic. The first means the uncovering of the layers of unawareness that Model I people have about discovering-inventing-producing-generalizing double-loop learning. The second means focusing continually on the dilemmas that arise while trying to move from Models I and O-I toward Models II and O-II. As one president put it, "The path toward II and O-II appears to be a life full of dilemmas." As we have seen, people programmed with Model I are not competent to deal either with dilemmas or the fears that arise when they encounter those dilemmas and realize their depth of unawareness. Life becomes a continual zig-zagging between Models I and O-I on the one hand, and II and O-II on the other.

The reader may question whether changing values and behavior is such a lengthy and complex process. We believe it is probably even more complex than we have suggested.

Embedded in the argument is the assumption that individual theories-in-use and organizational learning systems are preferred starting points for change in values. This does not mean that the macro-environment is unimportant; it means that people should begin change with the factors over which they have control. Unless they do so, focusing on the macro-environment could be a way to protect their Model I state, and hence, to use OD values as a new set of gimmicks serving the old theories-in-use. The illustrations that come to mind are the alternative schools and the attempt to decentralize the large corporation described previously. In both cases, they were espousing aspects of Models II and O-II—but they were not behaving according to their espoused theories, and they were unaware of this fact.

Under these conditions, "changes" toward OD values will not spill over into the macro-environment because they have not been produced in the micro-environment in the first place. This leads us to the second question of compartmentalization. It may be that there was no basic change in the theories-in-use or in the learning systems. The likelihood of a spill-over to the macro-environment is low when the organization cannot even make it work in the environment over which the members have some control—namely, their own.

It is our hypothesis that if Speer and his group went through the double-loop learning and encounter with the good dialectic that we propose, they would have shown a greater awareness of the incongruence between what they were doing and their nation's actions. It is not our hypothesis that they could then necessarily have done something about it. Nor would such action be evidence for our perspective. There were attempts made on Hitler's life (and on the lives of other dictators), but there is little evidence that the assassins were risking their lives for Model II values. Indeed, if history teaches anything, it is that most dictatorships are replaced by, at best, enlightened Model I worlds. We would hypothesize that in a society whose population held Model II theories-in-use, the confrontation of a despot would come early rather than late. The members would know, through the pain and frustration experienced during their learning processes, that Model II worlds are protected through Model II confrontations. The longer people wait to confront the emerging signs of dictatorship, the greater the probability that they will have to use Model I tactics—and the more the dictators' use of such tactics comes to seem like fighting fire with fire.

People following Model II theories-in-use will tend to relate them to the environment that surrounds them. They will strive to alter that environment toward Model II if they believe that they have the necessary control and if there is no evidence that their lives would be at stake. If their lives are at stake, and if they know that the probability of affecting Model II changes is nearly zero, then the choice they have is whether or not they wish to become moral heroes. Model II has little to say that directly informs the choice of endangering one's life and becoming a moral hero, but it has much to say about the world for which one would be dying.

Nord and Durand (1975) report another example of the difficulties created when learning at the espoused level is not differentiated from learning at the levels of the theory-in-use and learning systems. They describe a case in which participative management (PM) and management by objectives (MBO) were introduced, resulting, after an initial period of success, in a "blooming buzz of confusion" and mixed results. The program was well financed, the top executives were highly supportive (they attended many of the training sessions), and all managers were offered and attended several training programs. A process consultant was also hired as a member of the top management team to implement team management throughout the organization. The people were largely positive about their training experience (Managerial Grid). Some teams reported that they had greatly increased authority to get their jobs done; for example, the manager of a small plant reported, "We determine what needs to be done and have *carte blanche* to do it." Also, reports were obtained that barriers were beginning to be broken down and communication was becoming more open (p. 4). Finally, evidence was presented to show that in some areas the organization's performance was enhanced as a result of the more effective communications (p. 5).

After several months, however, difficulties with the program began to develop. The first complaint was that top management seemed to equate participation with abdication of leadership. They (especially the president) seemed to have removed themselves from the thrust of the company. Second: There seemed to be a proliferation of changes with a low degree of "follow through." Third: It appeared that some in top management were using participative management to avoid making decisions or taking action. Fourth: MBO and the holding of meetings ("We have meetings just to have meetings") were becoming ends in themselves. Fifth: The group dynamics during problem-solving meetings were not effective. ("We talk a decision to death; by the time the decision is made, it's too late to act.")

The first point to be noted about these complaints is that the respondents felt that not much could be done to resolve them. They made attributions that were not tested publicly with each other, that the activities were self-reinforcing. For example, one executive used PM to dominate others—a fact that was confirmed by many but seen as discussable by none. This executive was a top-down leader who saw himself as a counterbalance to the president's withdrawal leadership style. The authors described him as a person who would be a "winner" in face-to-face discussions; as one who enjoyed combat (win/lose situations) and who got a "real thrill out of winning or crushing someone" (p. 8). All these are characteristic of Model I.

Finally, the evolution of MBO indicates that it operated as a fad with a Model I theory-in-use. For example, many of the managers who used MBO also saw it as a technique to avoid taking action. Moreover, many managers were critical of the paperwork involved, which they felt was counterproductive. Also, there was agreement that people were not developing realistically challenging objectives. Again, although many of the people held these views privately, they were not discussed publicly nor did the people appear to see any sense in trying to alter them.

From these observations, we may begin to infer that the participative management program which espoused Model II was actually, at the level of theory-in-use, Model I and the opposite to Model I (withdrawal).

The pervasive attitude about PM and MBO was that they were not working and that nothing could be done about this state of affairs. This illustrates the sense of hopelessness found in a Model O-I learning system. Also illustrative of Model O-I were the games people played. Thus top management blamed the failure of MBO on the incompetence and lack of motivation of lower-level managers. The latter blamed the same failures on the top's blindness and incompetence. Another game that was played was that both sides apparently knew about these views, both sides knew that neither side would discuss them publicly, and both sides knew that neither side would discuss the undiscussability of the games. Finally, the double-bind that the managers reported to the authors also indicated a Model O-I learning system. For example, if top management excluded the lower-level managers from participation, it could be interpreted as insincerity on the part of the top in terms of their commitment to PM. On the other hand, engaging in participative efforts was interpreted as a sign of weak leadership. Under these conditions the upper-level managers were damned if they did and damned if they didn't. And again, none of these double binds were reported to be discussable and solvable.

The consultants to this organization may have manifested some of the same problems as their clients. The consultants documented that their clients did not behave according to their espoused theory. However, they did not attempt to discover their clients' theories-in-use. This would be critical if they were to explain the discrepancies that they observed.

Without the requirement to discover their clients' theories-in-use, the consultants defined their task as one of reducing the discrepancy between espoused theory and client behavior. They suggested that the way to reduce the discrepancy would be to change the organizational structure. Although they did not specify the changes, it appears that they were suggesting a change that would make power-equalization a genuine and not a manipulative tool of management (p. 8).

If we are correct that the clients' theories-in-use approximate Model I, and if Model I clients will create Model O-I learning systems, then a change in the organizational structure will not result in a world that approximates genuine participative management (Model II) because the clients will not be able to produce Model II theories-in-use or O-II learning systems. The discrepancy between espoused theory and behavior is in reality a discrepancy between espoused theory and theory-in-use. Without the alteration of the latter, genuine participation is unlikely to occur.

Nord and Durand assert that too often OD experts mislead clients regarding the degree of difficulty involved in producing genuine participation. They admonish (correctly, we believe) the all-too-quick tendency for OD specialists to blame failures of programs on the lack of client commitment, when in reality the clients may never have received the appropriate education to help them transform PM and MBO from espoused theories into theories-in-use. The danger is that without an alternative model to create the conditions for the good dialectic, they too would tend to create unrealistic expectations for the clients. For example, they imply that the change in organizational structure would help, but without alternative models such as Models II and O-II, it would not be possible to define change objectives. More importantly, the good dialectic would not be possible. In such a case, it also would not be possible to define the transformation processes required to move from I and O-I to II and O-II. Finally, without the existence of such transformation processes, it would not be possible to derive a set of learning experiences for the clients that would help them to learn the values and competencies required so that PM does not fade into a manipulative oscillating Model I.

In short, the consultants do not appear to differentiate between espoused theory and theory-in-use (they do differentiate between espoused theory and behavior); they do not appear to have alternative models for individuals and organization, which if achieved, would correct the errors they discovered; and they do not appear to have a model of individual and organizational learning that would be required to correct the situation. To this extent they have some of the blindness of their clients.

The consultants may also have unrealizingly played Model O-I games with their clients. For example, they concluded that one reason why the top wanted to introduce PM was so that the president could maintain his preferred leadership style of interpersonal withdrawal, coupled with intellectual inquiry. This was not reported as having been discussed with the president. Nor did they appear to have discussed with the top management their attribution that the top may have introduced PM so that they would not make other structural changes (p. 7). The authors apparently never attempted to help the participants to become aware of what prevented them from discussing the diagnoses and attributions they made of each other. Nor did the authors appear to confront the participants with the games they were playing.

CHAPTER ELEVEN

Summary and implications of part IV

We will summarize our analysis of each of the six approaches presented in Chapter 10, and suggest some implications for intervention toward good organizational dialectic.

CASE A

In the first case, the authors attributed an organization's inability to learn to vicious circles which inhibited corrective action at all levels of the organization—specifically, in relation to conflicts in the supervision and service functions of headquarters and field offices. The underlying strategy was to design new structures that reduced the vicious circles and increased organizational learning. For example, the researchers recommended that if a field office developed an innovation, then it, rather than world headquarters, should become the center for disseminating and teaching the innovation to other units. This should eliminate the necessity for the field offices to go to central headquarters (which would only have second-hand acquaintance with the innovation), and simultaneously permit direct contact with the branch that produced the innovation. The idea embedded in this strategy was that of bypassing the stultifying effects of the home office on the branches.

Our analysis suggests that such a strategy may work if it can be shown that the Model I theories of action of the participants and the O-I learning system of the organization would also have been

292

changed. Otherwise, these factors would operate in the new, more decentralized relationships. With time, the relationship of a particular innovative branch to its sister field offices would take on the same properties that presently characterize field office/home relationships.

Our analysis also suggests that Model I theories-in-use and O-I learning systems cannot be altered merely by eliminating structures that inhibit organizational learning. For people tend not to trust the assertion that a new structure represents a new organizational theory-in-use. They tend to be cautious, waiting to see whether new behavior matches the new espoused theory. But the new behavior tends to be opposite to Model I, or oscillating Model I. We predict that under mild stress, superiors will revert to Model I governing variables which will "prove" to subordinates that organizational change was at the espoused level. Hence, subordinates will become even more cautious.

If the subordinates act more cautiously, the superiors may interpret that behavior as evidence that they do not wish to change, or they are not able to do so, or that the subordinates do not trust the superiors. Any combination of these will tend to increase the stress, and thereby increase the probability that people will revert to Model I theories-in-use and O-I learning systems. Soon the changes that were designed to be double-loop settle down to single-loop alterations, relegating the espoused changes to the status perennially used in organizations, namely, a fad.

The second reason why lifting or eliminating the repressive structures will not produce change toward Models II and O-II is that people do not have the competence to behave according to Model II. The knowledge and skills required take a significant amount of time to learn.

Hence, conflicts in the supervision/service functions of headquarters are unlikely to be resolved through recourse to structural change alone. Change in structure will simply displace or proliferate such conflicts unless there are changes in the O-I learning system of the organization. And these cannot be brought about through change in structure.

CASE B

This case dealt with an attempt to change the structure of a very large organization toward increasing decentralization. The change grew of the CEO's recognition that the requirement for corporate gr in sales and in profits, was incompatible with the earlier pattern of centralized management.

But the move toward centralization generated a dilemma. Because the CEO recognized that the divisions must be the origins of innovation and growth, he tried to create the conditions for divisional autonomy. The divisional presidents, schooled in the O-I learning system of the corporation, reacted to these changes in ways that were conservative and risk-averse. And whereas corporate strategic planning would now require the cooperative inquiry of the presidents, they reacted to decentralization by increasing their competition with one another.

The CEO attempted to reduce these dysfunctions through massive educational programs which, although they were intended to increase feelings of autonomy and self-responsibility, had a Model I theory of instruction.

The result was that the students entered into learning environments where much of the substance was related to Model II and O-II types of concepts, yet what they experienced were Model I theories-in-use and O-I learning systems. This being the case, the discrepancies were rarely discussable. Since the undiscussability was reinforced by the CEO (who, when he lectured, gave no clues that he was aware of the discrepancies or the difficulties involved in overcoming them), the heads of the divisions quickly inferred that the changes were (at best) possible in their relationships with the CEO and his staff, and (at worst) had to be ignored in their relationships with their subordinates. This strategy assured that decentralization, if it were to occur, would be limited to a few layers at the top.

Again, the change-inhibiting forces identified in Case A were also operating in Case B. The majority of the people did not accept genuine decentralization as a theory-in-use, therefore they hesitated and were cautious. The hesitation and caution "proved" to the division heads that their subordinates were not capable of genuine decentralization; hence they found reason to continue their unilaterally controlling leadership styles. Both reactions enhanced the forces that discredited the validity of decentralization, which in turn relegated the idea to a fad. In this case it happened to be a rather long-lasting one, since the CEO, with the power and resources available to him, supported the concept.

Finally, we noted that, in attempting to overcome the division heads' disbelief in genuine decentralization, the CEO may have concentrated so intensely on decentralization that he ignored cues that some of the major causes of decreasing profitability were in areas such as poor strategic planning and financial analysis.

CASE C

The third structural example had to do with relationships among organizations. Central to it was a conflict between the maintenance of distributed power and the requirement that the system adapt to increasing socioeconomic pressures for change. The very system of secretive and restrictive practices which preserved the equilibrium of power among agents of the system also prevented the system from responding adaptively to these pressures for change. When the analysts asked whether the system could change, the agents of the system responded in the negative. This would be predicted from a Model O-I learning system. There should be a very low probability that double-loop changes can be instigated and carried on from within O-I learning systems. Indeed, there was so great a ridigity toward change in the O-I learning systems that existed within the network of towns, cities, regional bureaus, and the national government, that a new parallel set of relationships had to be created if the needs of the cities were to be fulfilled.

We noted that the only model of change mentioned as possible by the authors writing of the case was the emergence of new charismatic leaders. This meant that change, if it were to come at all, would have to begin with new individuals holding a new perspective. At this point, the authors—who are leading sociologists—unknowingly team up with those traditional industrial psychologists who maintain that the way to change organizations is to select new people with new ideas.

However, neither group helps to explain how effective the new people will be in the organization. Will not the O-I learning system impinge on their ability to help bring about double-loop change? If not, by what processes do outsiders overcome Model I theories-in-use and O-I learning systems?

CASE D

The fourth example also dealt with the relationships among organizations. The focus was on the implementation of state and national laws or executive orders primarily in the area of health, education, and welfare. Bardach's rich description of the implementation process made it possible for us to relate the win/lose, competitive bargaining activities, the quasiresolution of conflict, and the low trust to the Model I theories-in-use of the participants. The description of the group dynamics and the interdepartmental dynamics, plus the description of the many different types of games played among agencies, approximated the dynamics and the games identified in O-I learning systems. Hence we conclude not only that O-I learning systems may exist within organizations, but also, as indicated in the previous case and much more strongly illustrated in this case, that O-I learning systems can be created in networks among organizations.

Applying a theory of action perspective to Bardach's analysis permits us to conceptualize one of his major recommendations ("as little government management as possible") as an act that is opposite to Model I and O-I—and hence not an act that will appreciably alter the predisposition of the actors and their agencies to change the nature of the implementation game. Moreover, we predicted that the recommendation that politicians be required to write detailed scenarios of the implementation of proposed legislation (which makes sense to us) would be difficult to carry out because the O-I learning system would inhibit obtaining the very data needed to write the scenario.

We have suggested that some of Bardach's insightful recommendations assume that the planning process is not subject to dysfunctional activities, and that it may be possible to bypass the implementation game. We find this unrealistic in a world dominated by O-I learning systems.

Finally, we suggested that the reason the analysis may be incomplete is that Bardach (as was true for the other cases, also) did not have a map of another state of affairs which provided a different set of norms, governing variables, and theories-in-use. Without such a map, the good dialectic is not possible. Hence the recommendation will tend to remain within the confines of single-loop thinking and action.

CASE E

The next case was concerned with the use of management information systems to overcome some of the problems related to the search and production of valid and useful information for management.

First, given our models, we predicted that the introduction and effective use of MIS would tend to be inhibited when such systems threatened individuals or O-I learning systems. Hence, the finding that there was negligible resistance to MIS when they were used to solve single-loop problems was not inconsistent with our perspective.

Second, we predicted that whenever the resistance to MIS increased, it would be due to the fact that the MIS was threatening individuals, groups, intergroups, or organizational norms. We also predicted that the underlying causes of resistance would not be discussable. Any discussion of the difficulties would be in terms of such factors as MIS requiring assumptions that oversimplified reality, data-gathering processes that were almost prohibitive, and an understanding of the use of models rarely manifested by line executives, etc. All of these factors would be valid but not sufficient in and of themselves. If the resistance to MIS were to be genuinely overcome, and if truly new MIS were to be developed, it would be necessary to help line and staff specialists to focus on their model theories-in-use and the O-I learning systems of their organizations. Otherwise, well-intentioned actions may become counterproductive.

For example, a line manager might indicate lack of understanding of the use of the models. Education in the use of models might then seem helpful. However, even after learning to use models, the line manager would still be left with dilemmas.

Management information systems, with their emphasis on public formulation of objectives, performance criteria, and strategies, tend to restrict the space of free movement open to individual managers. Hence, organizations are confronted with managers' needs for free movement on the one hand, and, on the other hand, with the requirements for organizational rationality implicit in management information systems.

Finally, we noted that the underlying assumption of MIS is that valid information is basic to organizational effectiveness. However, line administrators embedded in O-I organizations know that valid information can be threatening, and since such information tends not to be discussable, it is rarely correctable.

More importantly, if for some reason these factors did become discussable, the tendency would be to design new features for the MIS that would be counterproductive to the production of valid information. For example, attempts at making MIS not fudgeable and resistant to distortion could lead to layers of devices that enhance unilateral control, which reinforces the O-I inhibiting loops.

CASE F

The behavioral intervention strategies did attempt to change behavior, but they did not focus explicitly on changing theories-in-use. Hence, if an authoritarian executive reduced his unilateral controlling behavior, the T-group experience was considered a success. There was a failure to recognize that the behavioral change was still informed by a theory-in-use that was as counterproductive as Model I, namely, the opposite of Model I.

A second possibility not recognized by the behavioral approach was that changes in Model I behavior may be informed by oscillating Model I theories-in-use. For example, as we said, the dynamics of personal-growth laboratories were similar to those of highly competitive business organizations. Yet the personal-growth faculty condemned such dynamics.

The second problem identified was that the behavioral approach rarely related possible changes in individual behavior to features of the O-I learning system in which the individual may have been embedded. Consequently, changes that might have occurred in a T-group, for example, would have been transferred into the organization only with great difficulty.

The lack of focus on changing Model I theories-in-use (not simply behavior) and the O-I learning systems led to several dysfunctional consequences. For example, when the people were learning to express all their feelings or to withdraw from controlling others, they were behaving according to a theory-in-use that we have described as the opposite to Model I. Such a polar opposite to Model I does not provide propositions about the limits of use of its recommended behavioral strategies. For example, should all feelings be expressed?

When can feelings be suppressed in order to accomplish tasks? Can withdrawing from a relationship characterized by unilateral over-control be counterproductive? Under what conditions do people following theory Y advocate strongly their positions?

The second dysfunctional consequence was the blindness people developed to the incongruities between the Model II theories of action they espoused and the Model I theories-in-use they utilized. Hence, in the case of the alternative schools, the available data suggested that where financial and political support was available, and where the teachers and students volunteered to attend, the schools eventually failed because the students and the teachers, lacking Model II theories-in-use, could not create O-II learning systems (which were the core of the espoused theory of most alternative schools). Moreover, neither the students nor the teachers could design ways to avoid becoming bogged down in the inhibiting loops and games of O-I styles. Finally, neither teachers nor students were aware of these factors, or, if they were, they could not find ways to make them discussable. And even when they did so, primary and secondary inhibiting loops made it highly improbable that the problem-solving would be effective.

IMPLICATIONS

Each of the six approaches recognizes the existence of fundamental organizational dilemmas whose confrontation is a starting point for what we have called good dialectic. Thus, in Case A, the conflicts surrounding the supervision and service functions of headquarters; in Case B, the CEO's dilemma concerning divisional autonomy and corporate strategic planning; in Case C, the competing requirements of systems adaptation and maintenance of the balance of power.

In each of the six cases, analysts advocate a selective approach to intervention based on structure, "new blood," information, or inter-personal behavior. But organizational dilemmas are embedded in organizational learning systems. In O-I learning systems, the dilemmas of organizational theory of action are fostered and rein-forced. Interventions which do not take account of O-I learning systems are likely, as we have shown, to exacerbate existing dilemmas or to create new ones. Organizations cannot be freed up to engage in good dialectic, to confront fundamental dilemmas and incongruities in their theories-of-action, except by confronting their O-I learning systems in their entirety. Yet each of the six cases represents only a selection of one or two facets of organizational reality.

First, in each case, whenever structure was focused on, it was organizational structure. In these cases, the human personality was considered as a black box—that is, no model of man was presented.

Second, almost no attention was given in the diagnoses to the connection between the individual level and the systems level. Although the writers in the first case made it clear that they saw these levels as intimately connected, we could not find statements specifying the connection. This gap meant that the cases did not provide insight into the mechanisms or processes by which the organizational level could influence the individual level and vice versa. Whatever the processes or mechanisms, they tended to be limited to those that described activities within a single level. For example, the description of the self-sealing processes in Case A was primarily at the organizational level.

Third, little or no attention was given by any of the studies to the distinction between espoused theory and theory-in-use. In Case B, although the executives undergoing the massive educational program knew that there was an enormous gap between the new espoused theory of management and the existing theory-in-use, they also realized early on that the top management and the educators did not seem to be aware of, nor did they wish to discuss, the gap. It appeared that the theory of intervention was based on the assumption that if a new theory of management could be espoused and taught, and if the top would support the new espoused management theory, then it would eventually become part of the organizational theory-in-use. Even the behavioral approach never focused on the theories of action in people's heads that informed their behavior.

Fourth, there was little focus on how the individuals and the system learn. In none of the cases were we able to find that any attention was paid either to the processes of error detection and correction at the individual and organizational levels, or to how these processes interconnected and reinforced each other to create a learning system which, in turn, influenced what the individuals, acting as agents, would tend to include in their problem-solving processes.

As we pointed out in Part I, individuals are the agents of organizational learning. Organizations learn when the organizational inquiry, carried out by individual members, becomes embedded in organizational theory-in-use and recorded in organizational memory through the media of maps and images. The learning system of an organization significantly influences the way in which individuals carry out the tasks of organizational inquiry.

From this description of organizational learning, there follows a set of requirements on a theory of intervention. These requirements correspond directly to the omissions listed above.

First, whatever intervention activities are derived from a theory of intervention, they must be doable by human beings. A theory of intervention ought not to suggest actions that human beings cannot perform, or cannot learn to perform.

Second, intervention activities must be feasible within the learning system of an organization.

Taking these together, it follows that an effective theory of intervention should contain a theory of human nature which is connected to a theory of organizational learning systems. Connecting the two levels means that one is able to specify the mechanisms or activities by which individuals may influence the organization, and vice versa. A theory of intervention that attempts to specify what individuals and organizations must do if they are to become capable of good dialectic must also show how these specifications lead to the intended changes.

Intervention theory must be amenable to the concept of personal causality and responsibility. Without such concepts, what is the point of saying that something must be done?

And intervention theory must take account of structure, in the sense proposed by Blau (1975) and Homans (1975); namely, patterns of interrelationships that persist over time. Without such patterns, how can one find a rational basis for the empirical generalizations that underlie theories of intervention?

As we see it, the theories of intervention that are explicit and implicit in the six cases do not attend to all of these requirements. Each may attend to one or two, but none attend to all. And as we understand the literature, these cases show no signs of attending to these requirements.

We believe that our perspective addresses itself seriously to all of these requirements. Ours is a theory-of-action perspective that provides a model of the human personality (the espoused theories and theories-in-use), plus a model of the organization as a learning system

(Models O-I and O-II). Secondly, we are able to connect these two models by making explicit the mechanisms by which the individual influences the organization and vice versa (i.e., primary and secondary loops and loops that inhibit deutero-learning).

We have shown in Parts II and III how an individual's theory-in-use cannot be said to exist apart from the environment in which it is embedded. On the other hand, we have also shown how individuals programmed with Model I theories-in-use interact with information in such a way as to create primary inhibiting loops, which, in turn, contribute to the secondary loops, games, and camouflage characteristic of O-I learning systems.

Our perspective has as a central concept the notion of personal causality. At the individual level, we assert that individuals are responsible for creating their own theories-in-use and that these theories-in-use define for them how they will deal with reality. Hence, individuals are personally causally responsible for their actions.

We make the same assumptions about organizations. We believe that the creation and maintenance of the learning system is the responsibility of the members of the organization. As well as we can, we design our comprehensive intervention strategy so as not to violate the concept of personal causality at the individual and organizational levels. As we have seen, this tends to create conflicts and tensions with clients right at the outset.

One of the most basic conflicts is that Model I theories-in-use inhibit double-loop learning and consequently produce individuals who are not competent to discover-invent-produce-generalize in this area. These people systematically hide their personal causality by projecting the blame for their inability to double-loop learn onto the environment. As we have seen, there is evidence that the environment (O-I) does inhibit double-loop learning; thus the projection is based partly on a rational diagnosis of reality.

It is our assumption that changes can be made in O-I learning systems if individuals first learn to behave according to Model II theories-in-use and then strive to create O-II learning systems. Hence, we hold that clients are causally responsible—which is another way of saying that either they can choose to change themselves and their system or at least specify why they don't. (For example, they may show that having learned Model II, the environment in which they were embedded made it possible for them to create an O-II environment.)

Our theory suggests that these differences in views about personal causality should not be submerged but be made a basis for learning and progress during the intervention.

Our theory is also concerned with structure, not in the sense of the organizational task/role system alone, but in the sense of relationships that persist over time. The concepts of theory-in-use and learning systems are structural concepts in that they map a set of interrelationships among variables that persist over time. Thus we intend to include in our notion of structural rationality what happens at the individual, group, intergroup, and systemic levels, because all of these factors and activities are critical for the design and production of effective interventions.

In closing, we should like to relate the implications for organizational learning embedded in these cases to the concepts described at the outset.

Individuals are agents who carry out the learning for organizations. There can be no organizational learning unless individuals learn in their agent's role. Individuals may learn and organizations fail to learn because the agency function is not fully or effectively carried out. Whether or not individuals can perform their agency function so as to produce organizational learning depends on the nature of the learning system.

Learning has been defined in terms of the detection and correction of error. Figure 11.1 depicts the four logical possibilities regarding detection and correction. In the first category, error is detected and corrected. We maintain that O-I learning systems enhance the likelihood that this will occur with single-loop learning and reduce the likelihood of double-loop learning. The second category (error is not detected but is corrected) we will consider trivial, because if error is corrected it must be through some chance factors and not through organizational inquiry, which we have taken as necessary to organizational learning.

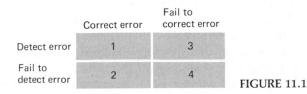

FIGURE 11.1

The third category exists when the error is detected but not corrected. The fourth category is when the error is neither detected nor corrected. All the cases we considered in Chapter 9 fell into categories three and four.

Several examples of category three come to mind. The internal faculty of the school knew that it was an error to make the educational program responsible for transforming decentralization from an espoused theory to a theory-in-use. They knew that it would take much more than that, but this was not discussable. Some appeared to fear that if they made this point clear to Cordiner, he might close the school. Others felt that he would seek a faculty who could give him assurances to the contrary. Turning to the strategic plans, one of us observed several top planning people who knew that the strategic plans had the gaps and could have the unintended consequences described by Baughman, but they found these issues undiscussable. In both examples, the actors chose not to discuss these differences and restricted their organizational learning to what they believed the learning system permitted.

This does not mean that the same actors did not, as individuals or cliques, think and learn about the undiscussable issues. It means that the thinking and the learning was not introduced into the organizational theory-in-use.

Another example is related to the cases in which OD specialists are aware that weekend workshops represent limited interventions and, at best, bypass the counterproductive factors of the O-I client learning system. Nevertheless, they design and execute the workshops because that's all the client will accept.

Examples of the fourth condition would include the consultants for the European organization who behaved toward the client in ways that were congruent with the way the client was behaving toward the subordinate, but which the consultants had found to be counterproductive. Also, the consultants suggested a new organizational structure but apparently did not design the learning environments that would be required to transform their recommendations from espoused theory to theory-in-use. They utilized a theory-in-use about learning that was similar to the one used by their clients (although the content differed). For example, the president believed that if management defined clear maps for the subordinates to follow, then the subordinates would indeed follow them. The consultants believed that if they could develop new and more accurate maps, then the clients would learn.

Two different examples of the fourth condition are the cases of the French governmental processes and the case of the U.S. implementation processes. The actors in the cases, as well as the authors of the cases, act and write respectively as if manipulation of others, covert strategies, deception, etc., are necessary because there are no other alternatives.

In all these examples, the actors in the cases and the social scientists making the analyses presented no significantly different models of any alternative learning systems, nor any explicit transformative process to transform the new model from an espoused theory to a theory-in-use. In other words, all the cases lacked the conditions for the good dialectic. Under these conditions, organizational learning will be limited to single-loop learning. Even when individual actors can see that double-loop learning is required, they will not produce such learning because to do so would be to violate the games and rules of the O-I learning system.

PART **V**

CONCLUSION

A fitting conclusion to this book seems to us to consist not of a re-affirmation of our main line of argument (which we hope has now become clear), but of a delineation of the questions we have generated through the research, criticism, and speculation which have gone into our writing. We believe it is a test of the vitality of the line of inquiry we have pursued that it leaves us with better questions than those with which we began and with ideas about the kinds of inquiry appropriate to those questions.

CHAPTER TWELVE

Directions for future research

TESTING THE O-I MODEL

We have built our models of organizational learning systems from case studies of organizations, from accounts of consultation, and from research on the scenarios of members of organizations. The formulation of the O-I Model has a strong empirical base, but the model has not been systematically tested.

We have advanced Model O-I to account for a range of organizational phenomena, most particularly for organizational learning phenomena. Having once established the *sense* in which organizations may be said to learn (or fail to learn) and the *kinds* of learning in which they may engage, we have noted through example and generalization the patterns of learning they do in fact exhibit. We claim, on the basis of the evidence we have gathered, that:

- Organizational learning is typically limited to single-loop learning.

- Changes in the norms of organizational theory of action, or in central elements of organizational theory-in-use, tend to occur through the eruptions consequent on ecological adjustment and in the face of change in organizational environments.

- Organizations typically do not engage in double-loop learning.

- Organizations do not deutero-learn, except in so far as such reflection is about single-loop learning (as in the example of industrial learning curves).

These claims are bounded in a variety of ways. Our sample of organizations, as reflected in the examples of earlier chapters, is drawn from many kinds of formal organizations (business firms, government agencies, universities) but not from all kinds of formal organizations. Our sample is drawn from North American, Latin American and European cultures, but not from all cultures. We have not sampled such organizations as families, voluntary associations, neighborhood groups, and the like. We therefore express our conclusions about organizational learning in the language of tendency and likelihood. We make claims about what is typical rather than about what is universal. We do not argue that there may not be somewhere an organization that engages regularly in double-loop and deutero-learning—only that we have not run across it.

Our research problem has been to account for the patterns of organizational learning and nonlearning as we have found them, and it is for the purpose of explaining these patterns that we have advanced our model of O-I organizations. It is the particular strategy of this model to link together the Model I features of the behavioral world of organizations with the processes of organizational error detection and correction, to take as central the interpersonal interactions in which Model I behaviors reinforce and are reinforced by conditions of error, and to show the interactions of these primary inhibitory loops with other processes (dysfunctional intergroup relations, games of deception, camouflage) which make an organization incapable of learning about its own learning system and of double-loop learning. We have also used Model O-I to account for the single-loop learning that organizations do engage in, distinguishing among the conditions appropriate to correctable and to uncorrectable error.

We believe we have shown that Model O-I can account for the patterns of learning and nonlearning described in our examples (and in many other examples we have collected but have not included in this book). However, we have not yet undertaken systematically to disconfirm Model O-I by deriving from it predictions central to the model and testing those predictions against experience under carefully observed conditions. To be more exact, we have attempted such predictions, and confirmed them, for parts of Model O-I (for example, the intervenor's predictions and findings as described in Chapters 7 and 8), but we have not yet done so for Model O-I as a whole.

The method described in Chapter 7 for mapping organizational learning systems lends itself to such a predictive enterprise. We believe it is possible to establish through such a diagnostic mapping that an organization's learning system conforms to Model O-I, and on that basis to make certain predictions. For example:

- The kinds of changes in organizational environment which the organization is likely to detect and respond to, and the kinds it is likely to ignore.

- The kinds of organizational errors that are likely to be detected and the kinds that are likely to go undetected.

- The kinds of errors that are likely to be correctable and those that are likely to be uncorrectable.

- The kinds of responses, including learning responses, that the organization is likely to make to various sorts of unanticipated or troublesome situations that may confront it.

Our orientation toward intervention offers yet another avenue for testing Model O-I, for that model permits us to predict how an organization is likely to respond to interventions of various kinds, and, in particular, to predict how it is likely to respond to the kinds of intervention we believe to be conducive to the transition to Model O-II. (To take only one small example, Model O-I allows us to predict how an organization is likely to respond to an intervention that takes the form of calling attention to a conflict which has been treated in the organization's learning system as undiscussable.)

In our testing of Model O-I as an explanation, we will be primarily concerned with its comparative resistance to refutation. For this purpose, we need theories that are plausible alternatives to Model O-I, so as to design crucial experiments. In Part IV we have considered several kinds of alternative approaches to organizational learning—the structural, information-system, behavioral, and political-science approaches—and we have criticized variants of these approaches, both from the point of view of their explanatory power and as theories of intervention. In a rigorous testing of Model O-I, we would have to take the most promising of these variants (indeed, to create new and more promising ones, if we can) so as to design crucial experiments which would distinguish between them and Model O-I. To take one instance, we can predict (as suggested in the analysis of Case A) how O-I processes will distort a merely structural change designed to promote improved organizational learning. The difference between what we have already done on this score and what we would need to do is that the prediction would be made on the occasion of a before-the-fact structural intervention (to take one instance of a kind of partial-intervention strategy), and observational follow-up would be made subsequent to that intervention.

TESTING MODEL O-II AND THE INTERVENTION THEORY

Perhaps the most fundamental test of Model O-I would be to show that the interventions based on an O-I diagnosis of an organization could lead to a more nearly O-II organization and that an O-II organization would yield the organizational learning consequences which we attribute to it. Such an experiment would test the O-I diagnosis, the claims for O-II, and the effectiveness of the proposed intervention strategy.

It is worth spelling out the components of such a process, and we do so in the next three subsections.

An O-II organization is possible

This requires, in effect, an "existence proof." We do not believe that the achievement of O-II status is an all-or-none affair. An organization may *approach* the good dialectic implicit in O-II without fully and finally realizing it, and may do so in several respects. For example, an organization may succeed in extending the zone of activity and experience in which it can exhibit good dialectic, thereby increasing the range of correctable errors with which it can deal.

Implicit in O-II and intervention theory is our belief that the approach to O-II is not likely to be continuous but to proceed in a staged or discontinuous way, as the organization becomes capable of extending good dialectic to deeper levels of its theory-in-use and to more central features of its learning system. The reason we hypothesize that progress toward O-II will be discontinuous is that (as pointed out earlier) no matter how much Model O-I learning activity there may be, it will not yield O-II learning.

In Chapters 8 and 9 we have described some of the examples available to us through our own consulting experience in which fragments of O-II, or partial approaches to O-II, have been achieved. Argyris's work with the presidents of six small firms, for example, describes how these presidents were helped to overcome primary inhibiting loops in their interactions with one another and in some of their interactions in their own firms, and further describes some of the organizational learning episodes consequent on those changes. Schon's work with the Mercury Corporation describes the diagnostic mapping that may be achieved through joint inquiry when a consultant enables members of the organization to side-step the primary loops which would ordinarily prevent them from such a mapping.

But we have yet to establish, in a full and sustained example, the feasibility of an O-II organization, nor are we aware of anyone else having done so.

An O-II organization has the organizational learning consequences predicted for it

Our claim is that, insofar as an organization approaches O-II, it will:

- Extend the range of errors and anomalies it can detect in its transactions with internal and external environments. Because organizational tolerance for perceived error will increase, members of the organization will become more able, jointly and publicly, to acknowledge the mismatch of outcome to expectation, and to acknowledge awareness of events which simply do not fit the categories of organizational theory-in-use.

- Extend the range of correctable error—that is, reduce the extent to which inaccessible and obscure information prevents members of the organization from attributing error to mistakes, incongruities, and inconsistencies in organizational theory of action. To put this in other terms, the effect of good organizational dialectic should be a clearer and more regularly shared awareness of organizational dilemmas. Because dilemmas are characteristically expressed through conflict, there is likely to be more public awareness and acceptance of conflict among individuals and groups in the organization, but there is also likely to be greater internalization (for individuals and for groups) of the conflicts that are experienced.

- Become progressively more able to engage such conflicts through collaborative reflection and inquiry—that is, through double-loop organizational learning.
- Reduce the double-binds experienced by individual members of the organization.
- Increase the shared awareness of the organization's own learning system and the incidence of joint inquiry into that system.

Again, we have described partial examples of all of these effects. But the more systematic example we believe it is necessary to create would be one in which a longitudinal study/intervention would map and describe the O-I learning system of an organization, describe and assess organizational learning phenomena of the kinds named above, trace the changes in the organizational learning system as it moves toward O-II, and describe the degree and range of changes in consequences for organizational learning as outlined above.

The intervention theory we have proposed is a workable means to Model O-II

The intervention theory and method described in Chapters 7 through 9 is a complex strategy which combines: (a) the mapping of an organization's O-I learning system, (b) helping members of the organization to make the transition from Model I to Model II theories-in-use, (c) guiding and facilitating the members' collaborative reflection on and restructuring of their own learning system, (d) modeling, and helping members to model, good organizational dialectic in their efforts to detect and correct error in the organization's instrumental theory-in-use.

The intervention strategy set forth is one which begins these processes at the top of the organization, engaging first those who have greatest power to set in motion or to block the transition from O-I to O-II. Further, as we have described it, the intervention strategy is iterative and cyclical, rather than linear. Work on individual theories-in-use proceeds in the context of interactions in which members of the organization seek to inquire into substantive organizational issues; the primary inhibiting loops which arise naturally in the course of such interactions become the focus *both* for the modeling of organizational inquiry *and* for work on individual theories-in-use. The intervenor, feeding back to members of the organization the map he or she has constructed of the organization's learning system, creates situations in which the primary inhibiting loops of the organization are likely to manifest themselves all over again.

We have described some of the partial and limited examples of intervention on which we base our belief in the workability of this strategy. In the previous section, we described a more systematic experiment in intervention which would test the feasibility of this approach to intervention as a means of effecting the transition from O-I to O-II. What we must now observe is the extent to which this theory of intervention requires development and fleshing out.

Among the themes of research in this direction are the following:

- Development of a typology of stages of movement from O-I to O-II, a typology which reflects important differences in type of organization, starting conditions, and context for intervention. At each such stage, we expect that different kinds of organizational issues become salient, different patterns of interaction among members of the organization become dominant, and different kinds of awareness and concern become manifest in the relations between intervenors and members of the organization.

- Analysis of extent to which members of the organization, as they succeed in moving from Model I toward Model II theories-in-use, become able themselves to discover, invent, and produce good organizational dialectic. To what extent does the transformation of individual theory-in-use assure this capacity for organizational dialectic? To what extent will the members still require help in conceptualizing good organizational dialectic in their own substantive organizational context?

Just as we have recognized the need to develop a theory of instruction for the transition from Model I to Model II at the level of the individual, so we envisage the need to develop a theory of instruction for the movement from Model O-I to O-II at the level of the organization. The sources of such a theory of instruction lie in reflection on the tacit, intuitive knowledge embedded in the practices of those who already possess some skill at intervention of this sort.

There are two domains, in particular, which seem to us to be fertile sources of investigation in this regard. One of these has to do with organizational structure, and the other with modes of organizational knowing.

Structures for organizational inquiry

In Part IV, we examined structural and information-systems approaches to questions of organizational learning. We argued there that the existing variants of these approaches are, in significant ways, incomplete. Nevertheless, we believe that organizational structures do matter. Some structures are more conducive than others to O-II learning systems and to good organizational dialectic, and the nature of these O-II structures will vary with the type of organization (for example, its profit or nonprofit status, its espoused functions, its cultural context), the scale of the organization, and the stage of development in its life-cycle.

In this context, moreover, we mean to designate by "structure" not only the patterns of roles implicit in an organizational task system but the patterns of information and of information flow by which the task system is informed and through which it evolves.

We believe, in short, that there are important interactions between organizational learning systems and organizational structure. Structural intervention is not sufficient to enable an organization to achieve an O-II learning system, but organizational structures may impede or facilitate that achievement, and the maintenance of O-II learning systems is likely to require new structural designs. Members of organizations who undertake the transition to an O-II system will themselves be confronting the problems of inventing and producing such designs. But research can provide useful frameworks for their efforts, along the following lines:

- In large-scale organizations whose tasks involve a high degree of variety, uncertainty or complexity, there are inevitable requirements for *decentralized* management, if only as a response to information overload as experienced by central managers. In O-I systems, decentralization tends to generate an incongruity between espoused theory and theory-in-use. Central managers espouse autonomy for divisional managers while maintaining a high degree of unilateral control over them through such devices as control of "P and L," program budgeting, and the like. The dysfunctional consequences of such incongruity have been illustrated in earlier chapters in cases A & B and the Mercury case.

O-II learning systems would not dispel the requirement of decentralization but would create the conditions for good inquiry into the dilemmas of decentralization (always related to the conflicting requirements for autonomy and control). What are the types of decentralized patterns of interaction which are most compatible with the norms of an O-II organization?

- The requirement for organizational deutero-learning is a continuing one, as internal and external environments continually shift out from under organizational maps. A continuing requirement for organizational learning about its own learning system sets up a further requirement for a design for organizational deutero-learning. Particularly in the case of large-scale organizations, there will be a need for designed interactions through which members can reflect on and map their changing learning systems. The rhythm and patterns of these inquiries must meet the always potentially incompatible requirements of full and accurate mapping *and* of noninterference with the essential day-to-day work of the organization.

- Management information systems, as we have pointed out, are characteristically based on a narrowly rational picture of organizational life. Their designers ignore the reality of O-I learning systems. In an O-II system, however, it would be more nearly feasible to design the sorts of information systems which would facilitate the detection and correction of error attributable to organizational theory-in-use. An O-II system would not obviate the need for such a design, but it would create the conditions under which such a design might be effectively developed.

There is a research program to be undertaken, therefore, which would consist in exploring management information systems compatible with and conducive to O-II organizations. What are the properties of management information systems conducive to organizational double-loop learning? To organizational deutero-learning? And what are the properties of the structure of organizational memory, of organizational "archives," which would most lend itself, in an O-II system, to good organizational dialectic?

Modes of organizational knowing

In this book, our focus has been on error detection and error correction, on the properties of information (inaccessibility, obscurity) which represent conditions for uncorrectable error, and on the learning systems which facilitate or impede the work of dispelling conditions for error.

But there is a domain of organizational knowing which lies, as it were, between error detection and error correction. In order to function as agents of organizational learning, individuals must set problems, construct models of organizational situations, and frame interpretations of error and anomaly. Their models, pictures, problem settings and interpretations display characteristic strategies for naming, framing, grouping, and describing the phenomena of organizational life. These strategies, which we call modes of organizational knowing, have not been central to our concerns in this book. (We came closest to engaging them, in Chapters 2 and 9, when we described in the Mercury story some of the typical ways in which problems were constructed and stories were told.) Nevertheless, we believe that modes of organizational knowing are centrally involved in processes of organizational learning. An organization's capacity to correct error depends, in considerable measure, on its members' ways of constructing the problems reflected by error. An organization's capacity to engage in good dialectic depends, in considerable measure, on the way its members model the phenomena of the organization's transactions with its internal and external environments.

For example: All problem-setting and modeling involves the simplification of complex phenomena. But *strategies of simplification* vary. They may be inherently counterproductive to good dialectic (strategies of decomposing an organizational task may ignore differences which are crucially important to effective performance), or they may be held so rigidly over time that they are impervious to error correction.

Organizations tend to develop *metaphors* which are generative of diagnoses, inventions, and actions taken in response to various kinds of situations. Such metaphors are more than decorative figures of speech; they are actually generative of the ways in which situations are framed, phenomena are modeled, and options for action are described. Often these metaphors are tacit, or have entered so fully and implicitly into organizational life that they no longer come to attention. Consider, for example, the cluster of notions surrounding the motivation of subordinates through "carrots and sticks"; the military metaphors of "chain of command," "front lines," "being a hero"; the machine metaphors of "production," "production line," and "productivity," as these are carried over to zones of the organization which are literally distant from production equipment. Consider the metaphor of "entrepreneurial gap" which served, in the Mercury story, to set the problem which gave rise to the New Business Division.

We believe that problem setting, through which error is interpreted, often takes its structure from such generative metaphors. We suspect that in O-I systems metaphors have evolved that shape, and are reinforced by, O-I processes. Perhaps the movement toward O-II systems will also depend on the development of metaphors compatible with those systems.

In our analysis, we have concentrated on the features of organizational learning systems which are conducive, or inhibitory, to the surfacing and testing of these ways of constructing problems and modeling phenomena. But the modes of constructing problems and modeling phenomena are themselves essential to good organizational dialectic. We suspect that organizations tend to develop characteristic modes of knowing; that organizations tend to differ from one another, in important ways, in their characteristic cognitive modes; and that individual members of organizations can learn to reflect on these cognitive modes, to extend their capacity for multiple viewing of organizational phenomena, and to develop the capacity for richer, more coordinated, and more adequate ways of representing organizational phenomena. We suspect, moreover, that enhancement of this capacity for modeling and problem setting is complementary to the development of a more nearly O-II learning system.

We recognize, of course, that our grasp of these notions is, at best, primitive. They represent an as-yet-unrealized impulse to transplant to the organizational domain certain developments in cognitive psychology which are, in their own right, embryonic. Nevertheless, we believe this impulse could lead to exciting and important developments in intervention-oriented research on organizational learning.

*Appendix**

A REVIEW OF THE LITERATURE OF ORGANIZATIONAL LEARNING:
THE THEORY-OF-ACTION PERSPECTIVE IN CONTEXT

There is a literature of organizational learning. We have attempted to describe that literature and to place our own approach in relation to it, but in doing so we have had to confront three sorts of difficulty.

Those who write about organizational learning ought to be grouped according to their views of what an organization is that it may learn and of what learning is that it may be applied to the things called organizations. Some writers, such as March, Kennedy, Dunn, and Bateson, actually use the term "organizational learning" and try to say what they mean by it. But for many other researchers, their approach to the study of organizations carries an implicit view of organizational learning which they do not put into words. In their case, we have had to construct the theories of organizational learning which seem to us to underlie their work.

A second difficulty has to do with the nature of the reason for taking up the idea of organizational learning in the first place. It is clear that one would not make use of the term unless he or she believed that an organization was in an important sense something

*   We are grateful to Scott Cook for his contributions to this review. We have also profited from reading an unpublished review of the literature on organizational learning by Bo Hedberg.

319

more than the individuals who happened at a particular time to be its members. But given that necessary starting point, we very quickly arrive at an important branching. For some researchers, organizational learning functions primarily as an explanatory notion, one that makes understandable some features of the history of organizational experience. For others (and we are among them), the notion is primarily important because of its normative relevance for intervention. The term "organizational effectiveness" has been widely used to describe the goals of intervention. But the notion of organizational effectiveness implies the correlated notions of organizational tasks, environments, and purposes. Increasingly, intervenors have had to recognize that their main challenge is not to help an organization become more effective at the performance of a stable task in the light of stable purposes, but rather to help an organization restructure its purposes and redefine its task in the face of a changing environment. A term like "organizational learning" then becomes necessary in order to define the goals of intervention.

From this point of view, the observation that organizations ordinarily fail to learn does not count against the utility of the term "organizational learning"; on the contrary, it is because organizations ordinarily fail to learn that we can arrive at the importance of interventions aimed at increasing the capacity for organizational learning. But it then becomes most important in examining the literature to distinguish efforts to explain organizational phenomena from efforts to build a theory of intervention.

A third difficulty has to do with the reality status* assigned to organizational learning. Some authors use the notion of "system" as a metaphor; they *see* organization *as* systems. For others, such as Simon or Ackoff, organizations really are systems. Similarly, "organization learning" is rather widely employed as a metaphor for certain kinds of organizational experience; but for some observers organizations really do learn. The two ways of using the term are associated with very different degrees of seriousness about theories of organizational learning.

Keeping these difficulties in mind, we believe it is useful to group theories of organizational learning into six categories. The categories are based on more or less conventional ways of describing what an organization is, but they are also associated with certain approaches

---

*   We owe this thought to Cook.

to the notion of learning and with certain ways of thinking about intervention. The categories are as follows:

Theories of organizational learning	Associated learning approaches
1. *Organization as group*	Social psychology
2. *Organization as agent*	Instrumentalism, management theory
3. *Organization as structure*	Sociology, theory of bureaucracy
4. *Organization as system*	Cybernetics, information theory
5. *Organization as culture*	Anthropology, ethnomethodology, phenomenology
6. *Organization as politics*	Political theory, theory of sociopolitical movements

Each category is an ideal type, a major theme around which there are many variations. The six-category scheme is a gross simplification of a very complex literature—a simplification justified, we believe, by the salience of the perspectives around which we have clustered different approaches. Many authors, including some of those most important for our purposes, must be understood as hybrids, but their views are illuminated by consideration of the pure types.

In our discussion of the categories, we will name authors who illustrate the prevailing tendencies, and we will identify some of those who have been dominant figures, but we will not attempt anything like an exhaustive inventory of researchers.

1. Organization as group

On this view, organizations are collections of persons who interact on a regular basis and share a sense of collective identity. The person is a salient element, but there are also group phenomena. Groups as such may be effective or ineffective in carrying out shared tasks in order to achieve shared goals, and groups have characteristic climates which may be described as open, competetive, trusting, and the like. An important focus of study is the relationship between levels of group effectiveness and features of group climate.

"Learning" is a term applicable to individuals within the context of a group, but when individuals learn to interact with one another so as to carry out shared tasks, one can speak of the group itself as learning.

The early students of group dynamics, such as Bales (1) and Homans (2) concerned themselves mainly with describing the phenomena of group behavior, the ways in which roles are sorted out and distributed among individuals, and the processes by which group climate develops and changes.

Kurt Lewin was a landmark figure, with his post-World-War-II studies of autocratic and democratic group climates. Some of the main features of Lewin's approach became central to the work of those who followed him: his fundamentally normative view (his approval of democracy and his distrust of autocracy, all very much influenced by his experience as a refugee from Nazi Germany); his recognition of the reality and life history of the group as things in themselves, unable to exist without individuals but irreducible to individuals; his belief in action research, in intervention as an approach to theory-building, and in theory-building as a guide to intervention.

Those who came after Lewin tended to adopt one of two approaches to group learning. Bavelas (3), Kennedy (4), and the Rome (5), focused on group performance of shared tasks and on sequential improvement in task performance. In Kennedy's "Cogwheel Experiment," for example, the intervention consisted of producing conditions of group structure and information flow which would yield the steepest learning curve for group task performance. On the other hand, those who have participated in the development and elaboration of the T-group movement, which also grew out of Lewin's work, have emphasized, in study and intervention, the ways in which individuals may learn to transform the character and climate of the group. (6)

Within this category, there is no clear distinction between the study of group dynamics and the study of organizational phenomena, for organizations are mainly understood as groups. Nevertheless, researchers such as Weick (7) and Katz and Kahn (8) have attempted to place the social psychology of groups within the larger framework of organizations.

2. Organization as agent

Here, organizations are seen as instruments for the achievement of social purposes. Although it is legitimate to speak of the collection of individuals who inhabit an organization at any given time, the organization is not reducible to them or to their interactions. The organization is itself a subject which is conceived as sentient, active, intelligent, and purposeful.

The viewpoint is instrumental and rational. Organizations-as-agents are involved in the effort to achieve objectives by the judicious selection of appropriate means. The focus is upon the acquisition and application of knowledge useful for effective performance of organizational tasks, and the organizational world is conceived as fundamentally knowable through scientific method—that is, through empirical observation, modeling, and experiment.

The salient elements are decisions, for it is through decision-making that knowledge is applied to the performance of organizational tasks. The organization acts upon its environment through the decisions made by individuals in key roles. The task system is a design for decision-making and the organization, in essence, is just such a design.

Organizational learning refers to experience-based improvement in organizational task performance, and is decomposable into the improvement in performance of individual decision-makers whose learning comes to be encoded in organizational maps, memories and programs. The task system itself may be improved through the increased problem-solving effectiveness of those who decide about *it*.

The organizational world is seen mainly from the perspective of a manager schooled in the instrumental rationality of engineering. Hence, it is not surprising that we find the precursors of this school of thought in the reflective manager, Chester Barnard (9), and in the evangelical engineer, Frederick Taylor (10). Barnard sought to map the functions of the executive as the principal decision-maker concerned with organizational effectiveness; and Taylor, who thought of the design and performance of work as an engineering problem, attempted by the measurement of output, and by an experimental approach to work design and worker training, to increase the efficiency of organizational task performance.

From these beginnings, it is possible to trace the development of the concept of organization-as-agent and the related school of instrumental rationality. In the work of Mayo (11), Roethlisberger (12), and others, Taylorism was subjected to critique from the viewpoint of human relations: worker performance was found to be conditioned by the worker's perception of and feelings about the meaning and context of work, and by the ways in which the work setting fulfilled or violated the worker's needs as a human being. In the writings of Peter Drucker (13), and in burgeoning literature on management effectiveness, Barnard's early insights were developed and elaborated.

Herbert Simon (14), along with Cyert (15) and the early March (16), sought to identify the limits of organizational rationality and to describe the character of effective decision-making under conditions of uncertainty and stress. For Simon, and for those who shared his view, instrumental rationality began to be described in the terms of computer science. Organizations could be seen as programs for action, mediated by the action of individual problem-solvers. One could intervene so as to improve organizational learning by increasing the organizational store of useful knowledge, by improving the design of organizational programs, and by increasing the problem-solving capabilities of individual decision-makers. In the end, organization theory could be seen as a branch of an emerging cognitive science.

In the work of Chandler (17), Thompson (18), Stinchcombe (19), and Lawrence and Lorsch (20), the basic idea of organizational instrumental rationality has been connected to theories of types of organizational structure, to further analysis of sources of uncertainty, and to analysis of the varying demands of kinds of organizational environment.

3. Organization as structure

This way of looking at organizations coincides with a popular view of them, one that regards organizations as what the organization chart signifies: an ordered array of role-boxes connected by lines which represent flows of information, work, and authority. It is unlikely that any researcher holds the perspective in quite this ethereal form. Most structuralists also think about people, their relations to one another, and their interactions. But in doing so, they seek to relate people to an abstracted order of positions and relationships in a task- and authority-structure.

Max Weber is perhaps the landmark figure (21). He singled out organizations of large scale, rountinized work, finely divided and uniform tasks, compartmented units, and rigid hierarchies of authority, and he called them bureaucracies. The study of organizational structure is by no means limited to bureaucracies, but it was in the context of bureaucracies that structuralism first emerged. Merton (22) and Parsons (23) drew upon and developed the Weberian tradition, treating whole societies in terms of the key notions of structure and function. The task of the student of organizations was for them one of identifying the latent and overt functions of organizations, analyzing the determinants of structure, and exploring the interactive evolution of structure and function.

Later organizational sociologists have elaborated the structural perspective. Blau (24) has used the concept of organizational structure to understand organizational dysfunction, bureaucratic rigidity and flexibility, and organizational development. Crozier (25) and Downes (26) have, in very different ways, attempted to build general models which account for the behavior of large-scale bureaucracies. Gouldner (27) and Perrow (28) have explored typologies of bureaucracies. Burns and Stalker (29) have distinguished "organic" and "mechanical" structures, and have attempted to relate these to organizational responsiveness.

From the structural perspective, organizational learning has to do with change of structure. An organization may be said to learn when it restructures itself in response to change in internal or external environment. Organizational restructuring may be placed within the context of evolution, as in the work of Edgar Dunn (30). But from the point of view of intervention, organizational learning has primarily to do with the ways in which members of the organization learn to select new structures and modify old ones so as to respond more effectively to changed conditions, or to create an environment more conducive to individual learning. Rhenman (31) is an example of a structuralist who writes explicitly about intervention for the sake of organizational learning.

4. Organization as system

With the growth of the idea of systems as an idea in good currency, some researchers have come to think of organizations as systems —that is, as self-regulating entities, as complexes which maintain certain essential constancies through cycles of action, error-detection, and error-correction. While basic theories of self-regulating systems have been developed by researchers such as Cannon (32), Wiener (33), Ashby (34), and Von Bertalanffy (35), the attempt to apply these theories to organizations has been carried out by others. We have distinguished three distinct groups of systems theorists of organization.

The cyberneticists have concentrated on organizations as systems of decision and control, seeking to apply the principles of control and communications theory to organizational phenomena. Deutch's (36) is the classical work in this field, but the writings of Beer (37), Ackoff (38), and Churchman (39) have been important. More recently, Steinbrenner (40) has combined cybernetic approaches with those of cognitive science.

Information theorists, drawing on the work of Shannon and Weaver (41), among others, have seen organizations as systems of information flow. Wilensky (42) has examined the features of the content and distribution of information which are conducive to effective organizational functioning. Galbraith (43) has offered principles to structural design based upon analysis of information flows, and Dunn (44) has attempted to apply a general model of information processing to organizational analysis.

Emery and Trist (45) have coined the term "socio-technical systems" to refer to the systematic interactions of human beings and technologies in the context of organized work.

For systems theorists, organizational learning consists of the self-regulating process of error-detection and error-correction itself, whether or not maintenance of the organizational steady state is mediated by the self-conscious efforts of individual members of the organization. Bateson (46), whose approach to organizations draws on systems theory and cybernetics among other sources, distinguishes levels of learning depending both upon the degree of centrality of the systems variables changed in the course of systems adaptation and upon the logical type involved (thus, "learning" and "learning to learn").

Approaches to intervention sometimes focus on the design of appropriate systems of information and control (as in Galbraith), on appreciation of naturally occurring self-regulation (as in Beer), or on self-conscious creation of conditions favorable to the more important kinds of organizational learning (as in Ackoff and in Bateson).

5. Organization as culture

In this category, we have lumped together researchers who think of organizations as small societies in which people create for themselves shared meanings, symbols, rituals, and cognitive schemas which allow them to create and maintain meaningful interactions among themselves and in relation to the world beyond their small society.

Some of these authors devote themselves primarily to describing the organizational culture itself, conceiving it as a kind of collective artifact which is continually formed and transformed as the organization seeks to balance the demands for maintaining its worn integrity with the demands for response which it detects in the world around it. The landmark figures in this tradition are the great figures of social anthropology, including, in recent years, Levi-Strauss (47). Cognitive anthropologists such as Douglas (48) and Van Maanen (49) conceive of organizational cultures as involving schemes for categorizing reality, schemes associated with decision processes by which phenomena may be categorized and processes for ignoring or interpreting anomalies which have the potential for disrupting the scheme. Vickers (50), though not an anthropologist, places great emphasis on the culture of organizations, especially on the appreciative systems which are the source of organizational norms, evaluations, and purposes.

A second group of researchers select for attention the representations of reality held by members of organizational societies and the cognitive processes by which these representations are used and transformed. The roots of this approach lie in the work of cognitive psychologists such as Kelly (51), Piaget (52), and Bruner (53). Thus, Whyte (54) analyzes the models of organization held by the members of an organization. March and Olsen (55) explore the cognitive processes by which individuals make choices in the face of ambiguity and uncertainty. Allison (56) shows, in his case study of the Cuban missile crisis, how the "conceptual lenses" used by members of an organization shape the organization's perception of a situation. Kolb (57) describes the "cognitive styles" which characterize whole organizations or their parts.

A third group of researchers concerns itself with the ways in which individuals construct for themselves, in the context of the societies to which they belong, the social realities in which they live. The sources of this point of view include sociologists of knowledge, such as Mannheim (58), but perhaps also the American social philosopher, G. H. Mead (59), who saw the creation of the self as an internalization of social processes. More recently, Berger and Luckman (60) have given a generic description of the social construction of reality. Goffman (61) and other ethnomethodologists have described in detail the processes by which social reality is constructed in situations of everyday life. Snyder (62), Hudson (63), and Parlett (64) have presented accounts of the social reality constructed by individuals within the milieux of academic institutions.

From these perspectives, there follow several different possible senses of organizational learning. For the first group, organizational learning may refer to the processes by which individuals become socialized to the culture of the organization. Or organizational learning, in a deeper sense, may refer to the processes by which organizational category-schemes, models, images, or cognitive modes are transformed in response to error, anomaly, or inconsistency. Finally, organizational learning might be taken to signify the process by which members of an organization become cognizant of the social reality they have jointly constructed, subject that sense of reality to critical reflection, and seek deliberately to transform it.

Most of the researchers we have mentioned choose not to discuss intervention. If they were to discuss it, their perspectives would seem to imply an effort to enhance individuals' consciousness of organizational culture.

6. Organization as politics

From this perspective, organizations are political systems. They are political both in the ancient sense of *polis* (that is, they are governments) and in the more contemporary sense of an interplay of contending interests and associated powers. For these researchers, organizations are primarily understandable as interest groups which contend with other interest groups for the control of resources and territory. Organizations are themselves made up of contending parties, and in order to understand the behavior of organizations one must understand the nature of internal and external conflicts, the distribution of power among contending groups, and the processes by which conflicts of powers result in dominance, submission, compromise, or stalemate.

The sources of this perspective are, of course, in political theory, and the variations in its development reflect both the various fields of conflict chosen for attention (conflict between line and staff, labor and management, branches of government, central and regional offices) and the various frameworks chosen for the analysis of conflict.

Among the authors who have employed this perspective to study organizations are Selznick (65), Simmel (66), and Long (67).

Lasswell (68) and Lindblom (69) are among those who have used the political perspective to illuminate the processes by which organizations have entered into the shaping of public policy.

Organizational learning, on this point of view, might have two very different meanings. The researcher may put himself in the position of one or more of the contending parties, asking himself how to play his part most intelligently in order to win. Game theory (70) provides a framework for such an analysis, and researchers such as Schelling (71), Kahn (72), and Shubik (73) have applied game theory and related methods to the problem of winning. Organizational learning might consist of the processes by which members of an organization learned to invent and apply, in concerted organizational action, the strategies most appropriate to the task of winning the game in which they are engaged with other organizations. Contexts for organizational learning, in this sense, would include the competition of business firms for market, of government agencies for resources, and of nations for hegemony.

In a very different sense, the researcher might ask himself how members of an organization might achieve collective awareness of the processes of contention in which they are engaged, gaining thereby the possibility of converting contention to cooperation. Organizational learning might consist of just such a process of converting organization politics to organizational inquiry.

THE SIX PERSPECTIVES ON ORGANIZATIONAL LEARNING, AND THE THEORY-OF-ACTION PERSPECTIVE

This review of the literature on organizational learning may seem to our readers, as it does to us, to be both extraordinarily comprehensive and extraordinarily incomplete. The essential difficulty of the review is that organizations are phenomena which may be, and have been, examined through the lenses of very different disciplines—social psychology, anthropology, sociology, and systems theory, to name only a few. The notion of organizational learning has a meaning, and we think an important meaning, from all of these points of view. But a reasonably adequate review of the literature requires that one reach back into the discipline in order to discover the sources of each perspective and then that one identify a sample of those who have used the perspective to study phenomena related in important ways to organizational learning.

As it is, we have left out of account perspectives which give a very different view of organizational learning—for example, the study of social movements in relation to which organizations may be seen as mere "precipitates" (74).

We have been guided in our selection and clustering of researchers by our sense of the perspectives by which we ourselves have been mainly influenced. In many different ways, we have drawn upon the six perspectives, have adopted parts of them, or have reacted against them.

We have held onto the traditional perspective of organization-as-agent, seeking to account for the fact that organizations act and may be held accountable for their acts. Like Simon, and other proponents of instrumental rationality, we have tried to analyze organizational action in terms of means and ends. But we have used the notion of organizational theory of action which lends itself to an account of organizational learning analogous to the ways in which individuals' theories of action are transformed through encounter with error, anomaly, inconsistency, and incongruity.

We also depart from the instrumental rationalists in our concern with the inhibitory loops—that is, with the intéractions between the organization's theory of action and its behavioral world. In our analysis of the primary inhibitory loops we have linked a cognitive analysis of group climate to a cognitive analysis of organizational action.

From the systems theorists, particularly from Ashby, we have taken the concepts of learning as error-detection and -correction, levels of learning, and organizational learning systems. Our O-I and O-II learning systems are, indeed, self-regulating systems, in very much the sense described by Ashby, Beer, and others; but we have attempted to include in our models of organizational learning the interactions between organizational and interpersonal variables which systems theorists often ignore.

Certain other perspectives we have opposed, ignored, or treated as subordinate. We have argued that questions of organizational structure are best understood in the context of organizational learning systems, and that structural interventions alone are unlikely to enhance organizational learning capacity. We have treated contending interest groups as phenomena which in O-I systems contribute to inhibitory loops and in O-II systems may be converted to organizational inquiry.

Our approach to the study of organizations is essentially normative and intervention-oriented. We give primary importance to organizational inquiry—to an organization's capacity for conscious transformation of its own theory of action, and to individuals' ability to appreciate and transform the learning systems in which they live. We treat other domains of organizational phenomena (politics, structure, culture, group dynamics) in terms of their interactions with organizational inquiry. Because we try to develop a theory of intervention, we focus on the links between individuals' theories of action and the larger systems of the organization. Because we try to develop a *general* theory of intervention, we tend to emphasize the common rather than the idiosyncratic features of individual, group, and organizational experience.

We have been less interested in making a rich description of the varieties of organizational cultures, cognitive styles, and individual constructions of social reality, than in describing those features of organizational and individual experience which lend themselves to a general account of the factors which facilitate or inhibit organizational inquiry. We recognize, however, the need to test and elaborate our general theories in the context of many different varieties of organizational and individual experience.

Not surprisingly, we have been most influenced by those researchers who have also tried to synthesize a variety of perspectives on organizations for purposes related to double-loop and deutero-learning. Among these are Vickers and Bateson, both of whom have attempted (although in ways very different from one another) to combine cultural, cognitive, social-psychological, and systems approaches with the notion of organization-as-agent.

The prinicipal challenge to present-day organization theory is to invent a productive synthesis of fragmentary approaches. We believe that such a synthesis is most likely to be achieved from a stance that is frankly normative, one that is grounded in the requirements of workable intervention.

REFERENCES

1. ROBERT FREED BALES, *Personality and Interpersonal Behavior.* N.Y.: Holt, Rinehart and Winston, 1969.

2. GEORGE HOMANS, *The Human Group.* N.Y.: Harcourt Brace and World, 1950.

3. ALEX BAVELAS, Communication Patterns in Task-Oriented Achievement Groups. *Journal of the Acoustical Society of America* 22, 6: 1950.

4. ROBERT L. CHAPMAN, and JOHN L. KENNEDY, *The Background and Implications of the Systems Research Laboratory Studies.* Systems Development Corporation, 1951. See also HAROLD LEAVITT, Some Effects of Feedback on Communication. *Human Relations* 4: 401–410; 1951.

5. BEATRICE and SYDNEY ROME, *Organizational Growth through Decision-Making: A Computer-Based Experiment in Eductive Method.* N.Y.: Elsevier, 1971.

6. This group includes Herbert Shepard, Douglas McGregor, Warren Bennis, Edgar Schein, Chris Argyris.

7. KARL E. WEICK, *The Social Psychology of Organizing.* Reading, Mass.: Addison-Wesley, 1969.

8. D. KATZ and R. KAHN, *The Social Psychology of Organizations.* N.Y.: Wiley, 1966.

9. CHESTER BARNARD, *The Functions of the Executive.* Cambridge, Mass.: Harvard University Press, 1968.

10. FREDERICK TAYLOR, *The Principles of Scientific Management.* N.Y.: Norton Library, 1967. (Original edition, 1911.)

11. ELTON MAYO, *The Social Problems of an Industrial Civilization.* Cambridge, Mass.: University Press, 1947.

12. FRITZ ROETHLISBERGER, *Management and Morale.* Cambridge, Mass.: Harvard University Press, 1941. Also co-author with WILLIAM J. DICKSON *Management and Worker.* N.Y.: Wiley, 1964. An account of the Hawthorne studies. (Original 1939).

13. PETER DRUCKER, *The Practice of Management.* N.Y.: Harper, 1954.

14. HERBERT SIMON, *Administrative Behavior.* N.Y.: Macmillan, 1947.

15. R. M. CYERT and J. G. MARCH, *A Behavioral Theory of the Firm.* Englewood Cliffs, N.J.: Prentice-Hall. 1963.

16. J. G. MARCH and H. A. SIMON, *Organizations.* N.Y.: Wiley, 1958.

17. A. D. CHANDLER, *Strategy and Structure.* Cambridge, Mass.: M.I.T. Press, 1962.

18. JAMES THOMPSON, *Organization in Action.* N.Y.: McGraw-Hill, 1967.

19. A. STINCHCOMBE, *Creating Efficient Industrial Administration.* N.Y.: Academic Press. 1974.

20. P. R. LAWRENCE and J. W. LORSCH, *Organization and Environment.* Cambridge, Mass.: Harvard University Press, 1967.

21. MAX WEBER, *The Theory of Social and Economic Organization.* N.Y.: Free Press, 1964. Translated by A. M. Handerson and Talcott Parsons. (Original 1947.) See also *From Max Weber: Essays in Sociology.* N.Y.: Oxford University Press, 1946. (Translated with an Introduction by H. H. Gerth and C. Wright Mills.)

22. ROBERT MERTON, *Social Theory and Social Structure.* N.Y.: Free Press, 1968. (Original 1949.)

23. TALCOTT PARSONS, *Structure and Process in Modern Societies.* Glencoe, Ill.: Free Press, 1960.

24. P. M. BLAU, *The Dynamics of Bureaucracy.* Chicago, Ill.: University of Chicago Press, 1955, and W. R. SCOTT, *Formal Organizations.* San Francisco: Chandler, 1962.

25. MICHEL CROZIER, *The Bureaucratic Phonomenon.* London: Tavistock, 1964.

26. ANTHONY DOWNES, *Inside Bureaucracy.* Boston: Little, Brown, 1967.

27. ALVIN W. GOULDNER, *Patterns of Industrial Bureaucracy.* Glencoe, Ill.: The Free Press, 1954.

28. CHARLES PERROW, *Complex Organizations.* Glenview, Ill.: Scott, Foresman, 1972. See also: DERECK S. PUGH, "Modern organization theory: A psychological and sociological study," *Psychological Bulletin* 66, 4: 235–251; 1966, and DERECK S. PUGH, D. J. HICKSON, C. R. HINNINGS, and C. TURNER "Dimensions of Organizational Structure," *Administrative Science Bulletin* 13, 1: 65–105.

29. TOM BURNS and G. M. STALKER, *The Management of Innovation.* London: Tavistock Press, 1959.

30. EDGAR DUNN, *Economic and Social Development: A Process of Social Learning.* Baltimore: Johns Hopkins Press, 1971.

31. ERIC RHENMAN, *Organization Theory of Long-Range Planning.* London: Tavistock, 1973.

32. WALTER CANNON, *The Wisdom of the Body.* N.Y.: Norton, 1963.

33. NORBERT WEINER, *Cybernetics.* Cambridge, Mass.: M.I.T. Press, 1965. (Original 1948.)

34. ROSS ASHBY, *Design for a Brain*. London: Chapman and Hall, 1966. (Original 1954.)

35. LUDWIG VON BERTALANFFY, *General Systems Theory*. N.Y.: G. Braziller, 1968.

36. KARL DEUTCH, *The Nerves of Government*. N.Y.: Free Press, 1966.

37. STAFFORD BEER, *Brain of the Firm*. N.Y.: Penguin Press, 1972. Also, *Decision and Control*, N.Y.: Wiley, 1966.

38. RUSSELL ACKOFF, *A Concept of Corporate Planning*. N.Y.: Wiley Interscience, 1970.

39. C. WEST CHURCHMAN, *Design of Inquiring Systems*. N.Y.: Basic Books, 1971.

40. JOHN STEINBRENNER, *The Cybernetic Theory of Decision*. Princeton, N.J.: Princeton University Press, 1974.

41. C. SHANNON and W. WEAVER, *The Mathematical Theory of Communication*. Urbana, Ill.: University of Illinois Press, 1949.

42. HAROLD WILENSKY, *Organizational Intelligence*. N.Y.: Basic Books, 1967.

43. J. R. GALBRAITH, *Organizational Design*. Reading, Mass.: Addison-Wesley, 1973.

44. EDGAR DUNN, *Social Information Processing and Statistical Systems*. N.Y.: Wiley Interscience, 1974.

45. F. EMERY and E. TRIST, "Socio-Technical Systems," in C. W. Churchman and M. Verhulst (eds.), *Management Sciences, Models and Techniques;* vol. 2. Oxford: Pergamon, 1960.

46. GREGORY BATESON, *Steps to an Ecology of Mind*. N.Y.: Ballantine Books, 1971.

47. CLAUDE LEVI-STRAUSS, *Anthropologie Structurale*. Paris: Plon, 1958.

48. MARY DOUGLAS, *Purity and Danger*. London: Routledge and Kegan Paul, 1966.

49. JOHN VAN MAANEN, "Observations on the Making of Policemen," *Human Organization* 32, 4: 1973.

50. GEOFFREY VICKERS, *Value Systems and Social Process*. London: Tavistock, 1968.

51. GEORGE KELLY, *The Psychology of Personal Constructs*. N.Y.: Norton, 1955.

52. JEAN PIAGET, *The Essential Piaget*. Howard Gruber and Jacques Voneche (eds.). N.Y.: Basic Books, 1976. Also *Structuralism*. N.Y.:

Basic Books, 1970. Co-author with BÄRBEL INHELDER, *The Psychology of the Child.* N.Y.: Basic Books, 1969.

53. JEROME BRUNER, *On Knowing; Essays for the Left Hand.* Cambridge, Mass.: Belknap Press of Harvard University Press, 1962. Co-author with JACQUALINE GOODMAN and GEORGE A. AUSTIN, *A Study of Thinking.* N.Y.: Science Editions, 1956.

54. WILLIAM F. WHYTE, "Models of Building and Changing Organizations," in *Human Organization* 26, Spring/Summer: 1967.

55. JAMES MARCH and JOHAN P. OLSEN, *Ambiguity and Choice in Organizations.* Oslo: Universitetsforlaget, 1976.

56. GRAHAM ALLISON, *Essence of Decision.* Boston: Little, Brown, 1971.

57. LAWRENCE KOLB (co-authored with RONALD FRY), "Toward an Applied Theory of Experimental Learning." M.I.T. Sloan School Working Paper 732-774; Sept. 1974.

58. KARL MANNHEIM, *Essays on the Sociology of Knowledge.* London: Routledge and Kegan Paul, 1952.

59. GEORGE H. MEAD, *Mind, Self and Society.* Chicago, Ill.: University of Chicago Press, 1934. Also *On Social Psychology.* University of Chicago Press, 1956.

60. P. L. BERGER and T. LUCKMANN, *The Social Construction of Reality.* N.Y.: Anchor Books, 1967.

61. ERVING GOFFMAN, *The Presentation of Self in Everyday Life.* Garden City, N.Y.: Doubleday, 1959.

62. BENSON SNYDER, *The Hidden Curriculum,* N.Y.: Alfred A. Knopf, 1970.

63. LIAM HUDSON, *The Hidden Curriculum.* N.Y.: Norton, 1968.

64. MALCOLM PARLETT, *Classroom and Beyond.* Cambridge, Mass.: M.I.T. Education Research Center, 1967.

65. PHILIP SELZNICK, *TVA and the Grass Roots.* N.Y.: Harper and Row, 1966.

66. G. SIMMEL, *Conflict and the Web of Group Affiliations.* Glencoe, Ill.: Free Press, 1955.

67. NORTON LONG, "The Local Community as an Ecology of Games," *American Journal of Sociology* 44, Nov. 1958; pp.251-261.

68. HAROLD LASSWELL, *The Analysis of Political Behavior.* N.Y.: Oxford University Press, 1947. Also *Politics; Who Gets What, When, How.* N.Y.: Whittlesey House, McGraw-Hill, 1936.

69. CHARLES E. LINDBLOM, *The Intelligence of Democracy.* N.Y.: The Free Press, 1965.

70. J. VON NEUMANN and H. MORGENSTERN, *The Theory of Games.* N.Y.: Wiley, 1953.

71. THOMAS SCHELLING, *The Strategy of Conflict.* Cambridge, Mass.: Harvard University Press, 1960.

72. HERMAN KAHN, *Thinking About the Unthinkable.* N.Y.: Horizon Press, 1962.

73. MARTIN SHUBIK, *Games for Society, Business and War.* N.Y.: Elsevier, 1975.

74. TOM BURNS, "Organization and Organizations." Unpublished paper.

Bibliography

Argyris, Chris (1962). *Interpersonal Competence and Organizational Effectiveness*. Homewood, Ill.: Dorsey Press.

Argyris, Chris (1976). *Some Causes of Organizational Ineffectiveness Within the Department of State*. Center for International Systems Research, Occasional Papers, No. 2.

Argyris, Chris (1970). *Intervention Theory and Method*. Reading, Mass.: Addison-Wesley.

Argyris, Chris (1971). *Management and Organizational Development*. New York: McGraw-Hill.

Argyris, Chris (1974). *Behind the Front Page*. San Francisco: Jossey-Bass.

Argyris, Chris (1976a). *Increasing Leadership Effectiveness*. New York: Wiley-Interscience.

Argyris, Chris (1976b). Theories of Action That Inhibit Individual Learning. *American Psychologist* 39: 638–654.

Argyris, Chris (1976c). Single-Loop and Double-Loop Models in Research in Decision Making. *Administrative Science Quarterly* 21: 363–375.

Argyris, Chris, and Donald Schön (1974). *Theory in Practice*. San Francisco: Jossey-Bass.

Bardach, Eugene (1977). *The Implementation Game: What Happens After a Bill Becomes a Law*. Cambridge, Mass.: M.I.T. Press.

Bateson, Gregory (1958). *Naven*. Stanford, Calif.: Stanford University Press. Bateson borrows the term from W.R. Ashby's *Design for a Brain*, New York: Wiley, 1960.

Bateson, Gregory (1972). *Steps to an Ecology of Mind*. New York: Ballantine.

Baughman, James P. (1974). *Problems and Performance of the Role of the Chief Executive in X Company, 1892–1974*. Cambridge: Graduate School of Business, Harvard University (mimeographed).

Blau, Peter M. (1975). *Approaches to the Study of Social Structure*. New York: The Free Press.

Chapman, Robert L., and John L. Kennedy (1956). *Background and Implications of Systems Research Laboratory Studies*. Rand Corporation Report.

Crozier, Michael, and Jean-Claude Thoenig (1976). The Regulations of Complex Organized Systems. *Administrative Science Quarterly* 21: 547–570.

Geertz, Clifford (1975). *Common Sense as a Cultural System. Antioch Review*, Spring.

Glazer, Nathan, and Irving Kristol (eds.) (1976). Introduction: The American Experiment. In *The American Commonwealth–1976*. New York: Basic Books.

Greiner, L.E. (1967). Patterns of Organization Change. *Harvard Business Review* 45, 3: 119–123.

Homans, George C. (1975). What do We Mean by Social 'Structure'? In Peter M. Blau (ed.) *Approaches to the Study of Social Structure*. New York: The Free Press.

Janis, Irving L. (1972). *Victims of Groupthink*. Boston: Houghton Mifflin.

Lewin, Kurt, Tamara Dembo, Leon Festinger, and Paul Sears (1944). "Level of Aspiration." In J.M.V. Hunt (ed.), *Personality and the Behavior Disorders*. New York: The Ronald Press, pp. 333–378.

Miller, G.A. (1956). The magical number seven, plus or minus two: Some limits on our capacity for processing information. *Psychological Review* 6, 3: 81–97.

Monsen, R. Joseph, and Anthony Downes (1968). A Theory of Large Managerial Firms. In P.P. LeBreton, (ed.), *Comparative Administrative Theory*. Seattle: University of Washington Press.

Nord, Walter R., and Douglas E. Durand (1975). Beyond Resistance to Change. *Organizational Dynamics* 4, 2: 2–19.

Olsen, John P. (1976). Choice in an Organized Anarchy. In James G. March and John P. Olsen (eds.), *Ambiguity and Choice in Organizations*. Bergen, Norway: Universitietsforlaget, pp. 82–139.

Rien, Marten, and Donald Schön (1976). Problem-Setting and Policy Research. Manuscript.

Schön, Donald (1971). *Beyond the Stable State*. New York: Random House.

Simon, Herbert A. (1969). *The Sciences of the Artifical*. Cambridge, Mass.: M.I.T. Press.

Singer, Ethan A., and Leland M. Wooten (1976). The Triumph and Failure of Albert Speer's Administrative Genius: Implications for Current Management Theory and Practice. *Applied Behavioral Science* 12, 1: 79–103.

Turner, Barry A. (1976). The Organizational and Interorganizational Development of Disasters. *Administrative Science Quarterly* 21, 3: 378–397.

Name index

Subject index